Design Management
for Architects

Design Management
for Architects
Stephen Emmitt

Blackwell
Publishing

Blackwell Publishing editorial offices:
Blackwell Publishing Ltd, 9600 Garsington Road, Oxford OX4 2DQ, UK
Tel: +44 (0)1865 776868
Blackwell Publishing Inc., 350 Main Street, Malden, MA 02148-5020, USA
Tel: +1 781 388 8250
Blackwell Publishing Asia Pty Ltd, 550 Swanston Street, Carlton, Victoria 3053,
Australia
Tel: +61 (0)3 8359 1011

First published 2007 by Blackwell Publishing Ltd

ISBN: 978-1-4051-3147-6

Library of Congress Cataloging-in-Publication Data

Emmitt, Stephen.
Design management for architects / Stephen Emmitt.
p. cm.
Includes bibliographical references and index.
ISBN-13: 978-1-4051-3147-6 (pbk. : alk. paper)
ISBN-10: 1-4051-3147-0 (pbk. : alk. paper)
1. Architectural design. 2. Architectural practice–Management. I. Title.

NA2750.E46 2007
720.68–dc22

2006037872

A catalogue record for this title is available from the British Library

Set in 10 on 12.5 pt Avenir
by SNP Best-set Typesetter Ltd., Hong Kong
Printed and bound in Singapore
by C.O.S. Printers Pte Ltd

The publisher's policy is to use permanent paper from mills that operate a sustainable forestry policy, and which has been manufactured from pulp processed using
acid-free and elementary chlorine-free practices. Furthermore, the publisher ensures
that the text paper and cover board used have met acceptable environmental
accreditation standards.

For further information on Blackwell Publishing, visit our website:
www.blackwellpublishing.com/construction

Contents

Preface

It was during the 1960s that the architectural profession in the UK started to take the issue of management seriously. This resulted in the publication of many guides, such as the RIBA Plan of Work and *Architect's Job Book*. This early work has been continually revised and updated over the years, providing architects, architectural technologists and technicians with essential guidance to the administration of projects. Interest in the management of design has also been growing, with the International Council for Research and Innovation in Building and Construction (CIB)'s research into architectural management starting in 1992. Parallel to this has been the growth and evolution of construction management literature, which more recently has started to expand into the areas of design management and briefing. Since the 1960s there have been considerable changes in our approach to the management of construction projects and despite many good examples of how to manage the processes effectively and professionally we still see reports urging us to do it better. In addition to the reports and initiatives aimed at the construction sector, there have also been a small number of reports aimed specifically at architects. These have emphasised the need for better management of design activities and design offices, while also raising questions about how, and what, architects should be taught. Whatever our view, it is difficult to ignore the fact that our fellow professionals leave university with a thorough understanding of how to manage projects and commercial enterprises. The result is that architects often find it difficult to relate to their fellow project members and frequently find themselves excluded from important decision-making stages at pivotal stages in the life of a project. Architects have a significant part to play in the realisation of creative and exciting buildings, but this is difficult to achieve when positioned outside the management culture. It is imperative in a highly competitive business environment that architects are able to demonstrate professional management skills and leadership competences to their clients and hence retain (or regain) an important place in the planning and management of our built environment. Similarly, it is fundamental that architects are able to communicate with fellow professionals in an environment of greater collaboration and integral working; this requires an understanding and appreciation of management.

As students we spend a great deal of time, effort and emotional energy on learning to design, only to find that on entering practice we are suddenly constrained by many different pressures and controls. Administration seems to be endless and managerial controls too restrictive. Frustration is immediate, not necessarily because there is less time to devote to design, but because we have inadequate grounding in the management of design activity. My own managerial skills were honed in architectural practice through experience (good and bad), combined with reading many books and articles on management, and, when time permitted, reflection on daily practice. At the time there were few publications that dealt with managing the complexities of design and/or creative architectural practices. Books aimed at architects were primarily concerned with the administration of individual projects, not with the management of creative staff, nor for that matter with the interrelationship between the project portfolio and the office – a situation that has changed little over the years. My aim was to write a book that would be pertinent, stimulating and above all useful for architects entering architectural practices, essentially the type of book that I would have welcomed when starting out. The approach taken is to address the synergy between the management of projects (Part One) and the management of design offices (Part Two). It is the interdependency of architects' and clients' businesses, represented in projects, which colours, shapes and determines the quality of our built environment. The premise is that to be successful we need to ensure that projects are managed professionally and are conceived and delivered within a professionally managed office. It is through effective management of the design office and the project portfolio that client values may be translated into construction with minimal loss of creativity.

This book has been a complex and lengthy undertaking, bringing together many, often disparate, areas under one set of covers. The ideas and concepts presented were first developed when I was working as a design manager in an architect's office and were subsequently refined through interaction with a wide variety of construction professionals in practice and academia. The academic environment has allowed time and space for the ideas to be researched, tested and developed further. Regular interaction and collaboration with practitioners and colleagues from the CIB's working group W096 Architectural Management has been insightful, enjoyable and stimulating, providing the incentive to push on with my work. I am also grateful for the opportunity to explore issues with practitioners, both through the professional Masters programme at the Technical University of Denmark (Management of Construction) and the professional doctorate programme at the Technical University of Eindhoven (Architectural Design Management Systems). It has made for a richer piece of work. A note of gratitude is also extended to Pamela for her patience and to the trustees of the Johan Hoffmann og Hustrus Mindefond, which provided the funding for my professorial chair at the Technical University of Denmark.

I am very conscious that the way in which architectural practices and projects are managed is heavily influenced by context and prevailing socio-economic conditions. There is no one best approach; no easy answer; no quick fix. Instead a lot of time and effort is required to build effective ways of working and demonstrate leadership. I encourage readers to take the issues presented here, think critically and apply and/or adapt them to suit their own, very special, context.

Stephen Emmitt

Chapter One
Creative Design Management

Architects play a pivotal role in the delivery of value to their clients, building users and community alike. The unique value architects add to their clients' lives and businesses is grounded in an ability to deliver something that their competitors cannot: design vision. Design ability is, however, not enough in a highly competitive market, as clients seek professionals who can provide a professionally managed service, effectively and quickly. This means that architects, like their competitors, need a thorough understanding of business and the leadership skills to develop new capacity and hence build a highly successful architectural practice.

The role and position of the architect have always been in transition, from early efforts to establish the profession to subsequent battles with other actors for influence over the quality of our built environment and market share. The architect's influence on our built environment has also tended to fluctuate over time as the fashion for different types of procurement has varied, and with it, architects' ability to control design quality and hence deliver value. In some cases architects have deliberately withdrawn from, or have been pushed out of, the construction process, providing design-only services. Here, the architect's influence over the design as it progresses through the various stages to a completed building may be negligible, as others with different objectives exert control and take decisions that can impact on the value, performance and image of the completed building. At the other end of the spectrum architectural practices have taken full control, managing design activities throughout the entire life of the project, from inception to completion (and often beyond into facilities management). In this business model quality is delivered through single point responsibility and the architect has a direct and continual interaction with the building sponsor. In between these two extremes there are many varied approaches to architectural practice, some of which prove to be more suitable, and hence more successful and profitable, than others.

The stereotypical view is that creative designers lie outside the bounds of managerial control. It is a convenient image for some to hide behind, but the reality is that the majority of architects and fellow creatives appreciate sensitive and appropriate management. Creative people do not respond particularly well to tight control and the tick-box mentality of many management approaches. The problem appears to be less with the concept of management *per se* and more with the right sort of managerial frameworks.

Creativity is usually defined as the ability of individuals to make unusual connections between ideas and/or combine ideas in a unique way. This is a mental process that is influenced by the cultural and social environment in which it takes place. In the context of design management the cultural and social environment is the design office and its interaction with individual design projects. The office culture and the project culture are unique social groupings, which are shaped by leaders and managerial frames. The leadership style adopted by the design firm's owners will affect the individual's perception of autonomy. This influences the individual's intrinsic motivation and hence their creativity. Similarly, the leadership style of the project manager may also affect the motivation and hence creativity of project participants. At the individual level, creativity comprises three components (Figure 1.1):

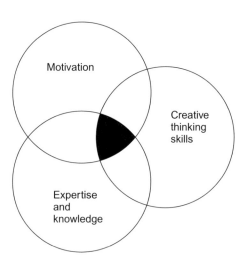

Figure 1.1 Creativity and the individual.

- *Motivation.* For architects intrinsic motivation is fundamental to creative work
- *Expertise and knowledge.* Design expertise and a wide range of technical and procedural knowledge
- *Creative thinking skills.* Highly developed in architects.

Creativity is not exclusively the product of individual action, but the interconnected actions of a community of people. This community of people is relatively stable within the design office, but more fluid within individual projects. Cultural and social influences include (Figure 1.2):

- Design office
- Clients
- Project culture
- Society.

The relationship between clients and architects is an extremely personal matter based on individual contact and personalised service. Management tools and techniques need to be sensitive and dynamic to allow for flexibility, individuality, intuition and creativity. Good management should support, not interfere with, the creation of stimulating architecture. Poor management will be time-consuming, inflexible and overly bureaucratic, and will detract from creativity – something that suppresses rather than generates, hinders rather than helps.

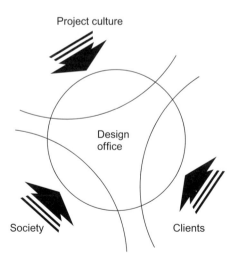

Figure 1.2 Cultural and social influences on creativity.

Design and its management

Architectural design decisions influence the artificial environment in which we live, work and play. Design is not about superficial styling or mere decoration; it is an expert activity that improves the usability, functionality and quality of the built environment, i.e. design adds value to our daily lives. Design is also a collective effort based on degrees of compromise and commitment, combining the skills and knowledge of a wide range of individuals to provide creative solutions to poorly defined problems. Problem-framing and problem-solving activities need to be undertaken within some form of framework, which is known as the design process. The design process is a series of iterative events undertaken by the design team to identify the nature of the problem, develop appropriate solutions and transfer the solution from the collective mind of the design team to those able to realise the design in a physical form. Design is a complex activity undertaken in close cooperation with many other professionals as part of a web of relationships we tend to refer to as a project team.

Design is difficult to explain in terms of value and also difficult to explain from a methodological stance. The purpose of this book is not to describe how designers design, or for that matter to try and define design. The aim is to address the managerial frames in which design activity is enabled and delivered. The starting point is that architects bring creativity and professionalism to projects, interacting with a wide variety of specialists who also contribute to the shaping and reali-sation of the design. Although the act of designing is a highly creative, intellectual, stimulating and personal process, it should be recognised that an increasing number of people affect the final design outcome. Architects remain the primary input to design, with engineers, tech-nologists and technicians contributing with specialist technical knowl-edge. Building product manufacturers and specialist contractors also make a significant contribution, bringing knowledge of production, assembly and construction to the design. Recognising that these 'designers' all have different values, objectives and motivation for real-ising the design in a particular way is a fundamental requirement for starting to manage design activities and hence control the outcome of the design process. Design is about discipline, flair and imagination. Architects pride themselves on their social responsibility for the built environment, putting people over and above profits.

Management

Management is a complex area and individuals must develop a wide range of skills and attributes to be effective in the workplace. The creative thinking skills encouraged in architectural education are also highly relevant to management. There is a growing recognition of the importance of people and a move away from production line thinking to more creative, dynamic and responsive approaches to management. The small but growing body of literature on creative management recognises the importance of creativity, culture, values and emotional intelligence (EQ), with a focus on people rather than systems. This softer approach has yet to find its way into the majority of construction project management literature. Techniques such as value management and relational forms of contracting are starting to become more widespread, although they are by no means universal. Integrated teams may be a better way of working and delivering value to clients, although this may not suit all contexts. Value-based management techniques are also being piloted and would appear to offer a more creative approach based on the ability of the actors to interact to the benefit of the process and the finished product.

Management is concerned with leadership and taking action. Creative management is less concerned with systems and procedures, more with individuals and their ability to apply their knowledge, skills and competences efficiently. Good managers know how to work with people and systems; they understand the importance of getting the right people for the required work, getting everything in place before work starts and providing appropriate leadership. Managers are concerned with designing appropriate operating frames that encourage innovation and creativity and applying sufficient resources to keep it all together. In service industries emphasis is on providing value for the customer and exceeding their expectations. The construction sector is not homogenous; it is a fluid and dynamic collection of specialists with temporary groupings of individuals and organisations. Many suppliers work across different sectors; for example the manufacturers of an energy-saving paint also produce skin products for the cosmetic industry. With a few exceptions of repeat building types and clients with very large property portfolios there are no established supply chains, unlike for example the car industry, and to apply the machine metaphor of lean production to the design and production of buildings may be misleading and inappropriate in many cases. Construction is also 'special' in that techniques applied elsewhere do not readily transfer to design and construction processes, which, despite the amount of off-site prefabrication, remain dependent upon site-specific conditions. There will always be a constant and creative tension between the design and production of buildings as the project team strives to deliver value.

Design management

Outside the architectural literature the term design management is used quite specifically to deal with the management of only the design element of a project, after which project management takes over. In this book the emphasis is on the management of design throughout the life cycle of projects and the relationship of projects to the professional design office. The term design management is used to encompass a wide range of activities, including project management functions and professional service firm management. A lot of the 'design management' literature is concerned with managing the production, creation and use of information. From the contractor's perspective information is the main concern since much of the design is codified in the contract drawings, schedules and specifications. Thus design management is often another term to describe an information management and coordination function. From the architect's perspective the main concern is in making sure that the enormous effort put into creating an exciting design is represented within the contract information.

Design management has been evolving since the 1960s as architects, engineers and contractors have sought to better understand the design process and the interdependency of the organisations and individuals contributing to construction projects. In 1964, chartered architects Brunton, Baden Hellard and Boobyer published a seminal work *Management Applied to Architectural Practice* (see Appendix 3), in which they highlighted the link between the successful management of the design office and the management of individual projects. They did not use the term design management; instead 'job management' was used to cover the management of individual projects and 'office management' to cover the management of the business (the main focus of their book). The term 'architectural management' was used to represent the synergy between the management of the office and individual projects. It is the synergy between individual projects and the design office that affects the health of an architectural business and thus the ability of architects to contribute to the quality of our built environment. More specifically it is the effectiveness of the relationship between clients and architects that is fundamental to the creation and delivery of exciting architecture (Figure 1.3). Engagement with the sponsors of building projects allows for the discussion of goals, opportunities, risks, values and business culture; the closer the interaction between the design office and the client, the better the understanding.

It is the tension between the decisions made within the office and those made at the individual project level that makes design man-

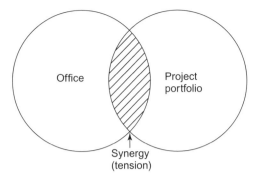

Figure 1.3 Synergy between office and project.

agement such a fascinating and challenging activity. Creative tension can help to stimulate innovation in product and process and fuel a proactive approach; conversely destructive tension can lead to a reactive 'fire fighting' mentality, which is not good for the health of those involved.

Managing creative projects

Building design and construction is a multimillion pound business, requiring the coordination of technological, design and management expertise to realise projects. Even the most simple construction project will require a small army of people to guide it from inception and development through to successful completion. Projects are temporary events that have an often poorly defined start and, by comparison, a clearly defined finish. The aim of a project is to bring about change; for example, in the case of a building project the change will be related to the physical appearance of the site and its use. Projects have a distinct characteristic; every one is unique. Every project differs from its neighbour to a lesser or greater extent. For architectural practices working on a mixed client and building portfolio, projects may differ greatly. For those that work for a limited number of clients with repeat building types the differences are much less, but the projects are still unique, partly due to the unique nature of the site and partly due to the actors that make up the project team. Construction project teams are most commonly set up for the life of a project and disbanded on successful completion of the building (or at specific stages of some large and complex projects). This creates new relationships for each project and provides the project manager with the immediate challenge of team building and establishing open communications between the project participants as quickly as possible. Further challenges relate to the timely exchange of accurate information and managing the web of interrelated and interdependent activities necessary to achieve project completion.

Project delivery objectives are primarily concerned with meeting time, cost and quality parameters. Project management literature has not managed to address the wider issues related to the life cycle of the building, which requires a much longer and arguably a different perspective to that afforded by project management tools and techniques. More recently attention has focused on maximising the project value, while at the same time reducing the cost of the work through the application of value management and value engineering techniques. The majority of projects are delivered on time, to budget and to defined quality levels, with problems dealt with quickly and efficiently as they arise through the lifeline of the project. Still, too many projects are haunted by poor communication, lack of coordination, inadequate and incorrect information, waste and hence failure to deliver value to the customer.

Emphasis on the process and the product has led to significant interest in product development techniques used in other industrial sectors. Product development encompasses the complete product life cycle, from inception through to after-sales service and marketing and is most commonly associated with mass-produced products. However, it is important to note that manufacturing processes are not projects (manufacturing a brick or a window is a process, not a project), and so care needs to be taken when trying to transfer process management techniques to a project environment. Although many buildings are bespoke and thus differ from their neighbours, the design and realisation processes can be modelled, regardless of the degree of repetition, as a generic framework (see Chapter 2). Design management is an evolving field in which the word design is interpreted widely to encompass the contribution of all designers, e.g. architects, engineers, technologists, technicians, product/component manufacturers, main contractor, sub-contractors, artisans and specialist suppliers. The creation and sharing of values is seen as key to the successful development, communication and implementation of design intent. Similarly, the measurement of performance should be an integral part of the design development process. Effective and transparent measurement can help to provide insights into the actual effectiveness of the processes used and is essential to the continual improvement of such processes.

Integration of design and construction activities can achieve significant benefits for all project stakeholders. Improvements in the quality of the service provided and the quality of the completed project, reduced programme duration, reduced costs, improved value and improved profits are some of the benefits. Traditional procurement practices are known to perpetuate adversarial behaviour and tend to have a negative impact on the product development process and hence the project outcomes. Focus has tended to be on limiting exposure to risk and avoiding blame, at the expense of creativity and innovation. The creation and maintenance of dynamic and integrated teams is a challenge in such a risk averse environment. Fostering collaboration and learning within the project-frame requires a more integrated approach in which all stakeholders accept responsibility for their collective actions. Project partnering is one approach that can help to bring the actors together, when combined with value-management techniques. Using new technologies and new approaches, such as off-site production, is another approach that significantly changes relationships.

Managing creative offices

In contrast to the management of projects, much less has been written about the management of design organisations and their symbiotic relationship with the construction sector. Architectural, engineering and surveying practices are project-driven organisations. They are dependent on the sponsors of construction projects for their existence and profitability: no projects, no business. Dependence on the building sponsors may be direct when the client engages an architectural practice, or it may be indirect, for example when the architects are employed by a contractor on a design and build scheme. Achieving synergy between the management of the design office and of individual projects is crucial to ensure a healthy business. The design office will be concerned with two interdependent issues:

♦ Design control within the office
♦ Design control within multiple projects.

Balancing the inspirational (esoteric, eccentric and fragile) world of design with the ordered (pragmatic, sober and robust) world of management is the intrigue of the architectural office. Management and design functions need to be integrated, yet also separated for operational purposes. Space must be provided for creativity, subtlety and quality of design, delivered professionally to consistently high standards within a managerial framework. As competitive pressures increase, so does the pressure to plan design work efficiently and administer projects competently. Due to its unique characteristics design needs to be managed in a particular way if creativity is to be encouraged and the client's requirements successfully delivered. The manner in which design is managed has far-reaching implications for the competitiveness of an architectural firm and indirectly for the profitability of others involved in the temporary coalition of the construction project team. The context in which designers work must be understood before it can be managed effectively. Designers should operate within normal managerial constraints; however, research and experience indicate that few are capable of constraining their creative pursuits. The problem stems from the design studio where architectural students rarely experience any time controls or budgetary limits on their creative endeavours. But to managers, design is just another resource and needs to be managed to ensure the profitability of the firm; there is clearly a difference in culture between designers and managers. As with business, the difference between good and excellent design is in the detail – small but important differences. Successful firms are committed to 'super pleasing' their clients through the provision of good design, technical expertise, delivery to programme and to budget; successful firms have clear business objectives through a balance of design, technology and management. Those who are over-enthusiastic about design (at the expense of the other elements) make design an end in itself – design for design's sake. The act of designing can be both intoxicating and addictive, but design is not the only differentiating factor when clients are making their choice of consultants. Clients require confidence in the control of costs, time and quality. This requires professional management skills and consistent quality of the information produced and the quality of the service provided.

Management of the firm is concerned with the management of people, physical space and finances. The working environment of the office, the organisational culture, will be determined by the interaction of the social characteristics of the staff employed, and the financial management of the business will create the character, or culture, of the firm – a unique culture that will directly affect the manner in which individual jobs are administered. The blood that runs through the veins of individual projects also runs through the veins of the firm. The culture of the firm, the manner in which it deals with individual jobs, staff and clients, will be unique to that organisation; whether the design-orientated professional service firm primarily comprises architects, architectural technologists or building surveyors in many respects is not important. The important point is to *design* the firm's culture, a process that demands as much care and skill as any building design; the firm must be capable of learning and adapting to changing circumstances and thus its management structure must also be adaptive.

Interdependent themes

The demand for better value from clients has resulted in the need for more efficient operating methods within the project team and the organisations contributing to them. There is no one best approach to the management of design projects or the management of professional design offices. Context is a crucial determinant, as is choice of appropriate processes, methods and tools. It is important to explore a number of potential approaches before deciding on the most appropriate 'fit' for organisations and temporary project organisations. The way in which people interact within the project environment and with their colleagues in their respective organisations will have a major influence on the success of individual projects and the profitability of the participating organisations. This is common to all projects, regardless of the managerial and contractual frames employed. This 'space' between organisations and the individuals working within them will influence the interaction practices and hence the effectiveness of individual project outcomes. This interdependency and associated uncertainty of relationships and position within projects helps to contribute to a dynamic and exciting environment. It also means that some effort is required in trying to map and then manage such relationships to the benefit of clients' projects and design office profitability. Underlying and interdependent themes are introduced here and addressed in more detail, both explicitly and implicitly, in the book.

Value

The prime goal of a project is to deliver maximum value for the customer, while making a reasonable profit on the resources invested. Architects play a pivotal role in helping to interpret the client's aspirations and create value through design, with other actors adding value through related services. Value is what an individual or organisation places on a process and the outcome of that process, in this case a building project and the resultant building. This is often related to price (e.g. value for money), although other factors relating to utility, aesthetics, cultural significance and market are also relevant. Values are our core beliefs, morals and ideals, which are reflected in our attitude and behaviour and shaped through our social relations. Our values are not absolute, existing only in relation to the values held by others and as such in constant transformation. In design and construction projects the management of value is dealt with through value management and value engineering activities. Value-based management uses face-to-face workshops as a tool to allow actors to discuss, explore and agree to commonly held values, often expressed in a written document as a set of value parameters and prioritised in order of importance to the project team. Working with shared values is a fundamental principle behind philosophies such as partnering and other forms of relational contracting.

Quality

Clients pay for, and expect, a consistent quality of service from their consultants. Clients also expect a finished building to meet predetermined and specified standards of quality. Depending on the contractual arrangements entered into, some issues of quality will be determined directly by the architect, but much is indirect. Quality, like value, is difficult to define and is usually negotiated with project stakeholders and subsequently confirmed in the brief and the written specification. Design quality cannot be achieved merely through the setting and achievement of technical specifications; it is also determined by the way in which people act (creating and solving problems as the work proceeds) and the manner in which quality controls are applied at various stages during that work.

Achieving high quality involves the use of appropriate systems and, most importantly, the right people: people with a commitment to quality (which is not to be confused with motivation). The philosophy is to design a building that can easily be materialised in a process where problems and challenges have been anticipated and actions taken to eliminate them. This is known as the zero defect approach and requires that actors/organisations:

- Commit to a continual search for improvement
- Resource activities in such a way that people feel valued and are thus encouraged to contribute to improvements.

Known as total quality management (TQM), the number one priority is customer satisfaction. Concurrent with this is the ability to see the process as an integral whole (not just a series of individual activities or steps) and to recognise the link between these activities (processes) and the end result (the product). This is also known as process-orientated thinking. Following a TQM philosophy, none of us should accept that the way we realise buildings is correct. We should be asking, 'Can it be done differently?' This means change (both incremental and radical), which is realised by empowered workers and effective leadership based on a clear purpose; it also implies measurement of performance and continual learning.

A lean philosophy

The lean thinking philosophy has also developed from manufacturing processes and there is growing application of the philosophy and tools to construction. Much of the literature on lean manufacturing and production is grounded in earlier quality management work, as are many of the tools used to minimise waste and maximise value for the end customer. One argument is that many of the lean tools applied to manufacturing processes are less applicable to service industries and project-orientated sectors such as construction. In some respects this may be true, but the development of the lean construction literature has shown that lean tools can be successfully used, sometimes with modification, in a construction project context. The same is true of the design process and the notion of lean design management (as something distinct from design management) has started to be discussed and applied in a small number of cases.

The lean philosophy of reducing waste by getting everything right before work starts is a good one, assuming the context is adequately addressed. Architectural businesses need to be designed to maximise the value of their resources and reduce waste in their processes to stay competitive. Similarly, projects need to be designed to maximise the value of the resources invested and reduce waste within the supply chains. This means that a lean approach should be taken to both:

- Management of the design office
- Management of the project portfolio.

For lean projects to be implemented successfully the participating organisations must use lean ideals and tools within their organisation. Most of the work relating to the application of lean thinking to construction has been focused on site-based construction activities and factory-based lean production of building components; there has been little recognition of the importance of lean organisations. The philosophy of eliminating waste and maximising value must be applied to the processes within organisations too.

Communication

The efficacy of the project and the financial health of the design business will be affected by the way in which individuals communicate. Communication involves the use of the most appropriate communication technologies, such as project websites, and the assembly of organisations and people who are able to communicate effectively. Interpersonal communication is required for effective team-building and the undertaking of daily tasks.

The management of project communications will come under the remit of the project manager. The management of information and communications within the office will come under the remit of the design manager. Organisations have control over the type of people who make up the office culture. New staff can be selected not just on their technical ability, but also on their ability to fit into the existing social system of the office, i.e. their ability to communicate with their colleagues. In a project environment the composition of organisations and hence individuals will be undertaken by the project manager; thus relationships are imposed on (sometimes reluctant) individuals. There is an old saying that you can choose your friends but not your family, and there is certainly some truth in this in construction projects. It is quite likely that we may find ourselves interacting with individuals in other organisations that we do not like, find difficult to trust and/or struggle to communicate with. Value management techniques and partnering initiatives seek to address this through careful selection of actors and team-building exercises. Working with competitive tendering may carry a higher risk of incompatibility within the project team, although this can be mitigated through preselection procedures.

Integrated teams

Information technology (IT) has transformed the way in which we design, manufacture and use buildings. Improvements in the visualisation of designs and communication between the participants have also helped to provide a better understanding of the management of intricate processes through process modelling. In particular, the development of IT and information communication technology (ICT), such as project websites, has made it easier to work as part of a virtual team from remote locations. Integrated design, supply and production processes are facilitated by cooperative interdisciplinary working arrangements. Integrated teams encompass the skills, knowledge and experience of a wide range of specialists, often working together as a virtual team from different physical locations. Multidisciplinary teams may be formed for one project only, or formed to work on consecutive projects. Although there has been a move towards more collaborative working arrangements based on the philosophy of project partnering and strategic alliances, it is difficult to see evidence of real integration; instead there are pockets of collaborative work within and between projects. Collaborative working may not suit all situations, and sometimes it is necessary or even desirable to work with a certain degree of separation.

For real integration to work there needs to be social parity between actors, which means that professional arrogance, stereotypical views of professionals and issues of status have to be put to one side. It also means that, in many cases, project teams need to be restructured and the project culture redefined through the early discussion of values. Management approaches such as value management and value-based management tend to encourage and promote integration by bringing together individuals in managed workshops and associated managed interaction. Creative clusters are another example of integration, although these tend to be set up primarily to tackle a particular problem, after which they are disbanded. Emphasis is on maximising the knowledge of the actors to the benefit of the project through improved interaction and communication. Knowledge transfer from one project to the next (and between concurrent projects) is crucial to the ongoing health of the design office. Learning from projects through feedback and constructive critical analysis is another fundamental component of good management and can be improved through integrated working.

Innovation

Innovation in projects is closely linked to the characteristics of the actors contributing to the project and the characteristics of the project and client. Similarly, the innovativeness of the architect's office will be influenced by the characteristics of the staff and the culture of the office in which they work, be it a physical or virtual office environment. Innovation will also be coloured through the interaction of office and project environment. Innovation means change, and the process of change needs to be carefully managed within the organisational setting and between projects. Project managers have a fundamental role to play in the establishment of the project culture and hence the innovativeness of the project team. Design managers also contribute to the innovativeness of their organisations, through the way in which they interact with external agencies and how work tasks are managed on a daily basis. The frameworks used to manage design activities and the amount of control exerted by managers will also influence the innovative climate of the office, i.e. whether innovation is encouraged or suppressed.

Trust

The concept of trust has become a topical issue in a sector renowned for its adversarial culture and general inability to trust others. As actors start to work in a more collaborative way, for example through partnering arrangements, the issue of transparency and trust takes on more significance. We have to trust the people that we work with and they have to trust us. This state is not achieved overnight;

the development of trust has to be earned and this usually takes a long time (and trust can be lost in an instant). Trust is not unlimited; we trust some people more than others and with different aspects of work and business. Trust is largely about our confidence to trust others' commitment, and commitment to shared project goals and values. So we do not trust an organisation *per se*; we trust the individuals working in the organisations with which we have contact on a regular basis. When actors fail to live up to expectations, trust starts to erode, and it is very difficult to regain the same degree of trust once it has been damaged. Once trust has gone there are two choices: either to fall back on systems and procedures for control or to cease the relationship. This means that some tough decisions may have to be made.

The development, learning, testing and reaffirmation of trust will require personal contact. Within the design office there is regular interaction between staff and the degree and levels of trust are usually well understood; indeed many architectural offices rely on trust and mutual respect in preference to rules and regulations to achieve their objectives. By contrast, management by trust is not easy to achieve in a project context. With people interacting only occasionally and holding different organisational values and objectives, the development of trust is far more challenging because people have little opportunity to get to know each other well enough to develop trust. This is why we have contracts.

- Within the office, trust will develop over time as relatively stable relationships are developed.
- Within the project environment, relationships are less stable and participants work in different organisations on a daily basis. Thus the opportunity to interact is less compared with the office. Thus trust is more difficult to develop.

Risk and uncertainty

Underlying all of these factors is the amount of risk an individual and their organisation is prepared to take. This is primarily related to the amount of uncertainty and risk tolerance of the individuals and their immediate managers. This is coloured by organisational culture and rituals as well as the interaction with a diverse range of project stakeholders, some of which will be more risk averse than others. Risks can be managed using a variety of risk management techniques and uncertainty can often be dealt with via clear communications and identification of roles and responsibilities. Risk management should be linked to value management.

Agenda

All organisations need to keep up to date with current management thinking and its application to everyday practice if they are to remain competitive. Management literature varies enormously in its scope, drawing on disparate fields such as labour economics, sociology, human resources and industrial psychology. Each of these interrelated fields helps to provide a set of lenses through which to view the world, but no one model or theory transfers easily to the professional service firm. Managerial principles and techniques applicable to industrial production or mass-consumer markets, based on standardised processes, products and repetitive tasks, may be inapplicable to multi-project-orientated businesses. Thus some adaptation is often required if ideas and tools are to be borrowed from other sectors. Management literature is also full of instant solutions to rather complex sociological problems. So we should not be too surprised when many 'new' approaches are found to be rather poor solutions when viewed with the benefit of hindsight.

The philosophy behind this book is that creative design management depends on two interrelated areas: the management of the creative organisation (practice management) and the management of creative projects (project management). Emphasis is primarily on the softer issues underpinning the management of design with a focus on how people behave within the design office and within the project environment. The argument is for better integration between creative organisations and creative projects through a better understanding of how we interact with others. As a starting point the book adopts the philosophy advocated by Brunton et al. (1964) (see Appendix 3) and explores the synergy between design offices and their project portfolios. In recognition of the distinction between design management in projects and design management within the design office the book is presented in two interdependent parts. The first part of the book looks at the management of design projects from the perspective of architects. The argument here is concerned with designing the most appropriate project culture to stimulate creative design and realise value in exciting and functional buildings. Chapters are organised by key stages in the life of projects with emphasis on how people interact within the project frame. The second part explores the management of the professional design office. The argument here is concerned with designing the most appropriate office culture and implementing flexible systems that allow creativity to flourish and the office members to enjoy the act of creating architecture. Although there is some degree of overlap between the two sections, each chapter concludes by looking at the synergy between project and office from the perspective of the design manager.

Projects and businesses require the right attitude, great leadership and passion for design excellence. Good management is about delegation, responsibility, ownership, vision and leadership. It is about common sense and a consistent approach to decision making and problem solving within a creative environment. It is also about taking informed decisions and enabling positive action in an ethical and professional manner. Creative design management puts creative people at the centre of the process. The principles and tools outlined in the chapters that follow aim to show that creative management can offer considerable benefits to all architectural businesses, regardless of size and market orientation. It is through a professional approach to management that design organisations are better positioned to make a positive input to building design and construction. Similarly, it is through creative design management that design excellence can be promoted and sustained from inception to completion, reuse and eventual disposal of the building.

Part One
Managing Creative Projects

Chapter Two
The Project Context

Design and construction teams are a loose grouping of interested parties brought together for a specific project. The team is composed of specialists operating in a disaggregated sector, each carrying different values and intentions to other team members. These individuals and groups enter and leave the project at different times, working towards individual and group goals in a temporary social system that for convenience we term the project team. Construction draws from many different disciplines, with many organisations also operating in other sectors, thus construction is not a particularly homogenous sector. Similarly, organisations are not as homogenous or stable as we would like to assume. Contractors tend to rely very heavily on sub-contracted and sub-sub-contracted labour. So do architects and engineers, outsourcing non-core activities to other professionals in an attempt to stay competitive. It would be misleading therefore to assume that the suppliers of sub-contracted labour share the same values as the main contractor. Similarly, it would be unreasonable to assume that the suppliers of sub-contracted work share the same values as the architects or engineers; they do not. Discussing and sharing values, with the aim of establishing common project values early in the project, is crucial to the successful development and delivery of projects. Recognising that differences of opinion may emerge as interests and values are developed and challenged, and hence values and priorities may change as the project proceeds, is also crucial. To recognise and respond to the values of others, and to align and reinforce the values of the project team, there is a need for effective communication skills.

The primary function of project management is to manage the project participants with the sole objective of completing the project to agreed targets. This means managing people with different professional backgrounds from different organisations; hence, the function crosses organisational boundaries. The architect's position in the project system and the extent to which they are able to influence design quality, and hence the value delivered to clients, are connected. There are no set recipes for achieving successful projects and great design; merely some approaches prove to be more effective than others for specific contexts.

It is evident that the philosophy and approach to the management of design projects varies between architectural offices. Some architectural offices adopt a relatively flexible approach to the management of individual projects, responding to the context creatively and flexibly. Although this may suit certain types of design office and projects, to the casual observer an emergent approach may appear rather chaotic and other project participants may be uncomfortable with the perceived lack of structure. Project management literature urges a standard approach to all projects in an attempt to ensure consistency for all contributors. Adopting a consistent approach to projects can help to provide clarity and certainty to projects, and is in line with TQM thinking. The danger lies in becoming too prescriptive; for example, some of the methods taken from industrial sectors that have a production line mentality represent the antithesis of creativity and are not popular with designers. Badly designed and implemented frameworks will not help the organisation to maximise its resources, nor will they help with the efficient delivery of creative projects. Individuals will work around the system to maintain working practices with which they feel comfortable. The challenge for managers is to find a model or approach that is consistent and applicable to the culture of the design office, and to which other project members can relate.

Understanding projects

Projects are a vehicle to deliver the client's requirements, and architectural projects are no different to projects in other settings; each is unique. Each project must be tailored to suit the individual requirements of the client and the context of the site, which will vary significantly between projects. Projects are characterised by the:

- Values of the client
- Values of the project team
- Values associated with the site.

The values of the client need to be explored and defined through a well-managed briefing process (see Chapter 4). The values of the project team are defined by the way in which the team is assembled

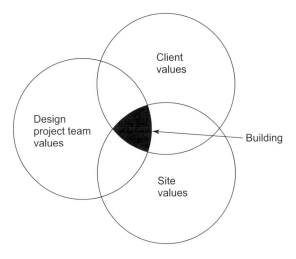

Figure 2.1 Architectural project values.

(individual values and competences), the procurement route used (which influences the attitude of actors) and the way in which the team is managed (which influences interaction). Figure 2.1 illustrates the interaction between client and project team values and the learning that takes place as values are explored and agreed. This is influenced by the experience of the client and of the project team, be it assembled for the first time or a relatively stable grouping of individuals and organisations. The values associated with each site also have a role to play – a complex mix of values associated with use, context and community. Together these values combine to make a unique formula for each architectural project.

Roles and responsibilities

The design manager and project manager roles may well be interchangeable within small organisations and small projects; however, it is becoming common to separate the roles into specific functions since different skills and abilities are required. Separation is identified in process models although the roles will be defined differently within organisations, sometimes varying to meet specific project requirements. In the context of this book the roles of the project manager and the design manager are defined as follows (see Figure 2.2):

♦ *Project managers* are responsible for the overall management of the project and are often employed directly by the client organisation. Their prime responsibility is the project.

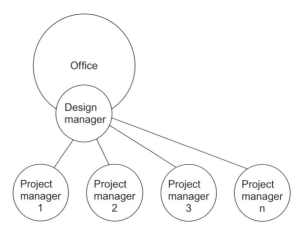

Figure 2.2 Design manager's relationship with project managers.

In simple terms, the project manager could be seen as an 'external' agent. Project managers are usually employed to work on one project at a time to ensure that it is delivered within agreed time, cost and quality parameters. This is a challenging role since the project manager usually has very little control over the organisations and individuals contributing to the project. The project management role is responsible for the smooth running of the project. This requires skill in coordinating the work of others.

♦ *Design managers* are employed directly by organisations to coordinate and manage design-related work. Their prime responsibility is the design. In simple terms, the design manager could be seen as an 'internal' agent, responsible for managing the office resources and coordinating design chain activities. The design manager will be responsible for a number of projects running concurrently within the office, all at different stages in their life cycle, i.e. he or she is concerned with multiproject management. The design manager is responsible for ensuring the realisation of design quality in the office and balancing the requirements of many projects. The design manager must earn the trust and respect of his or her architects, technologists and engineers working in the design office. Similarly, the design manager acts in an organisational boundary-spanning role, responsible for communicating with others, contributing to the design and through interaction building relationships based on trust and mutual respect. The design management role is crucial to the interface of projects and office environments.

Project management requires particular leadership skills and an understanding of a broad range of management techniques and systems. Many architects move into management roles as their career progresses, developing the appropriate managerial skills through experiential learning and educational/training programmes. The architect's ability to integrate disparate areas into a whole and maintain the overall vision helps to make many designers very good project managers, and project managers with a design background are highly valued.

The role of project manager is separate and distinct from the architect's traditional role and should not be confused with administering the project. Project management is concerned with the planning, coordination and control of complex, diverse and interrelated activities. The project manager role may be internal to the client organisation, provided by the lead consultant or provided as an external function (e.g. by a firm of project managers or architects).

Skills and attributes

The experience and personal characteristics of the project manager will have a significant impact on the development of the project culture. Emphasis should be on appointing the most appropriate project manager for the project. For example, a fast-track commercial project will need project managers with very different experience and skills sets from those managing sensitive refurbishment work. Successful project managers understand how participants interact during construction projects and how they communicate within the context of the construction team. Time spent on making and maintaining contacts is an effective strategy and is explored further in Chapter 3. Communication networks, the system architecture of the project, need to be designed with the same care as is expended on buildings. This involves implementing appropriate ICTs and trying to assemble the most suitable people for the project. These tasks should be undertaken as soon as practicably possible after a decision to engage in a project has been taken. In some situations it is possible to consider the system architecture before briefing starts, although it is more usual to do this concurrently with the early client briefing stages. It is also common to leave this until later in the process, which means that many of the connections are already made and the communication networks tend to develop organically, which may make the management of the system more challenging than it needs to be.

Leadership

Leadership is an emotive subject. For some authors it is the inter-relationship of a client's needs and the restrictions of the site that 'ensures' the position of building team leader to the architect, but recent trends have seen the leadership role pass to other management-orientated professions. Leadership is important, first because it is the most active link with the building sponsor, an important link if business opportunities are to be maximised. Leadership is also important in terms of delivering value through design, and consideration must be given to contractual arrangements that allow architects to control design quality rather than abrogate it to others. Leadership skills are particularly important in developing an effective communication culture throughout the project life. Projects represent a temporary overlap of authority and there may be rivalry for power within the project team, which is associated with the allocation of resources. People tend to remain loyal to their employer, not the project, which can cause difficulties for the project manager. Managers should have the experience, competence, ability and energy to:

- Provide appropriate, clear and consistent leadership
- Develop and maintain project values
- Compose and hold disparate groups together
- Develop empathy and establish appropriate extent of trust with all contributors
- Communicate effectively within and between different levels
- Design effective project communication structures
- Encourage interorganisational and intergroup communication
- Implement systems and tools that enable participants to collaborate effectively
- Arrange and chair meetings
- Develop relationships with informal leaders and organisational gatekeepers
- Map and facilitate value-chain activities
- Establish and develop the project attitude to risk and innovation
- Communicate and reinforce project goals, safety culture and quality standards
- Benchmark project performance
- Deal with crises quickly and openly
- Manage conflict to the benefit of the project
- Maintain an ethical approach
- Maintain and develop the project culture (avoid entropy)
- Provide regular opportunities for feedback and learning.

The importance of early decisions

Far too often projects are rushed into without adequate understanding of the importance of the early phases. Research in business management has consistently revealed weaknesses in the front end of poorly performing projects. This can be found in design and construction projects, with problems encountered in the realisation and use phases traced back to poor decisions early in the life of the project. The recipes for successful building projects appear to be related to the assembly of the most appropriate team and comprehensive briefing to determine project parameters. Here the creation, retention and realisation of the design vision throughout the life of a project are of paramount concern. Building sponsors must accept that too much haste in the early days of the project life may have severe consequences for the project. Architects, project managers and other key consultants must demonstrate the value to their clients of starting projects from a solid foundation.

Research findings and direct experience of practice show a strong correlation between successful projects and the time spent assembling the most appropriate people and organisations to work together collaboratively. Time invested early in the life of a project can make a significant impact on the future ability of the actors to interact efficiently and effectively. In some respects it is common sense, yet far too often projects are conceived and launched without pausing to think of the consequences. Sponsors of building projects may be reluctant to invest resources (money and time) in preliminary team composition when the likelihood of the project progressing is uncertain. Early discussion of values is a fundamental prerequisite, and this may be achieved by getting key actors together to explore possibilities and discuss preferences: an approach central to the partnering philosophy and lean production ethos. It follows that the person responsible for putting the team together and implementing managerial frameworks has a crucial role to play. Selecting the right project manager and design manager for a project is therefore a critical first step.

Design teams (in the widest sense of the term) bear a great deal of responsibility for the outcome of building, their collective decisions influencing the efficiency of realisation, project duration, cost and quality. Figure 2.3 represents the relationship between making decisions and the ability to influence cost over the life of the project. As the project progresses the ability of the design team to influence cost decreases relatively quickly. This curve is also representative of the ability of the design team to influence quality and project duration (by substituting these for cost in the figure). Thus detailed planning at the start of a project is essential to enable the design team to take full account of downstream activities. From this figure it is evident that as the project develops, the cost of design changes will increase. When designing to allow innovative techniques to be used by the contractor it is important that the contractor is involved early

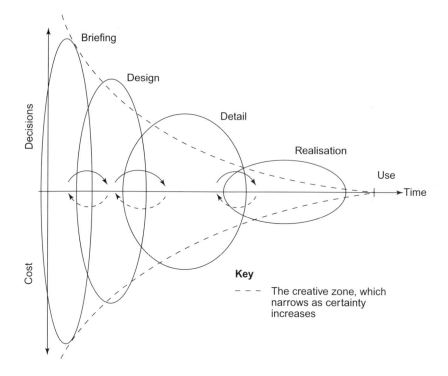

Figure 2.3 Duality of decision-making and the influence on cost.

and that the performance parameters are not set so tightly that the ability to innovate is negated.

Tasks must be completed by a set time, otherwise delays will occur, and so it is necessary to establish key milestones in projects for major decisions to be made and to set intermediate dates when the last responsible moment for decision-making can be made without adversely affecting the progress of work. Problems must be resolved if the building is to be completed within the scheduled duration, and problem solving is subject to the pressure of closure. Closure is defined as the desire for a definite answer to a question, issue or problem.

Project deliverables

Project management literature has identified three project deliverables that compete for attention and hence place a degree of tension in the system. These are cost, time and quality, represented in Figure 2.4. The theory is that placing emphasis on one project

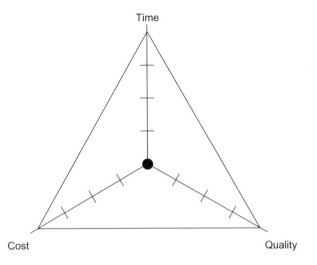

Figure 2.4 Project deliverables.

deliverable, e.g. time, can cause the other deliverables to suffer. This would equate to fast project, high cost and low quality. Of course, with adequate forward planning and excellent design and realisation teams, it is possible to deliver high quality buildings quickly and at reasonable cost. It is essential that the design manager takes a proactive role in relation to the development of the design within known cost limits.

Total project economy

Financial control of individual projects is paramount in the minds of clients and a natural focus of project management. Although financial control and monitoring is important throughout the project any decisions should be taken with due consideration for the building design. A cost-orientated project manager may be concerned with the project cost and not the implications for the cost of the building in use. Thus the design manger may have to argue strongly to retain the agreed design solution if pressure on time and/or cost starts to mount. One of the most unnerving aspects of the construction sector is the inability of the construction team to guarantee cost certainty. Given the number of professional advisers contributing to projects it is difficult to believe that so many projects are delivered late and are over budget. For the vast majority of building projects this is unacceptable. Advances in building technologies have allowed for a considerable amount of work to be completed away from the site, unaffected by the weather and problems with coordination of works packages. This has helped to increase cost certainty of major elements of the building, and in some cases the whole building. Greater attention to life-cycle costing has also helped to (re)emphasise the relationship between design decisions, cost and value.

Overall responsibility for cost control will rest with the project manager. Design managers contribute to project cost certainty through management of the design decisions made and encoded in project/contract documentation. Quality of decision-making and of the information produced is a fundamental requirement; if information is compatible and error-free there is less chance of rework and errors occurring during assembly. Clients want and often demand cost certainty. They do not trust contingencies funds and many clients have insisted on no contingencies monies. Computer software has also become more sophisticated, allowing instant costing of alternative design solutions. This is transparent for the client and other team members. Open, transparent and honest discussion and reporting of costs is a prerequisite of relational contracting-type agreements.

Total quality

A lot of work has been done in manufacturing to ensure processes are defect-free, thus ensuring a quality product each time. Such approaches are common with building product manufacturers, the vast majority of whom can guarantee their products satisfy a certain quality standard. Artisans would guarantee a similar level of assurance through application of their craft. Site work is more difficult to control and there is a very persuasive argument for moving production completely off-site. The current trend is for increased use of off-site assembly and a reduction in the number of operations undertaken on the site. Where high levels of prefabrication and off-site assembly are employed, there is less need for site operatives and with it a change in the type of management function required on the construction site. The site has become a place of assembly, with little need for complex management of site operatives trying to work with and around climatic variations. However, such an approach does not suit all building projects.

The time dimension

Time is the most precious resource and the one that no one ever appears to have enough of. No matter what the task, we would all like longer to complete it or to do it better. Time has an economic value, and for commercial concerns the sooner clients receive their building the greater the financial return. Similarly, building designers and builders able to minimise the amount of time required to assemble a building, from inception to occupancy by the client, have a competitive advantage over those who cannot: a service many clients are willing to pay a premium for. To do this requires extensive knowledge of design, manufacturing, assembly and managerial skills. Too many decisions are taken in haste on projects and subsequently turn out to have an undesirable effect on the finished building. The design manager must be able to protect the integrity of the design throughout the entire project. Ensuring that the project is well planned, well resourced and coordinated will go a long way to ensuring a happy client.

Procurement and influence

The procurement of design and construction services is paramount in the successful delivery of the client's goals and values. The client is not only faced with a variety of formal contractual routes from which to choose but also a wide variety of professionals from which to seek advice, all competing for the client's attention and apparently offering the best service. The initial choice of professionals will strongly influence the outcome of the project because of the social interactions set up. The lean philosophy of getting everything right at the start, before procurement routes are decided, should be noted here, i.e. getting the right people, the right communication networks, the right supply chains, the right culture and the most appropriate managerial framework. Clients need to consider a number of factors before a decision on procurement is made, ranging from timing and flexibility to make changes, through to risk management, cost certainty and liability.

The type of procurement system used will influence the manner in which the design and construction phases are organised, and hence how individuals interact and communicate through formal (and informal) communication channels. The type of system used will also dictate the responsibilities of the actors and their individual level of control over the process or parts of the process. In some respects the choice of procurement route is about control and power over the project, information flow, communication routes, decision-making and finance. There are four approaches:

♦ *Client-led relationships* are common on very small projects (e.g. house extensions and some self-build projects). The client appoints consultants and contractors to carry out specific works packages through separate contracts. Interaction between professionals and builders tends to be rather minimal.

◆ *Design-led relationships* are known commonly as 'traditional' systems of procurement. The client appoints an architectural practice to design and oversee the construction of the building. Contractors are usually selected through competitive tendering, with the lowest tender being selected, although it is possible to enter into negotiation with preselected contractors. In this relationship, the architect is responsible for putting the team together and managing the project.

◆ *Construction-led relationships* typically take the form of design and build (design and construct) contracts. Originally the contractor carried out the design work in-house and managed the construction of the building using directly employed labour. With the vast majority of main contractors now sub-contracting all of the work packages it is questionable whether or not this is a construction-led or management-led relationship. In this relationship architects are dependent on contractors for their business and may have little or no contact with the building sponsor. As sub-contracted suppliers of design services to the contractor, the architects may have rather limited control over the design during realisation and hence little influence over design changes and hence the overall quality of the completed building.

◆ *Management-led relationships* cover management contracting as well as design and manage. In this relationship there is no prime contractor; instead a manager oversees the integration of works packages. Architects in this relationship will supply a works package to the management contractors, sometimes referred to as design and manage. With increased use of prefabrication and off-site production, and a reduction in the number of activities and trades to manage on the site, this form of procurement may be attractive to a growing number of architects and building sponsors keen to improve design quality.

Attitude

Contracts are concerned with formal communication routes, ideal situations that few participants follow to the letter. Informal communication routes are required to make things run smoothly and are regularly used. Indeed, many actors may be quite ignorant of contractual arrangements until something goes wrong; they simply have a job to do. Although new contractual arrangements have been developed (and no doubt will continue to be developed), the construction sector still operates with different organisations (or different departments) dealing with specific tasks, hence actors have to communicate over organisational boundaries, and communication barriers may exist. The attitude of the building sponsor and the team assembled to deliver the project will influence the choice of procurement route. Attitudes towards adversarial or relational approaches and the willingness of the client to become involved in the project will affect the behaviour of the actors and the way in which they communicate. Concurrent working and fast-track construction also require a different attitude from the team members compared with more traditional approaches.

Project frameworks

Design and construction projects differ from one another in type, size, complexity, time and financial constraints as well as site-specific constraints. They also differ in terms of the actors involved in each project. Even with repeat clients and repeat projects the individuals involved are likely to differ from the project that went before. The differences between projects add to the excitement of managing projects, but they also help to demonstrate the need for a familiar framework to help guide actors towards the project goal. Architectural offices tend to use some form of standard approach to the management of projects, with procedures and protocols set out in an office or quality manual. Similarly, engineers and contractors use their own management frames, which can sometimes lead to compatibility problems when working together. Many of these models are formalised by the use of a quality management system which, if designed to suit a creative office culture, can be instrumental in helping architects and the collaborating partners to achieve consistent standards of service provision.

A number of well-known frameworks and models exist for the administration and management of projects, their suitability dependent on ensuring the best fit between project and office culture. Models represent a rational (and often prescriptive) approach, although the reality is that considerable flexibility is required in practice. Frameworks help to give a degree of formality to sub-sets of work and help to formalise the interface of work and workers. The formality of the framework is such that it is sufficiently understood by those contributing to the process to enable informal interactions within and around the frame, i.e. it is interpreted liberally. It can be misleading to put too much emphasis on the framework model. It is more important that everyone understands the project, roles and responsibilities and a simple

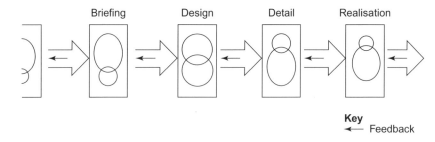

Figure 2.5 Simplified conceptual model.

graphical illustration of the project stages is a very effective way of achieving understanding (see Figure 2.5).

Managerial frameworks should facilitate design work, communication, knowledge-sharing and information flow. The process needs to be mapped and a suitable operating structure devised to manage the various activities in an efficient manner. It is a sensible policy to assemble the main actors, discuss how the project should be planned and agree on the most appropriate framework in which to work collaboratively (a bottom-up approach). This tends to be a more effective approach than implementing a system and expecting everyone to be comfortable with it (a top-down approach). From the perspective of the architects, the model must allow space for spontaneity and creativity. Frameworks should be customised to suit the project context and as a minimum should contain:

- ♦ Clearly defined stages, roles, tasks and responsibilities
- ♦ Value and risk management workshops at strategic intervals
- ♦ Project milestones
- ♦ Last responsible moment for decision-making
- ♦ Control gateways to coincide with the end/start of different phases
- ♦ Learning opportunities and feedback loops.

One of the best-known guides for managing design projects is the Royal Institute of British Architects (RIBA) Plan of Work. This was first developed in the early 1960s as a tool to help architects manage their projects; since then it has been revised to reflect changes in how we build. The guide continues to be used extensively by architectural firms and has parallels with guides produced by architectural bodies in other countries. The Plan of Work has been criticised (mainly by non-architects) as being a linear model that promotes a segmented approach to the management of projects. Although this may appear to be the case when read literally, it fails to recognise the way in which architects use the model. The Plan of Work provides a familiar guide that helps designers navigate their way through highly complex and interwoven activities. The guide is not followed strictly, since design activity requires constant iteration and reflection as the design work develops. A fluid approach is possible because of the guide, forming a backbone to decision-making and delivery of work to defined milestones.

The Plan of Work and similar frameworks give a formality to the process that is understood by other actors. The process is a number of sub-sets of formality (stages or phases) held together by a number of loose joints. It is the positioning and control of the joints that determine the framework of the work plan and the subsequent effectiveness of the process. The actors interpret formality differently, but there is enough common understanding to make the process work. Care is required when implementing new (unfamiliar) frameworks, as time is required for the actors to engage in communication and hence develop a common understanding. The main phases are the inception phase, the design phase, the detailing phase, the implementation phase and finally the post-occupancy phase.

Other models are also available that claim to be less linear, although these too break down functions into discrete work packages and/or areas of responsibility. Process models can help to illustrate, or model, a web of relatively complex activities under a generic framework applicable to all projects. These models are more suited to large and complex projects, and application to small projects may be unnecessary and inappropriate. Emphasis tends to be on integration of activities, concurrent development of work packages, knowledge transfer and change management. Value management and value-based management models are based on the discussion and agreement of values via facilitated workshops. Consensus and the creation of trust are fundamental components of these models. Workshops start with team assembly and continue to project completion and feedback. Workshops encourage open communication and knowledge-sharing while trying to respect and manage the chaotic nature of the design process. Cooperation, communication, knowledge-sharing and learning as a group help to contribute to the clarification and confirmation of project values. Getting to know fellow actors and the development of trusting relationships is an essential feature of the model. The model is suited to partnering-type arrangements and relies heavily on the skills of the process facilitator to drive the work forward.

Often the frameworks are implemented in a pure form, although it is also relatively common for architectural offices to take different elements from models to suit their work ethic. Flexibility and some degree of latitude for change are essential requirements of good frameworks. Allowing some tolerance between well-defined stages or works packages is a familiar and effective way of allowing for some degree of uncertainty. For example, buffer management techniques have proven to be successful in helping to manage the interface between different work packages.

Control gateways and learning opportunities

A feature of good design-management models is the inclusion of control gates (see Figure 2.6), alternatively referred to as approval or sign-off gateways and design reviews. These events bring key stake-holders together to discuss, agree, approve and 'sign-off' the project at key stages. For small to medium-sized projects these evaluation events are often arranged at the end of a RIBA stage. For larger projects the control gateways are also arranged within stages to reflect the approval of key works packages. The project plan should clearly identify when and why evaluation activities are to be held, and this should be reflected in the project programme. Evaluation of the project allows the project team to evaluate the progress of the project against specific targets set out in the project brief. Progress to the next stage should only be approved if the project is progressing as planned. Learning opportunities also need to be designed into the project programme; these are discussed in Chapter 8.

Effective use of meetings

Potentially one of the most effective mechanisms for ensuring pro-ductive communication is the forum of the meeting. Meetings are

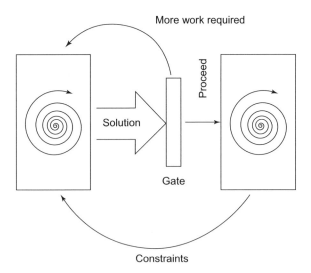

Figure 2.6 Control gateways and constraints.

held because people who have different jobs have to cooperate and communicate to accomplish tasks. Meetings provide a forum in which people can discuss issues face to face and reach mutual understanding, i.e. the interaction helps people to get things done. In addition to facilitating the exchange of information and decision-making activities, meetings are also used to:

♦ *Control*. Meetings allow managers to stay appraised of progress and in command of the tasks to be completed. They also allow those attending to follow up information requests, allocate scarce resources, agree action and set deadlines. All decisions should be recorded in the meeting minutes.
♦ *Coordinate*. Face-to-face discussion may help coordination of works packages and the clarification of roles and responsibilities. The aim is to ensure that adequate resources are allocated to allow operations to take place effectively and safely.
♦ *Appraise*. Meetings are used to appraise progress and the performance of organisations and individuals.
♦ *Bond*. Meetings fulfil a fundamental human need to communicate and bond, and hence help foster team relationships. They create a sense of belonging and reflect the collective and cultural values of the temporary project organisation. Meetings can also be used as a tool to help motivate the project team.
♦ *Resolve*. A timely meeting can help to resolve problems, differences of opinion, minor conflicts and disputes.

Meetings should not be considered as isolated events where decisions are made; instead they need to be seen in a wider context. This includes the incremental cycle of social interaction that is used to share and process information, make and confirm decisions and develop and maintain relationships. Many different types of meetings are convened during the project to serve a variety of complementary functions. These range from the informal to the formal and the impromptu to the strategically planned, the main ones being to:

♦ Start projects
♦ Build and maintain effective teams
♦ Explore values and agree value parameters
♦ Discuss and review designs
♦ Discuss project progress
♦ Resolve disagreements
♦ Exchange knowledge

◆ Close projects
◆ Hand over projects
◆ Analyse projects.

Whatever framework is chosen for a project it will involve a number of meetings, and these need to be planned to be effective. There is little point in holding a meeting for the sake of it; equally there is little point in holding a meeting without clear aims and objectives. The vast majority of us would readily complain that we have to attend too many meetings and hence we do not have sufficient time to do our work. This reaction is grounded in the reality that too many meetings are badly managed and coordinated, and hence wasteful of resources. When meetings are strategically planned (part of the project plan), well organised and appropriately directed they have been proven to be a major benefit to the progress of projects and the development of organisations.

Managers should also recognise that many decisions are made outside the meeting forum, either before people start the meeting, in discussions during refreshment breaks or after the closure of the meeting. These tend to be face-to-face discussions between two or three individuals anxious to reach consensus over a particular issue in order to present a united view and thus help avoid conflict later. Some managers will ensure that participants have adequate time to meet before the start of the meeting, for example by walking around the site to discuss progress, and that refreshment breaks are long enough to allow individuals to reach agreement over contentious issues.

Value and risk management

Value must be explored and clearly expressed as early as possible in the life of the project. Similarly the risks and uncertainty associated with the project must be identified and the consequences managed, otherwise value will be compromised. Value management techniques aim to articulate value for the project as perceived by the key project participants. Risk management techniques aim to identify risks and uncertainty and mitigate their adverse impact on the project. Value management and risk management are complementary activities that inform the design team, and should be incorporated into the project framework. Apart from helping to maximise value and minimise risks the techniques help participants to develop a deep understanding of the project and a sense of ownership. By working together the opportunity to develop the team culture and share knowledge through interpersonal interaction is also enhanced. Although it may be difficult

to quantify all of the benefits of integrating value and risk management within the project framework, it would appear that such efforts
are instrumental in determining project success.

Both value and risk management techniques rely on the interaction
of key project participants to discuss the value and risk associated
with the project at key stages, which is usually done in facilitated
workshops. The number of workshops will be determined by the size
and complexity of the project and the attitude of the key participants.
As a minimum, workshops should be held at the start of the project
(inception and client briefing), at the interface between design and
realisation, at commissioning and during use.

Value-based approaches

An essential feature of interaction between project participants is
the sharing of values, experiences and knowledge. Participating individuals and their organisations bring differing values, knowledge and
interests into the construction team and differences of opinion will
emerge as interests and values are developed and challenged. This
has been recognised in the value-based process models, which seek
to explore and agree values to aid team development and enable a
smoother process. Discussion and sharing of values is largely achieved
through face-to-face discussions within facilitated workshops. Agreed
values are then prioritised in a list of value parameters that forms the
basis of a partnering agreement.

Method

Some flexibility in programming may be required to accommodate
the inherent uncertainty in knowing exactly how many workshops will
be required to reach a consensus. When problems with understanding and attitudes exist, additional workshops are convened to help
explore the underlying values and tease out creative input. Bringing
people together and facilitating workshops is time-consuming and
expensive, but proven to be cost-effective over the life of the project.
The workshops are an essential tool to maximise value and to reach
agreement, which helps to reduce uncertainty in production, thus
reducing waste. Different cultures will exist from concept through to
production and the workshops provide a vehicle for addressing potential difficulties. Workshops can also be used to help select appropriate
consultants and sub-contractors based on the values they bring to
the project.

Workshops are value drivers and are concerned with problem-
framing and knowledge-sharing. Delivery of client value is achieved
between the workshops, where the problem-solving takes place. Design

alternatives that reflect the client's values are presented on the realism and criticism workshops. Project team meetings are used between the formal workshops to discuss and agree progress. A standard value agenda is used as a framework for decision-making in the workshops, and will include key areas of value, for example:

- Beauty
- Functionality
- Durability
- Suitability
- Sustainability
- Constructability.

This value hierarchy addresses the primary project objectives and breaks them down into further sub-objectives as part of an iterative process carried out within the workshops. Each area is explored until the value parameters have been mutually agreed using the value tree. Tools like quality function deployment (QFD) can also be used to weight options (values) in a decision matrix to help find the solution that provides the best value. A process facilitator guides participants through the discussion of values in a systematic and objective way.

Challenges and problems

The small amount of research collected from the field has revealed a poor understanding of the role of the design manager and of the skills required. It appears that the term 'design management' is rather all-encompassing and it is undertaken by a variety of individuals including architects, technologists, engineers, building surveyors, construction project managers and general managers. Inherent in the research find-ings is the observation that professionals with limited practical design experience do not make good design managers, simply because they find it difficult to empathise with the designers' milieu. Design man-agers must appreciate how designers design. They must possess the appropriate experience and skills necessary to lead the development of the design and ensure its successful realisation. This is a dynamic and interactive role requiring a love for design and the stamina to see good design implemented. Design managers must be able to balance the requirements of the project with those of their organisation. This involves a deep understanding of the client's needs, project goals and limitations. It also involves a thorough understanding of the design and construction environments so that value codified in design information is transferred from design to construction as seamlessly as possible without compromising design intent. Fundamental to the discipline is a clear definition of the organisation's mission and the mission of the temporary project team. A good design manager should be concentrating on realising the potential of those being managed and at the same time removing the fear and stress that often arise through poor management and working to unachievable deadlines. Workflow must be continuous and not obstructed by inefficient communication or unnecessary bureaucratic barriers.

All projects, no matter how well designed and planned, encounter problems during their life span. Many problems are trivial and easily resolved; however, some may have serious implications if not dealt with quickly and professionally. Inconsistent management processes, including poor planning procedures, inadequate design reviews, problems with resource allocation and poor quality of information, are common complaints of project teams. The inability to coordinate design information can lead directly to increased construction costs, unnecessary changes to the design, rework and programme overruns. This may have a detrimental effect on the success of the project and the profitability of those contributing to the project. Problems that arise in the design office are usually easy to deal with in-house before they affect other project members. Problems that arise outside the design office may be more challenging to deal with and will require a high degree of tact, diplomacy and strong leadership skills. The ability to deal with unexpected problems effectively and clearly communicate decisions are fundamental skills of the project manager. Such skills must also be underwritten by a clear understanding of the client's and designer's intentions: failure to communicate these to other actors may lead to compromise of the quality of the finished product, which has long-term implications for the user. Problem identification and resolution are affected by the framework used, the formal mechanisms for dealing with disputes, the legal contract and the attitude of actors involved and their organisations. Many problems are rooted in the early team assembly stages and briefing.

The project to office interface

Successful design organisations are good at establishing a synergistic relationship between the office and the individual projects that fuel it. Projects appear to 'fit' the organisational culture of the office, and the subsequent development of projects helps to grow the organisational knowledge and business acumen of the office. Project management is a natural vehicle through which to deliver a quality service. It should be seen as an extension of the marketing activity since it involves close contact with clients. Similarly, the manner in which design activity is managed within individual projects will have a significant impact on the effectiveness of the design office as a whole. Consistently delivering good-quality design information on time will help to enhance the reputation of the practice and should help in acquiring new commissions.

Consideration must be given to the link with the client and the likely effectiveness of communications within the project team. Architects need to demonstrate the value of architectural knowledge and explain their services to clients. This is much easier to achieve if the project manager role is integral to architectural practice. Choice of procurement route will determine the formal communication routes, power relationships, roles and responsibilities, decision-making and hence design quality. Worldwide, architects have withdrawn from, or have been pushed out of, this crucial area. From a business viewpoint detachment from the client is potentially disastrous, because design practices must rely on others for their work (which is likely to be for design services only). The architectural office's 'client' is the client's representative, not the sponsor of the building project. Detachment from the client is also problematic when it comes to developing a comprehensive brief.

All projects have to be resourced adequately by the design office. On the surface, this may appear a relatively straightforward activity. However, even when clear dates and budget have been agreed it can be a challenge for the design manager to resource the project given the capacity of the design office and the demands of other projects. It is unusual for a professional design office to work on one project at a time and complete it before starting on another. Normally many projects are running concurrently, all at different stages of completion and all with context-specific characteristics. This provides a challenge for the effective management of resources within the office, but also creates a dynamic environment in which knowledge is created and shared. Value of time in relation to the decision-making that occurs during the project must be understood if programming is to be effective. The history of past projects can help to establish the amount of time required for similar projects, thus helping the design manager to match resources to the project portfolio.

Chapter Three
The System Architecture

Effectiveness of communication is a significant factor in the successful completion of projects. Over the years a number of government-led reports have consistently drawn attention to the difficulties caused by the organisational systems in which construction teams operate. More recently concepts such as integrated teamworking, project partnering and strategic partnerships have become fashionable in response to the criticism. The inadequacies reported seem to stem from poor interaction practices during the life of the project. Interaction affects the strength of relationships between the actors and ultimately colours their ability to transfer knowledge and appropriate task-based information to complete projects successfully. Teambuilding, the discussion and subsequent sharing of values, resolution of minor differences and conflicts, question asking and the creation of trust between construction team members are just a few of the factors that are crucial to the smooth running of projects and are reliant on the ability of the actors to communicate effectively and efficiently. It follows that the interaction of individuals and organisations should be the primary concern of those charged with managing projects.

It is in the early stages of a project that the majority of opportunities are generated (or lost) and the risks minimised (or generated). Early decisions also influence the health and safety culture, attitude to quality, and social and economic conditions that are subsequently infused within the project. Studies have shown that investing in early teambuilding can be beneficial to the smooth running and successful completion of projects, with the time and effort invested upfront recouped as the project progresses to completion. The establishment of the project team is an area most associated with the project manager, although design managers also have a role to play since the system architecture of projects will contribute to the design agenda. Building the project's system architecture is a highly complex undertaking, requiring an understanding of interpersonal communication traits and an appreciation of how groups and teams function effectively. Research on professional interaction in live construction projects has found that communication does not always follow formal channels. Professionals pursue social structures that benefit the individual organisation, i.e. they will use informal communication routes to achieve their objectives.

Communicating to achieve project objectives

Construction projects are undertaken in a dynamic social system; nothing is particularly stable for very long and uncertainty and interdependence are constant factors of all construction projects, regardless of size or complexity. Projects are not hermetically sealed or static; they are dynamic, temporary groupings of individuals and organisations. Contributors have different degrees of influence over the project outcome and vary in the amount, type and timing of their contribution to the project. It is this dynamic interaction of the various actors to a construction project that constitutes a process of communication. Effectiveness of communications will have a major effect on the project outcomes and hence will affect the profitability of the organisations contributing to the project. Without effective communications it is unlikely that the participants will succeed in realising the project objectives. The word communication in the majority of the communication literature means the sharing of meaning to reach a mutual understanding and to gain a response. This involves some form of interaction between sender and receiver of the message via synchronous and/or asynchronous communication:

♦ *Synchronous communication* involves team members communicating at the same time through face-to-face dialogue and interaction in meetings, telephone conversations and video conferencing.
♦ *Asynchronous communication* is the term used when parties do not communicate at the same time, e.g. by email and through intranets, by post and facsimile. Messages are sent and responded to later, and this can be a quick and highly effective way of exchanging information.

The creation of meaning between two or more people at its most basic is an intention to have one's informative intention recognised. Simply informing someone by any action that information is to be disclosed is considered to be an act of communication. There are many ways in which people make their introduction and let others know information is about to be disclosed, or by their non-verbal actions set a context for discussion. The message and clues can be very subtle but still convey considerable information to the receiver of the message. When people communicate they intend to alter the cognitive environment of the persons whom they are addressing. As a result, it is expected that the receiver's thought process will be altered. Communication performs much more complex tasks than simply letting someone know that we are about to send information. For understanding to take place most theorists claim that a background of shared social reality needs to exist. To engage in meaningful communication we need to build on information and develop a context supported by cues and clues. These guide us to use sub-sets of knowledge and help us to link information together. Clues used come in many different guises. The appropriate mode of referring to something or someone in conversation depends on what common ground a speaker and addressee share. It is this common ground and the development of a shared understanding that make communication possible. Similarly, a lack of common areas of understanding can create difficulties in communication and lead to misunderstanding.

Communication in any group has social and task dimensions. Task roles are those that determine the selection and definition of common goals, and the working towards solutions to those goals, whereas socio-emotional roles focus on the development and maintenance of personal relationships among group members. Open and supportive communication is conducive to building trust and facilitating interaction between project members. Unfortunately, when communication between team members is most needed, during times of uncertainty and crisis, relationships often break down through the development of defensive behaviour and hence ineffective communication. Open exchanges of information and sharing task responsibilities are essential for effective teamwork. Interaction that builds and maintains the fragile professional relationships necessary to accomplish tasks is fundamental to project success.

Face-to-face interaction is essential for addressing contentious issues, problem solving, conflict resolution and building relationships. Improvements in the effectiveness of communication between individuals and groups can help to increase the performance of individual organisations and hence that of the project. Poor communication is the root cause of many problems in building projects (see Appendix 1). Poor communication, lack of consultation and inadequate feedback are among the primary causes of construction defects. Research has also shown that the most important skills for a project manager are communication and listening skills followed by the ability to negotiate, influence and persuade. Best practice in construction teams is characterised by open exchanges of information and good communication, enabling responsibilities and ownership of tasks to be negotiated and shared.

Interfaces and language

There is a need for effective communication on two levels: intra-organisational (within organisations) and interorganisational (between organisations). Organisational and cultural boundaries within construction projects are constantly changing; individuals enter and leave the team at certain stages (i.e. they have separate goals) and the team changes in size and format. It is at boundary conditions that individuals may well use different language to express themselves. Obvious cultural boundaries are the interfaces between client and brief-taker; brief-taker and design team; design team and contractor; and contractor and sub-contractors. Other more subtle boundaries, for example between architects and engineers, also exist. In many cases the interface is effective and projects progress well, delivering a building that satisfies both client and end users; conversely, interaction difficulties are experienced and may quickly spiral out of control into a dispute.

Professionals have developed specialist languages, using words that are specific to their professional background to enable them to communicate specific facts and ideas quickly to fellow professionals. This professional jargon is a codified language that is difficult to understand for those lying outside the professional culture. Use of certain words or phrases may lead to confusion if not supported with sufficient background information and explanation. Some words will carry more meaning and information when used in a specific context and when exchanged with actors who share the same language. Confusion can also arise when workers from different parts of the UK use different words for the same thing and regional dialects offer the potential for further misunderstanding. Add in the increasing migration of construction workers in Europe and it is not uncommon to find construction sites with a multinational workforce using their native tongues to communicate. The potential for misunderstanding is never too far from the surface in such environments, even where everyone's intention is to do a good job.

The project communications infrastructure

All actors need to collaborate, share, collate and integrate significant amounts of information and knowledge to realise project objectives. To do this well requires a combination of good management, committed people, supporting ICT networks and the opportunity to regularly communicate on a face-to-face basis. Many of the problems inherent in construction have been attributed to the separation of the design and realisation teams. The rapid development of ICTs provides the technology to work in a more integral manner. In architecture the increasing sophistication of technologies and computer-aided manufacturing has allowed more exciting designs and in some cases a redefinition of how buildings are procured. Current emphasis is firmly on digital information and improved communications through project web technologies, which provide a tool for better exchange of information between project participants. Care is required when planning and implementing ICTs to ensure that the system(s) meet the needs of the users. The use of new technologies does not necessarily ensure better performance, especially when the fit between the system and the people is not adequate. The interpersonal, often informal, communication that forms the glue between individuals and organisations is also crucial. The dominant factor is the temporary interaction of people and our collective ability to use communication media effectively in dynamic situations. It is the social life of construction projects, the formal and informal relationships that help and sometimes hinder the delivery of a successful project.

One lesson that can be learned from lean manufacturing is the importance of getting everything right before production commences. Lean manufacturing aims to eliminate waste at all stages in the product life cycle, thus helping to enhance value for the customer. Other approaches such as 'total design' have similar aims, although they use different terminology. When applying the lean philosophy to the design and realisation of buildings, it is a fundamental requirement of the project that the main actors are identified and some attention is given to their ability to interact to the benefit of the project. Emphasis should be on creative dialogue and effective communication, i.e. emphasis on contact rather than contract. Recognising the way in which people communicate within projects can help in the planning and implementation of an appropriate communications infrastructure for the project. This tends to imply a bottom-up approach to the design of the project delivery system.

Project websites are an important tool for design teams to share information and develop design work concurrently. Members of the design team are able to share information files and access current work of other designers, but to be effective the project website needs to be designed to suit the needs of the designers and managers using it; and once it is implemented, training will be required to allow all project participants to use the system effectively and efficiently. Failure to follow accepted protocols may result in problems with coordination activities. The quicker that information can be accurately produced, exchanged and understood by those dealing with it, the better. Much attention has been given to the transfer of information within project environments, since the timely exchange of information is a key factor for effective coordination and hence control of project information. A considerable amount of information can be processed at remote locations, e.g. in the office where all the tools, equipment and information are to hand, and information produced can be easily sent via email or web-based technology. Increased use of intra-webs and project-extranets has made a significant impact on the way in which information is exchanged between project actors. It would be prudent, however, to remember that *people* produce information, and we often make mistakes, especially when working under pressure. Subsequently some form of interaction between sender and receiver of information is required to resolve discrepancies in the information received.

Team-building

The one task that has a major influence on the success of the project is the assembly of the most appropriate organisations and individuals to work on the project. The ability of the team members to work together towards a common goal is not always given the attention it deserves early in the process. Ideally, the assembly of the project team should be started before the briefing stage commences, although this may not always be possible or desirable. The manner in which the various actors interact will create and shape the project culture. The design of this dynamic and constantly changing social system should not be left to chance. Socially engineering the project team is an important task for the project manager. Selecting the team members and massaging their egos to the collective benefit of the project takes a lot of skill, experience and sensitivity.

In the vast majority of construction projects the participants are brought together to work on one project only. Following completion of the project, or more accurately completion of a participant's work package, the relationship between the individual and the project stops. This means that, with the exception of large and repetitive projects, it is common for a project team to be composed of different actors to the previous one. This is often true even where the same organisations are involved, simply because different individuals within the organisation have been assigned to the project according to internal workload commitments. Thus communication is required to support industrial relations and hence provide the means by which teams can develop quickly and effectively. Relationships can be volatile and adversarial, making it difficult to form and thereafter maintain interorganisational relationships. To a certain extent initiatives such as partnering, strategic alliances and integrated supply-chain management help to mitigate the effects of fragmentation, although, as with more traditional approaches, there is still a heavy reliance on the ability of the team members to interact and communicate effectively. Thus, regardless of the approach adopted, the basic tenets of running a project remain the same, i.e. we are reliant on getting the right people together for the right job. Competences and the development of competent practices are a key factor in the success of the construction team. The attributes and actions of key construction personnel strongly influence the success or failure of the project.

Team selection

With a shift from procedures to people has come a greater emphasis on the competences of the actors involved as well as their emotional and social intelligence. Preselection or prequalification of project managers, architects, engineers and other key actors has become more widespread. In some cases project managers are asked to undergo psychological tests in an attempt to determine their suitability for major projects. In many cases the selection will be based on past experience, which is explored through a series of interviews to see if the individual is compatible with the client. Similarly, clients are paying greater attention to the people who will work on the project and it is relatively common for clients to ask to see CVs of the project team.

- ♦ *Experience.* The experience of the team members will colour the type and extent of interaction. In an ideal world a mix of experienced and less experienced participants would provide a well-balanced team. Project teams comprising a large number of inexperienced participants should be avoided.
- ♦ *Values.* The discussion of values is also related to the roles undertaken by individuals and their individual and collective responsibilities. Early discussion and agreement of roles and responsibilities are necessary to avoid, or at least mitigate, problems later in the process. Consultants should be invited to discuss their values with the client and project manager. Appointment of the consultant should take place after some degree of compatibility has been established.
- ♦ *Attitude.* The attitude of organisations and individuals to others must be addressed to ensure compatibility. Levels of trust and distrust are influenced by attitude.

Building effective relationships

Start-up meetings or workshops may be used to bring together representatives of the main stakeholders. These early meetings should include the client and/or the client's representative, architects, engineers, project managers and, if known at the time, the main contractor and/or specialist contractors. Representatives of user groups may also be present for some building types such as social housing. These 'getting to know you' meetings should be used to explore the values of the stakeholders. Various approaches are taken to start-up meetings and workshops. It is common practice for the project manager to take responsibility for arranging and directing the meetings and workshops. Another approach is for an independent person (someone with no contractual responsibility for the project) to act as a facilitator. The facilitator's primary aim is to encourage open communication and the development of working relationships based on shared values and mutual trust. This takes time and a number of workshops and activities may be needed to help build a team spirit. Subsequent workshops should focus on improvement of team interaction and further development of relationships based on trust.

The intention is to build the system architecture for the project, thus allowing actors to engage in open and effective communication during the life of the project. In addition to trying to engineer the project culture and hence make the events that follow run smoothly, the outcome of many teambuilding events and workshops is the signing of a partnering agreement (or similar document). Such agreements commit the project stakeholders to a working relationship based on open communication, knowledge sharing and trust.

Team maintenance and development

A related concern is the ability of managers to keep the team functioning effectively during the life of the project. A well-known characteristic of projects is the enthusiasm and energy that greets new projects and the tendency of people to drift away towards the end as other projects within their organisation become more important and hence more demanding of their time. This is common to all projects, regardless of sector. The construction team has an ephemeral character, with the temporariness of the arrangement prone to breaking apart. The project manager and key actors must put considerable effort into maintaining informal communication and avoiding entropy. Approximately 1% of effort is needed for team assembly, with 99% required to keep the team functioning effectively.

A relatively free and open atmosphere characterises interactions during the early stages of a project. Everyone is optimistic and positive and the amount of information in the system is relatively low and largely unstructured. As the project develops, the level of information increases and relationships mature, with informal and formal structures emerging, which create implicit rules of engagement. Goals and targets are set and as deadlines become more urgent the pressure to develop and exchange information builds. This can, and often does, result in higher levels of conflict between actors. The pressure resulting from limited time, a large amount of information and increased workload can affect the ability of team members to work with each other, leading to changes in communication patterns. This may either impede or help to improve project team performance.

The small teams, groups and individuals that constitute the construction team are dominant at different stages in the project. Thus, although dependent upon the work of others, many of the participants will not meet other participants during their period of involvement with the project. Relationships form, evolve and disband throughout the life cycle of the project. This is an important point to make, because newly formed groups exhibit different characteristics to established groups. In a newly formed group, members must simultaneously find their place within that group and socialise with one another. Each construction project embraces a new grouping of actors who must attempt to develop social relationships that support the project. Research on group interaction and socialisation processes found that in new groups the exchanges present a two-way process of social influence, changing others' ideas and opinions through communication. It is claimed that the norms that govern group members come into force as each actor's objectives become apparent. The group norms regulate group behaviour. As groups develop, their members get to recognise the importance of individual professional roles. The group regulatory forces are then used to control interaction of individual members. In construction, as the tasks change from feasibility to design and then construction, the power, importance and involvement of the professionals will change. The challenge for project managers is to try and lead this dynamic process. As the project develops and the specific demands of the situation change, the actors with the most relevant skills become more influential and powerful. Those with relevant skills emerge or are nominated by other members of the group to be the most dominant for a particular period of time, during which they are central to the information-processing and decision-making because of their expertise.

Any social situation is a sort of reality agreed on by those participating in it, or more exactly those who define the situation. Everyone who enters a situation does so with preconceived definitions of what is expected of him or her and the other participants. Such beliefs, which include expected interactions, are established from experience of previous groups to which the individual belonged. Thus, each situation confronts the participant with specific expectations and demands. Such circumstances generally work because most of the time our perceptions and expectations of important situations coincide approximately. Culture, society and individual power play an important part in the norms that govern the way social groups act. The same aspects will also influence the behaviour of professional groups, but the group may draw on those members with nominated roles, perceived expertise, skill and experience to determine who is allowed to interact, make decisions and play lead roles. However, some people, regardless of professional skill or experience, can use communication techniques to exert influence, enabling them to gain power over elements of group behaviour and decision-making.

Group development

The development of the construction team will have an effect on the group's interaction and vice versa. Similarly, the strength of the professional relationship between designers and managers and their ability to resolve problems will also be functions of their interaction behaviour. Achievement of a group's goals depends on concerted action and so group members must reach some degree of consensus on acceptable task and socio-emotional behaviour before they can act together. Interaction has been described as task-specific and social. The social element of interaction is developed through emotional exchanges that are used to express a level of commitment to the task and other members. To accomplish group tasks relationships need to be developed and maintained. The level of interaction associated with maintaining, building, threatening and breaking up relationships will be a function of socio-emotional interaction and will be subject to group norms.

A group's behaviour develops and changes over the period of interaction. As task groups attempt to solve problems they undergo changes in terms of their attitude and behaviour towards each other. Groups go through a process of learning, which can result in changes to structure as the group moves through a range of social, emotional and developmental stages. Two variables said to affect group development are the length of time that a group has existed and the number of occasions on which the group has previously met. When people have taken part in a series of meetings on related subjects and different people were present in each of the previous meetings (a common occurrence in construction meetings), group participation is the same as if the group had met for the first time. This phenomenon is due to the group's socio-emotional development. Individuals are not aware of the group's social and emotional norms, nor does the group know how the individuals will react to the group norms. Thus, a socio-emotional framework develops and re-establishes itself when new actors enter the group.

Early group meetings necessitate the formation of socio-emotional structure and a participation strategy that will be used to access information, develop group knowledge and make decisions. When actors have experience of the subject being discussed, but have not experienced interaction in that group setting, they are more likely to use task-based interaction rather than socio-emotional interaction. Socio-emotional communication emerges later once the newcomers are familiar with the group members and the group norms. Agreeing and disagreeing are socio-emotional communication acts. Equally, emotion is used to show support and concern. In groups it is the socio-emotional interaction that regulates interaction and provides the framework against which decisions are made.

Not all teams are totally new and group norms and behaviour may be influenced by previous relationships and experience of those relationships. Although the project is often a one-off and teams will disband, some groups will maintain relationships with the aim of working together on future projects. Clients, developers and consultants usually have a number of preferred contacts (individuals within organisations) that they will use if given the freedom to do so. Alternatively parties may contact those they have previously worked with for advice or help without entering into a contractual arrangement. Working with known actors through informal strategic alliances or formal strategic partnering may save time and improve knowledge transfer because relationships have developed, a level of trust exists, some formalities have been dispensed with and the skills are known (and to some degree have already been tested). In these situations emphasis will be on team maintenance and development activities.

Work-orientated groups need to maintain a balance between task and social demands. As groups address problems emotions start to develop and, as a result of disagreement, tension is built up between members as they focus on the problem rather than relationships. Conflict, even when constructive, leads to tension that can damage the cohesiveness of the group and threaten group maintenance; yet too much attention to cohesion tends to stifle constructive conflict and threatens the group's ability to solve problems. In order for a group to be effective task issues must be discussed, conflict will emerge, and relationships must be managed so that they are sufficiently sustained to bring the discussion to a successful conclusion. Functional conflict can help to avoid 'groupthink' and improve the decision-making process, but conflict may also damage relationships between group members if not managed with sensitivity.

Influence and persuasion

A factor affecting social interaction is the power of each side to affect the other. Influencing skills enable the development of relationships and are a key skill of good managers. People with a high persuasive ability can use their skill to handle conflict constructively and hence to promote openness and constructive debate. To perform effectively construction project managers need the ability to negotiate and persuade others to take action. One way to view negotiation is as a struggle, in which concealment and competitive tactics feature strongly. An alternative view of negotiation is as collaboration, a process in which parties make sacrifices rather than demand concessions in the pursuit of some (mutually beneficial) overriding project goal. Where parties use collaborative strategies during negotiations it is more likely that a mutually agreeable solution will be produced. In situations where negotiators or project managers feel that they have to satisfy tough demands (for example, negotiations with stakeholders within a project) they will adopt a more competitive approach. Both the collaborative and competitive styles of conflict involve positive and negative socio-emotional discussion. The collaborative method would have a tendency to maintain and repair relationships during discussion. The competitive style would be prepared to threaten the relationship and have a greater tendency towards extremes of the negative socio-emotional traits. Both approaches would also use task-based logic to explain the rationale; however, getting mutual understanding would be far more important in the collaborative approach than the competitive approach.

Rational persuasion is often used during negotiations. The most common form of rational persuasion consists of logical arguments and factual evidence to help develop understanding and explain the situation. Rational persuasion is most appropriate when the opponent shares the same task objectives, but does not recognise the proposal in its current format as the best way to attain the objectives. In a situation where the opponents have incompatible objectives or end-goals, this type of influencing tactic is unlikely to be successful for obtaining commitment or partial agreement.

Disagreement and agreement

Disagreement is usually seen as a negative term, yet it is found in most group interaction. A certain amount of challenge, evaluation and disagreement is necessary to appraise alternatives and reduce the risks. Emotional expression helps others to recognise an individual's preferred beliefs, behaviours and actions. It exposes the structure and routine in which the individual would like to work. In groups such expressions are needed to establish what is acceptable and what is not and in which areas conflict is likely to occur. The decision-making structure of a group is dependent on individuals expressing their agreement and disagreement and working through any variance. As individuals work through their differences they develop a much deeper understanding of others' beliefs and values. However, people may choose to avoid disagreements to enable them to pursue relationship goals, believing that disagreeing would weaken the relationship. Clearly it is important to expose differences of opinion and explore issues in depth, but it is equally important to identify and respond to an individual's values and beliefs.

During difficult tasks and stressful situations, members of the group are more inclined to pursue relationship goals, supporting each other rather than dealing with the problem and enquiring about the risks involved. Pressure to agree may be so strong that group members may continue to agree blandly while unwittingly consenting to their own destruction. Such attributes are associated with groupthink. Groupthink occurs when members of a group do not agree with statements that are made although they do not make their view known to others, which results in the group members believing agreement is reached. Ways of avoiding groupthink include asking questions, noting an absence of disagreement (which serves as a warning to group members to reassess alternatives) and being aware that the risk of illusory agreement heightens as external stress increases. Seemingly unanimous agreement by the group may disguise a silent minority.

Defensiveness and barriers

Defensiveness can be defined as the behaviour of an individual when he or she perceives threat in the group. A person who perceives threat may communicate in a guarded or attacking way. Defensiveness of this nature will manifest behaviour patterns that are either consciously or subconsciously recognisable to other parties. The inner feelings of defensiveness create outwardly defensive postures. If such actions take place without question an increasingly circular destructive response may occur. Defensive signals are said to distort the message. When a receiver attempts to understand a communicated message they also extend their efforts towards understanding the motives behind defensiveness, attempting to understand why someone is behaving in this manner. Excessive defensive and aggressive behaviour distracts those engaged in the interaction from rational discussion. Defensive arousal prevents the listener from concentrating on the message. The defensive behaviour increasingly distorts as the circular defensive behaviour continues. The conversation moves from the subject matter to defensive action and reciprocal attacks. Defensive and supportive communication can be accommodated without changing the content of the statement. For example, enquiring rather than demanding information reduces defensiveness and aggressive responses. Good communicators develop flexible interaction techniques that enable a greater appreciation of the other's perspective.

Help seeking and question asking

Help-seeking behaviours are fundamentally interpersonal, i.e. one person seeks assistance from another. Individuals are more likely to seek help from equal status peers and others who have helped them earlier; cooperative patterns are reciprocal. Help-seeking behaviour implies incompetence and dependence, and many professionals are reluctant to ask questions for fear of being perceived in such a manner. It is likely that high status professionals will avoid situations where they need further information, in order to avoid asking questions and to defend their status. Serious and costly errors have been made in multidisciplinary projects, which could have been prevented by seeking expert help that was available at the time.

Conflict

Conflict has been found to develop in design and construction teams as the group members discover their team objectives and then attempt to enforce them on others. During a group's development a relatively defined structure of interaction evolves through the group's regulatory procedures. Through experience, group members learn to expect conflict in certain areas between certain members, and also expect to gain support from others. As the group's socio-emotional awareness develops, the members anticipate where conflict could occur and use supportive reinforcement interactions to overcome it. This allows participants to engage in task-related elements and control discussions with socio-emotional interludes. People tend to be more inclined to express their emotions when they are more familiar with each other, thus the longer groups have been together the more likely it is that negative emotions will be shown. Established groups may not necessarily experience less conflict than newer groups, but they tend to be better equipped for dealing with it. There are two types of conflict:

♦ *Natural conflict* is the intended or actual consequence of an encounter, resulting in stronger participants benefiting from the clash. This is inevitable and thus some plan to deal with it can be made in advance.

♦ *Unnatural conflict* is where a participant enters into the encounter intending the destruction or disablement of the other, usually with the intention of making a financial or personal gain. This is quite a well-known strategy of less scrupulous contractors looking to increase their profit margins on a project.

Conflict needs to be managed so that it does not suppress information or become personal and dysfunctional and damage relationships. Most conflicts are managed by exploring alternative solutions and different perspectives, and encouraging all participants to engage in discussions and, hopefully, reach agreement. Conflict may be beneficial or destructive to team performance:

♦ *Benefits* include increased understanding of issues and opinions, and greater cohesiveness and motivation. When group members disagree and explore why they disagree, they expose key issues and points of misunderstanding. Groups that experience tension and conflict often feel closer and stronger after working through a crisis.

♦ *Disadvantages* include decreased group cohesion, weakening of relationships, ill-feeling and destruction of the group. If conflict goes on too long and is not resolved, it will decrease cohesiveness within the group; conflict between people can be distasteful and personalised, having little relevance to the task or problem. Most people do not like to be criticised and all conflict has a negative socio-emotional impact, which must be recognised.

When conflict takes place it is important that the impact on individuals is tempered with some form of positive socio-emotional support. The support does not need to come from the person who initiated the criticism, but the group's relationships must be managed. Groups that do not work through conflict and repair relationships will fall apart. Some conflicts may turn into disputes and this involves considerable cost and inconvenience for all parties. The negative perceptions that develop from public dispute often serve to damage all parties.

A certain amount of conflict within any organisation is inevitable and the existence of communication problems will make the management of conflict difficult. The management of conflict within organisations needs to concern itself with the reduction and eradication of dysfunctional conflict and the manifestation and management of functional conflict, which will help discussions to remain creative and useful. When there is more than one organisation affected by conflict, such as in a project environment, each organisation will attempt to secure its own goals before addressing those of the temporary construction organisation. A supportive group climate should be developed so that when conflicts emerge, as they inevitably will, the group is able to repair emotional damage and continue with the group task.

Conflict often emerges from perceived failure. When the failure level is high there is a greater chance that people perceive the task to be impossible or the chance of failure so high that it is not worth the effort. Very low levels of failure may be taken as a job achieved, but not done too well. Moderate failure, where the task is considered tough but achievable, may present a challenge and a chance to prove to oneself and others that the task can be achieved. Thus, moderate levels of conflict (being related to perceived failure) may be productive. Negative feedback can be stressful and group members need to be aware of the development of socio-emotional tension. Debate and negative emotional exchanges may threaten relationships; however, negative emotion can be useful if positive socio-emotional interaction is also used to maintain relationships. Any socio-emotional tension that develops is removed by positive emotional acts (such as showing support, joking and praise) and negative emotional acts (such as disagreements, an expression of frustration and even aggression). If socio-emotional issues are not addressed in a timely fashion the increase in tension may inhibit the group's work. Groups must maintain their equilibrium, moving backwards and forwards between task and socio-emotional related issues. Negative and positive socio-emotional interaction is interlinked with the group's task-based interaction. The task-based interaction will provide information about possible ideas, action and direction of the group. The positive and negative emotional signals will provide clues on how group members feel about the suggestions, and will encourage others to provide further information. Through suggestions and ideas, the subsequent testing of them and the reaction of the group (conveyed in rational and emotional responses), members are able to learn what is acceptable behaviour for the group. Too much attention to task interaction may limit the communication required to build and maintain relationships. If groups are to perform effectively positive reinforcement (agreeing, showing solidarity, being friendly and helping release tension) are needed to offset negative reactions (showing tension, being antagonistic, appearing to be unfriendly and disagreeing). The majority of project teams will need help, thus separate team-building activities need to be included in the project schedule.

Group members feel comfortable in a positive socio-emotional environment. Members prefer positive feedback, and interaction that suggests the group is effective can help to increase morale, but too much may be counterproductive and result in groupthink. Socio-emotional interaction is important in the accomplishment of tasks. The combined effort of the group requires exchanges that develop and maintain the group and provides a social structure capable of decision-making and task accomplishment.

Common problems

It is easy to overlook the social context in which design and realisation activities take place. Project failure is often a result of a breakdown in communications, fuelled by cultural differences and divergent values. The greater the empathy between participants, the closer they are in communication terms and the greater the potential for effective communication; conversely, the more distant they are in communication terms, the greater the chance of ineffective communication. It is natural that businesses prefer to work with those they know and can trust (based on previous project experience), via informal and formal alliances. However, because of requirements for competitive tendering on many projects the project relationships may be quite unexpected. Team assembly, maintenance and development stages should not be taken for granted since it is during this unpredictable and dynamic stage that many problems take root. The reluctance of the project manager and key stakeholders to deal with team assembly and maintenance may be related to:

- ◆ *Attitude*. Problems often relate to the project stakeholders having the right attitude to design and construction projects and the willingness to recognise the importance of social relations within projects. Failure to explore the attitude and values of key stakeholders before they are appointed may lead to problems as the project develops.
- ◆ *Inexperience*. Problems may be caused and/or go unnoticed if the main parties are inexperienced. Teams should not be

led by inexperienced project managers without support from more experienced colleagues.

♦ *Ignorance.* The softer side of project management tends to be overlooked in many education programmes. Thus we have to learn through experience.

♦ *Failure to learn.* Failure to learn from previous project experiences is inexcusable, but unfortunately too common as key actors rush from one project to another and priorities override common sense.

♦ *Priorities.* Even when the attitude is correctly aligned, knowledge of social relationships in projects is good and the ability to learn is exploited, the project priorities may make it difficult to apply some of the knowledge. Lack of time and finances are obvious factors and these relate to the attitude of the client.

♦ *People skills.* Not everyone is able to communicate and/or relate to others effectively, thus managers must be sensitive to personal traits.

Other problems commonly experienced are:

♦ *Assuming too much.* We tend to assume that all actors are knowledgeable about the project, but the reality is that actors may have only a partial understanding of the entire project, and so it is important to explore the boundaries of understanding at the start of discussions.

♦ *Failure to ask questions.* Assuming too much and concerns over professional reputation both combine to limit the amount and type of questions asked in face-to-face encounters.

♦ *Ineffective communication between groups.* This is often difficult to spot until there is a problem. Regular design reviews and meetings can help to identify some of the more obvious problems. All actors need to remain vigilant, especially the project and design managers.

♦ *Personality clashes.* These may be obvious from the start (and can be dealt with easily by substituting one or more individuals), but often personality clashes develop as people start working together and new actors enter and leave the team. It is impossible to prevent personalities from causing difficulties, but once evident they need to be quickly tackled. Failure to deal with differences may lead to ineffective communication and problems within the team.

♦ *Adversarial attitude.* Even within relational forms of contracting, such as partnering and alliancing, there may be individuals who adopt an adversarial attitude to others. Sometimes this is evident from the start of projects, but the attitude tends to develop or be revealed as the project proceeds and problems are encountered.

The project to office interface

At this early stage in the life of projects it is difficult to predict with any certainty whether the project will proceed as planned. The energy and excitement of the early meetings with clients can be misleading as projects get delayed or do not proceed for reasons completely beyond the control of the office. This means that any predictions of resources required for individual projects will be, at best, rather sketchy. However, this cannot be used as an excuse for not making a provisional plan (with appropriate contingencies). Resources will be needed and this will impact negatively on other projects unless some form of (fluid) plan is in place. Architects have to take a view as to how much time they are willing to expend without receiving payment in the hope that the project proceeds. In many cases architects are working as enablers, helping the client to put various initiatives in place before the project can proceed. This work is of considerable value to the client and architects should charge a fee for their involvement. Clients appreciate open discussion on such issues and need to enter into an agreement with the architectural office regarding the scope of the work and the fee.

A small, but increasing, number of clients and project organisations are starting to take the team assembly stage more seriously, aware that resources invested very early in projects can help to reduce uncertainty, improve communication and assist in the efficient delivery of projects. This can lead to improved performance, fewer errors and disagreements, and reductions in project costs, from which all participants benefit. Clients are also starting to realise the benefits to be gained from earlier involvement of key actors. Architects and project managers have a responsibility to explain the importance of effective team assembly to their clients.

Chapter Four
Exploring Client Values

Architectural programming, architectural planning, client briefing and design briefing are terms commonly used to describe the phase in a project when the sponsor engages professional advisers to discuss and explore their dreams and aspirations. Briefing is a creative process comprising a series of activities concerned with exploring client requirements and values. Collectively these activities should result in a clear, unambiguous and concise list of project requirements, codified in the written briefing documents. Emphasis is on data collection and analysis, the discussion and agreement of values and the confirmation of requirements. These activities inform the design and are an essential element of the design process, requiring excellent communication skills. The briefing documents are in effect a specification for the building, expressed as a set of performance and prescriptive requirements. These requirements are subsequently questioned, challenged, revised and restated and reaffirmed during the design phases, hopefully, resulting in a set of production information that reflects and enhances the client's needs and aspirations. This is an iterative and dynamic process that poses a number of challenges for the design manager. Although process maps show relatively distinct stages for briefing activities, the reality is that the process may be difficult to map given the relatively fluid nature of projects at an early stage. It is also extremely difficult to separate briefing activities from design work in many projects, with many designers developing conceptual designs as a means of exploring the client's milieu and hence developing the brief. And the written brief has a number of different, sometimes conflicting, uses. For example, briefing documents form the basis for communication between the client and the project team, and as such they form part of the contract between client and project team. The brief also forms a benchmark for post-project evaluation, in which the aim is to try and match client and user satisfaction with the original brief.

Articulating client needs through the briefing process is one of the most important events in a project. The project brief sets the scene for design decision-making. Good design and satisfied clients tend to be related to a well-managed briefing process. Vague project briefs waste time because additional effort is required at a later stage to define and redefine client requirements. A poorly managed briefing exercise can lead to poor information and hence the inability of actors to adequately determine the client's requirements. Uncertainty may lead to the development of an unsuitable design and subsequent redesign in the conceptual stages to match client values. Worse, the disparity between what the client wanted and what is being provided may not become evident until later in the project, with requests for expensive rework during construction and the possibility of disputes and conflict arising as a result. Briefing is often rushed into without adequate consideration for the consequences, and as with team assembly, time spent here can result in significant savings later in the process, helping to reduce uncertainty and mitigate wasted efforts. Better understanding of the briefing process is a fundamental requirement for better management of the client briefing and hence the actions that follow.

Briefing is a major communication channel that relies on effective communication and excellent listening skills. Effectiveness of communication between the client and the brief-taker(s) is a critical factor and it is here that empathy between client and briefing team needs to be established and maintained for the briefing process to be effective. Empathy between the client and the brief-taker is crucial to the development of effective dialogue, the sensitive and considered exploration of values and the development of a working relationship based on trust and openness. The persons best qualified to take the brief should have an excellent understanding of the value that design can add to the client's business or life, and also understand and empathise with the client's business values and/or lifestyle. The briefing process can be helped by the use of visualisation techniques, brainstorming and group/team exercises. The effectiveness of the process may also be linked to the procurement method and the early selection of advisers. The manner in which the briefing process is managed will be influenced by the size and complexity of the project. The effectiveness of the briefing process will be influenced by the ability of the individuals involved to tease out the salient points and record them for others to use as the basis of the design phases.

Understanding the briefing phase

Client expectations place considerable pressure on professional advisers to seek feasible and economic solutions to the client brief. For major projects, a project manager or client's representative will normally assist the client with the development of the brief, and it may be difficult for the designers to have direct contact with the client and building users. On smaller projects it is more common for the architects to be fully involved in the briefing process, working closely with client and users. Management of the briefing process is determined by project context as well as the attitudes, values and habits of the team assembled to work on the project. There is no doubt that the briefing process is a creative activity during which the client and the designer need to develop a close understanding, mutual respect and trust. From a management perspective it is important to recognise that the briefing process is a dynamic and iterative process. Controls are required to fix the brief at certain stages to make the design process easier to manage. There are two schools of thought relating to briefing, both valid depending on context.

The first school claims that client values should be fully explored, discussed, agreed and written down in a project brief before any design activity commences. Thus the project brief is a 'static' document, from which the design is subsequently developed. Changes to the brief can only be made with the consent of the client. In this approach briefing is separate from the other stages in the design process. This may be the most sensible policy from a design management and client relation perspective, since it is one way of narrowing the gap between client expectations and those of the design team. This approach is also required for public projects to allow for competition, with the brief developed by professionals who will not take part in the project. Developing a static brief is also central to a well-designed quality management system, in which the brief is agreed and signed off by the client. From a management perspective a static set of documents is the easiest to deal with, but given the time pressures brought to bear on projects (by the client) it is rarely possible to fix the whole of the brief before design activity commences. Thus parts of the brief are fixed and signed off by the client, with areas of uncertainty left for agreement at a future date in accordance with a project programme. Thus the term static may be a little misleading, since there is opportunity to reassess, agree, restate and approve the project requirements at predetermined points. This can help to save time on the overall programme, but still complies with quality management systems. The biggest challenge is that the client's requirements change as the design activities reveal alternative approaches and options, thus the document can become outdated and no longer read by designers unless it is updated. The static approach also assumes that the brief-taker is capable of expressing the client's needs in a written document; the reality is that communication between client and designer is necessary to explore the issues fully, during which time the briefing documents will need to be reassessed.

The second school argues that the briefing process should continue into the conceptual design phases and beyond, covering RIBA Plan of Work stages from inception, feasibility and outline proposals to scheme design (and some would argue into construction). The philosophy here is that briefing is a process that occurs throughout the design process, i.e. it is an iterative process that extends throughout, and is part of, the design process. Often, especially in very small projects, there is little distinction between briefing and design activities and in some cases there may be no written brief, merely a set of drawings and diagrams that reflect the client's agreed requirements. Design as a means of exploring client requirements can be a powerful tool and can be a very efficient approach for certain types of projects and clients. The 'end' of the briefing process coincides with a set of completed design drawings. In many respects this view represents the classic creative and chaotic stereotype of design as a creative process. Such an approach may suit some clients, certain projects and architectural offices, but it does make it very difficult to manage the briefing process in line with quality management procedures. If things do go wrong later in the process it is almost impossible to trace design decisions back to clearly defined client requirements, since the two became blurred during the process.

Effective and efficient briefing relies on several interdependent and generic areas, starting with the definition of an appropriate framework for the process, the project plan. This may be a simple bar chart following the RIBA Plan of Work, identifying key dates, responsibilities and last possible moments for decision-making, or a more sophisticated schedule of activities. The first task is to discuss and agree an appropriate programme for the project, taking into account the client parameters and the design office resources. The programme should clearly indicate critical dates and establish a schedule for design team meetings, strategic reviews and approval gateways. The framework sets the agenda for communications and information flow, which should be clear, concise and timely and include knowledge from other projects and products. From this, informed decisions will be made and fixed progressively through the briefing period. Given the iterative nature of briefing all decision-making should be delayed until the last responsible moment in an attempt to maximise value for the client and minimise risk. It is during the briefing exercise that major risks should be identified, discussed and recorded. When more than one professional is involved it is essential to establish responsibilities for certain aspects of the briefing process. It is also necessary to incorporate evaluation opportunities – control gateways – at strategic points in the project to coincide with the fixing of decisions. This helps to clarify decisions and re-emphasise roles and responsibilities. The aim is to explore and better understand underlying agendas and drivers behind the project and hence articulate client values and needs, through both prescriptive and performance requirements.

Understanding the client

The design and construction process is the interplay between two complex, emergent and highly dynamic systems: the client and the project participants. Capturing client values and goals in a structured manner is necessary and to do this effectively architects must understand their customer and their needs. Value management and lean thinking both aim to maximise value for the customer and minimise waste. Without understanding the customer the concept of value is difficult to define, and without a tangible concept of value waste is equally difficult to define in a meaningful sense. This is an important point to make in the context of design management, since it is the customer values that are being managed. The route to a leaner design and construction process should thus begin with a deeper understanding of the client.

Most textbooks tend to take it as a given that the client is a well-defined entity that has some very clear and well-defined value parameters that can be expressed in clear terms. Although the term 'client' appears to indicate a single person or a well-defined group of persons, each client entity is a complex system. On small domestic work the client may be the wife or husband, representing the interests of their family unit. In this situation the client is committing their own finances and a considerable amount of emotion to the project. Capture of the family's needs and aspirations can be undertaken on a face-to-face basis with all family members. On larger residential developments and other projects such as commercial schemes, the client is a business organisation. In this case the client's representative may be one or more people (hence the term client team), charged with doing a job. Rarely are they themselves the investors, owners and users of the building. This makes the capture and communication of 'client values' particularly difficult to achieve in practice and necessitates representation of, for example, user groups.

Architects should represent the interests of three distinct groups: the building owner, the building users and society. These three groups value different things at different times in the life of the building. The predominant focus is on when the building is completed and taken into use, where durability, usefulness and beauty may be used as expression of the primary view of each of the three groups. But there also exists the perspective of the value of the building in the future or for future users, and the value while the building is being realised. Value cannot be measured or expressed and communicated explicitly, but must be learned and understood through a process of interaction and exchange. This transaction is most evident in the briefing process, a learning process for all participants.

Client owner

Clients are usually defined as being first-time clients (inexperienced), occasional clients (some experience of construction) and repeat clients (experienced). Clients may also be defined as having short-term (developer) or long-term (owner) interests in the completed building.

- *First-time clients.* The first-time client will need guiding through the design and construction process. This client may only commission design and construction services once, for example a house owner wishing to provide more space for a growing family. Here the brief will be a bespoke document. Effort may be required to ensure that the client fully understands the implications of the decisions being made. Visualisation techniques and simple graphics are very helpful in this regard.
- *Occasional clients.* The term 'occasional client' tends to be used to describe people or organisations that commission design and construction services on a relatively infrequent basis. The gap between commissions may be lengthy and the type of project may be very different to the first, thus learning from previous project experience may be challenging. The brief is likely to be a bespoke document.
- *Repeat clients.* Repeat clients tend to be major institutions, businesses and organisations with a large property portfolio. Typical repeat clients would be food retail businesses, hotel chains, etc. Here the commissioning of buildings is more likely to be part of a strategic procurement strategy, closely linked to the business objective of the organisation and their facility/asset management strategies. There may be an opportunity to establish integrated teams that move and learn from one project to the next. Similarly, the ability

to make improvements to how design and construction activities are managed is also present with repeat clients. With repeat clients the brief may include elements common to previous projects that represent the values and knowledge of the client organisation and are codified in a standard brief.

Client user

User involvement is another key element of successful briefing. Building users can make a significant input to the data collection exercise since it is they, rather than the building owners, that interact with specific areas on a daily basis. Soliciting their views and listening to their requirements is a fundamental part of the briefing process. Identifying users can be problematic for many building types since users often constitute a disparate mix of people and groups. It is often impractical to try and capture the views of all potential users; instead representatives of specific user groups are identified and brought into the project-briefing phase. For example, personnel managers, facilities managers and building maintenance managers all have a part to play in representing the interests of a wide cross-section of building users. User consultation processes, via for example questionnaire surveys and workshops, help to provide essential information and knowledge for analysis, the results of which can be taken forward as a set of value parameters. This is 'first generation' user involvement and some flexibility (and vision) needs to be considered so that the second and subsequent generations of building users are also considered in the development of the brief.

Client society

The term 'client society' is used to refer to stakeholders who have an involvement in the project but are not part of any contractual agreement. Neighbours, local interest and pressure groups, town planners and building control officers will all be stakeholders, although in many cases these individuals may never use the building. Small extensions to residential properties may be of little concern to the community at large, but may have a significant impact on the immediate neighbours. For larger and more prominent developments there is often a need to engage in some form of public consultation exercises. These may be linked to the town planning process, or may be initiated by the building sponsor in a proactive attempt to hear the opinion of the local community. Public consultation exercises need to be carefully organised to allow members of the community a chance to contribute in a positive and timely manner. Similar to user involvement, there must be consideration of future societal needs since the building will still be around long after the current members of the client society.

Empowering the client

Briefing is, in many respects, an educational process. Clients can learn more about their organisational requirements by being encouraged to consider and articulate their values and requirements. Similarly, architects will learn a lot about specific clients and their business values. It is important that values and ideals concerning sustainability are discussed as early as possible since they represent a particular philosophy that must be present in the brief to be effectively implemented. For example, stating in the strategic brief that the project is to encompass sustainable design may influence the selection of the design and realisation teams, i.e. organisations and individuals that can demonstrate their commitment to sustainable design.

For the briefing process to be effective the client and/or the client's representative must be knowledgeable about their organisation and its values. Failure to create an effective dialogue with the brief-taker(s) is likely to result in problems later in the process. Involvement tends to be beneficial for clients. Involvement can, for example, help the client to get a better understanding of the project dynamics and lead to a feeling of ownership and empowerment. Early involvement is also essential for developing open communications and trusting relationships within the project team. Early involvement of key actors also provides the opportunity to discuss important issues, such as sustainable design, whole life costing, adaptable designs and innovative approaches, at the outset of the project. Greater involvement of the client and user groups can also help to limit the number of design changes later in the process. Some clients are unwilling or simply unable to get involved in the project. They prefer a 'hands-off' approach and this can cause problems with communications and decision-making if not handled sensitively. Client values, for example family values or business values, should be expressed in the value parameters for the building.

There is also a strong recommendation to include the building users in the early briefing process, although this is not always possible for all building types. However, some form of 'user' representation should be included in the briefing process and maintained throughout the duration of the project. The use of visualisation techniques, such as sketches and digital models, can help to tease out the client's likes and dislikes. This is particularly important for clients new to building that may be unable to read 2D drawings or fully appreciate the intricacies and implications of a written project brief. This should not be confused with the early design process; it is more a case of testing design ideas through precedent studies.

Client design advisers

In 2005 the RIBA started a register of Client Design Advisers (CDAs). The register lists experienced professionals that have been accredited by the RIBA to guide clients through the process of procuring a building. The aim is to provide clients with direct, independent advice so that value and quality can be maximised. CDAs are most likely to be architects, but they are independent of the design team, engaged by the client to interpret values and aspirations for the building. CDAs provide advice and assistance in the early stages of projects, with setting up projects and trying to ensure that design quality and value is achieved. The aim is to ensure that design is an integral part of public sector procurement programmes, helping to create high quality architecture for clients, users, society and the environment. The CDA will first and foremost champion design quality, advising the client team on the client's business case and project initiation, through briefing to post-completion. Value and risk management, as well as advice on topics such as partnering and team assembly, feature strongly. CDAs will help to champion the importance of good design and its relationship to excellent buildings.

Establishing value parameters

Clients vary in their ability to express their wants and needs. Some are able to do this well; others need some encouragement and prompting. Similarly, architects and other professional advisers vary in their ability to listen to their clients, interpret the meanings and express requirements in the written briefing documentation. The language used by clients is likely to be linked to their trade. For example, the sponsor of a supermarket may use very different language to the sponsor of a swimming pool or a family house. Architects need to be able to adapt to different languages, read between the lines and to a certain extent second-guess what the client wants. The development of a relationship through the briefing process will help both the brief-taker and the client to explore many issues and start to understand the idiosyncrasies of the various languages. The exploration of values and goals will also be enhanced through face-to-face communication. In some respects this is also linked to the client's level of experience and sophistication. Clients need to be empowered and encouraged to take 'ownership' of the project, although not all will be willing or able to become involved. Throughout the briefing process the emphasis should be on the development of a shared vision between the project stakeholders. The term stakeholder is used to describe a representative of groups, for example a member of the client's organisation, a member of the project team or a member of a local interest group, who hold a stake in the project. Some of these stakeholders will be employed to make decisions, some to shape decisions and others to try and influence decisions to suit their own interests. To discuss the stakeholders' values and explore the aims and objectives for the project requires the use of meetings. It is at these meetings that the dreams and constraints can be discussed and critical dates identified. Pressure to start as quickly as possible should be resisted until the value parameters have been defined and the methods of working agreed.

There are a number of strategies and tools available to help explore client values and hence identify the value drivers for the project. In the majority of cases there is a considerable amount of data that could be collected, but time and cost constraints make it necessary to limit the data collection exercise to a manageable, and affordable, task. The data must be relevant, and experienced brief-takers almost instinctively understand what is relevant and what is not, unlike those less experienced. The aim is to explore and hence define the client needs. These can be expressed as performance requirements, statements of need and/or value parameters. The temptation to offer solutions at this early stage should be resisted.

An experienced brief-taker is able to extract the salient points and communicate them clearly to others. However, written briefing documents do not, and cannot, convey the more subtle messages expressed by the client during interpersonal exchanges at briefing meetings. Some of these may well turn out to be important points that with the benefit of hindsight should have been stated clearly within the project brief. From a designer's perspective, the ability to see for oneself how the client expresses his or her requirements, the level of enthusiasm shown for certain aspects of the building and the response to questioning is paramount to producing a design that reflects the client's values. Senior partners are the normal contact with clients and it is they who often take the client's requirements and develop the brief before handing the document over to designers in the office, sometimes via the design manager. This indirect communication is liable to misinterpretation and relies on good communication between client, partner, design manager and designer. Inability of the partner and/or design manager to pass on the client's requirements in the form of a written document and accompanying verbal explanation may cause problems with interpretation and result in abortive work. Needless to say, some partners are better at this than others. It is helpful if the designer allocated to work on the project can be present at some of the meetings with the client, although for practical reasons this is not always feasible. It is through interaction with the client that subtle messages rarely captured in written project briefs are picked up by designers. To ensure a degree of balance it is advisable that two people, preferably with different skills, are present in briefing meetings to ensure that client values are clearly defined and separate from the brief-takers' personal wishes for the project. Essential characteristics of the brief-taker are:

- Being an excellent listener
- Ability to explore sensitive issues with tact and diplomacy
- Ability to record client requirements succinctly, yet without losing the spirit of the discussions
- Ability to communicate requirements clearly to others
- Willingness to separate the client's requirements from those of the brief-taker.

Collecting data

Briefing is primarily a research exercise and, as with all research exercises, success is determined by the manner in which questions are framed. The brief-taker will interact with a small number of stakeholders during this phase. Most design organisations use a standard checklist for typical building types to help guide the data-gathering and analysis process. It is difficult to provide precise guidance on this; however, depending on the size and complexity of the project, one or more of the following data collection techniques may be used. With all of these techniques it is important to set out clear objectives and timescales.

- *Workshops.* The use of workshops can be time-consuming, but they are an invaluable tool for bringing people together to communicate on a face-to-face basis. To make the workshops effective key project stakeholders should be represented and an experienced facilitator should manage the workshops. Various tools can be used to explore issues in a group environment, such as brainstorming, scenario planning, etc. It is the facilitator's job to tease out information from the client, not to add his or her own views. Workshops allow the discussion of values and the establishment of value parameters. It is not possible to know client values in depth at the start of a project, so workshops are primarily concerned with exploring values and establishing a common vision. Knowledge and experience from other projects may be brought into the workshops, for example from facilities management, to better inform the whole life costs.

♦ *Value management (VM) exercises.* These are workshop-based meetings in which the client and key stakeholders explore how value can be added to the building design. A facilitator, independent of the design team, manages the workshops. By discussing relevant issues it is possible to explore and confront potential problem areas early and also identify areas where value for the client can be added. Clients are looking to achieve the best value possible from their investment and this has to be set against the whole life costs of the building.

♦ *Interviews.* Face-to-face interviews are a useful way of developing the client's requirements and are often used in addition to workshops. Interviews with key personnel and selected building users or building users' representatives can provide useful data in addition to that gleaned from the client. Standard questionnaires and/or checklists can help to guide structured and semi-structured interviews. Unstructured interviews may be a better tool to explore hidden agendas. The purpose of the interviews should be explained to interviewees prior to the interview to allow them some time to prepare for the interview.

♦ *Focus groups.* These are an effective means of exploring the views and needs of stakeholders from different backgrounds, and are often used for collecting information from representatives of users and community groups.

♦ *Questionnaires.* These are best administered on a face-to-face basis, but can be a relatively cheap and quick way of collecting data from several stakeholders if distributed by post or email. Questions should be carefully framed and simple language should be used to avoid confusion with professional language and terminology. It is common practice to include some form of face-to-face interaction with some of the questionnaire respondents and/or to test the findings in a workshop-type environment.

♦ *Documentary evidence.* A lot of information can be gleaned from existing information sources, such as plans, maintenance logs, existing user surveys and facilities management data. Annual reports, business plans, management structures and action plans can also be helpful.

♦ *Activity surveys.* Visual surveys of existing space usage over time may provide data that both supports and contradicts the perceptions of how space is used within the organisation. Space usage surveys need to be undertaken over a period of at least one working week, and hence tend to be expensive in terms of the resources required.

- *Post-occupancy evaluation (POE)*. Knowledge gained from previous projects completed for the current client and for other clients can reveal a considerable amount of knowledge about the product and the process, which can be fed into the briefing process (see Chapter 8). This data will have been collected from user questionnaires, interviews and observation of space usage and records from facilities management/maintenance, etc. regarding running costs, serviceability.

- *Precedent studies and visits*. A lot can be learned from others and it may be prudent to visit buildings, with the client and key decision-makers, that represent different approaches to the client's needs to similar budget and quality parameters. Permissions will need to be obtained first, and this can be time-consuming and not always forthcoming. Visits to buildings are invaluable in gauging the client's reaction to internal space, something that is difficult to achieve even with the best 3D digital modelling packages. Visits can be supplemented with photographs, drawings and digital presentations of similar building types. Simple techniques such as measuring out areas on the floor to give an impression of actual sizes can also be very effective.

- *Simulation*. The presentation of designs to gauge the reaction of the client to, say, three different design solutions can help too. The initial response from the client, be it delight, shock or disappointment, can help to establish the client's preferences and thus guide the process – sometimes linked to precedent studies and visits, sometimes forming part of early design work. Gaming techniques can also be used in workshops to tease out the values of clients and project participants.

Analysing data and prioritising values

The main focus of the data collection and analysis effort is the establishment of client values. The better these are known, the better the team can deliver. The general consensus is that values should not be agreed and confirmed until the latest possible moment within the programme. Face-to-face dialogue helps to explore and develop relationships that can (or conversely cannot) develop into effective and efficient working alliances, essentially the preparation for the construction of efficient communication networks. Critical connections between decision-makers are explored so that everyone is certain before going into production, thus reducing downstream uncertainty. The outcome of the data collection and analysis phase is the establishment of basic values for the project, a very pragmatic document that does not contain any drawings. These values should be prioritised to help make the decision-making easier in the design and detailed design phases. A number of tools exist to help prioritise values, including value management and quality function deployment (QFD).

The written brief

The brief is a written document (sometimes supported with graphics) that aims to capture the client's requirements. The design team will develop the conceptual and detailed design to meet the requirements as stated in this document. A good brief should contain the client's objectives, the project timescale, the cost limit and an indication of the client's expectations of the finished quality of the building. The written brief must be able to communicate the client's requirements to individuals who were not party to the briefing process and who may never actually meet the client. Any questions that develop during the design phases will usually be directed to the design manager or the project manager.

It is the written brief that sets out the client's image for the building and the lifestyle of the building users. The design team use this document, or group of documents, to develop a number of conceptual design proposals. The contents of the brief should be set out logically and clearly. The brief should tell a story, describing what is to be achieved, why it needs to be achieved and the evidence (from data collection) to support the dialogue. Drawings, charts, diagrams and photographs may be used to support the story. The document should present information that can be acted on by the design team. A typical project brief would have a structure similar to that outlined here:

- ◆ *Mission statement.* The reasons for the project, a statement of intent
- ◆ *Objectives.* Statements that set out how the intent should be realised
- ◆ *Priorities.* Objectives prioritised so that resources can be targeted
- ◆ *Performance parameters*

- *Responsibilities* of all key actors
- *Timeframe for the project*, including milestones and completion date
- *Supporting information*, e.g. charts, illustrative diagrams, photographs and drawings.

Statement of need

The first stage is the identification of need (Figure 4.1). Once identified, the need will be presented to senior managers for approval prior to proceeding further. If the decision to proceed is positive then plans are put in place to develop a strategic brief, followed by the project briefing documentation.

Strategic brief

The term strategic brief is usually used to encompass the primary drivers for the project and hence the project brief. This relates to the inception stage of the RIBA Plan of Work, the start of the information-gathering stages. Information-gathering relates to the type of organisation, its managerial structure, its policy towards change and future business growth, etc. The client's core business will relate to its organisational culture and its value criteria. Values relate to quality, cost and time. Design values relate to aesthetics, image and esteem. These values need to be articulated and measured for them to be meaningful. The preferred or anticipated procurement route should be discussed at the strategic briefing stage because it will affect the relationship of key actors, and in some cases the way in which the briefing process is managed. Procurement decisions will affect who develops the project brief and the type of interaction between client and brief-taker. Stakeholders will be keen to impose their values on the strategic brief. The strategic brief will contain text and be supported by charts, tables and diagrams.

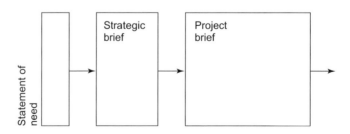

Figure 4.1 Development of the briefing phase.

Project brief

The project brief should reflect the broad strategy explored and established in the strategic brief. The project brief relates to a specific site and its environment and project needs. The project values should relate to the client value criteria set out in the strategic brief. The outcome of the various data collection and analysis exercises needs to be stated in a written document. This should concisely and clearly describe the project objectives and priorities. Concisely written documents are less likely to be misinterpreted by others. Ambiguity must be avoided and superfluous information excluded. Values must be explicit. Typical areas to be explored and articulated in the project brief are discussed later. On a more detailed level it is common to develop briefs for related areas such as the fit-out and furniture. Project briefs may contain prescriptive and performance requirements. Performance requirements tend to be preferred because each requirement allows alternative design solutions to be explored within the defined performance parameters. The project brief will contain text and be supported by charts, tables, diagrams, drawings and photographs. Physical and computer models may also be used.

The project brief is a specification of client values and needs, not solutions. The conceptual design will then seek to reflect these needs. The design brief should be a concise document that clearly outlines the client needs and states essential project parameters and constraints. This will help the client and the client's advisers to consider the best approach to the design and construction phases. The aim is to reduce uncertainty relating to the project. A number of checklists exist for different building types. Typical areas to be explored and articulated in the project brief are:

♦ *Context*. Site location factors, relating to physical and environmental factors and to social, cultural and political factors. Urban design management. Location will colour contextual factors, such as community involvement.
♦ *Design*. Functionality, flexibility and adaptability of design. Space usage related to activities. Esteem and image.
♦ *Comfort*. Internal and external environments, user satisfaction.
♦ *Environment*. Approach to sustainability, environmental impact, energy usage, recycling strategy, etc.
♦ *Finance*. Sources and allocation of funding. Projected cash flows and provisional project budget. Design to target cost. Capital costs, operating and environmental costs, whole life costing. Transaction costs.

- *Legal matters.* All legal aspects of the project, including contractual arrangements.
- *Risk.* Statement of significant risks to the project and stake-holders. Scenarios and contingency plans.
- *Statement of quality level(s).* Expected quality levels of the building and building elements. Expressed as a performance specification.
- *Time.* Key dates and significant milestones identified and set out in a provisional programme. Realistic dates and deadlines agreed and committed to by all key actors.
- *Responsibilities.* Identification of actors' key roles and responsibilities and establishment of lines of communication. Key actors need to be identified and boundaries of responsi-bilities discussed and established. Mapping key stakeholders and their role in the project can assist with the identification of clear communication routes.
- *Procurement route.* Identification of an appropriate procurement route given the parameters outlined above.
- *Resources.* Parameters and limits.

Standard briefs

Many corporate clients use a 'standard' brief for their repeat building projects, such as fast food units and retail units. These briefs set out, in varying degrees of detail, the technical and functional requirements for a typical building and reflect the corporate values and market image of the organisation. Some standard briefs are very prescriptive, listing, for example, materials that can and cannot be used, even the refer-ence number for the paint colours to be used. Standard client briefs are essentially documents representing preferred solutions based on the client's previous experience. As such they represent an important source of knowledge. Standard briefs are not static documents; the contents are constantly being tested and revised with new project experience and feedback from maintenance and facilities manage-ment departments. Thus standard briefs are gradually evolving and represent an excellent source of expert knowledge developed by the client organisation over time, revised to suit changing circumstances and improvements to their standard requirements. They provide an excellent briefing document and detailed design guide from which to work. Some clients will include some elements that are performance based in an attempt to allow greater choice and encourage creativ-ity and innovation within projects. These documents will contain text and be supported by diagrams, tables, drawings of 'standard designs' and (often prescriptive) specifications for materials and finishes. Lists of products that should, or must, be used and possibly a list of prohibited products may also be included. Where design organisations carry out repeat projects for clients, it is standard practice to develop a bespoke master specification and architectural details in response to the standard brief. Although many design organisations take client specifications as a definitive list, some designers will question the content from time to time, especially in situations where there is discrepancy between what a client wants and what other organisations/control agencies may require to ensure conformity. The client brief will be instrumental in steering both the conceptual and detailed design phases.

Communication of the brief

A clear understanding of the actors expected to read and act on the written project brief may assist in the writing and communication of the project values, i.e. the brief should be written for a target audience. The target audience may influence the language used within the brief; however, the golden rules of clarity, brevity and consistency should always be followed. Some commercial clients may impose restrictions on who is allowed to see written briefs when, for example, security and/or commercial advantage are paramount concerns.

Client approvals and common problems

Care should be taken to ensure that the project brief is to the client's approval before proceeding to the design phase. Alternatively, if the brief is being developed concurrently with the conceptual design it will be necessary to introduce a number of opportunities at which the client is able to approve the current status of the briefing documents. The usual tool for bringing the client and other participants together is a series of managed meetings at which the brief (and design) is reviewed. Reviews should be relatively straightforward events, where the brief is 'signed-off' at appropriate control gateways in accordance with standard quality management procedures and the project plan. The review affords the opportunity for client and consultants to check and agree that the brief is complete (the problem formulated) and is an accurate representation of the client's aspirations before proceeding to the design stages. When discrepancies are uncovered it may be necessary to undertake further work before proceeding further. In some cases it may be possible to proceed, with the understanding that some issues have not been resolved but will be tackled in subsequent stages. If an intermediary is involved in the briefing stages (for example an independent project manager), it is important to ensure that the scope of the architectural firm's input is clearly defined and approved by the client. Such procedures are central to quality management. The interface between the project manager and the design manager should be established and roles defined before proceeding with the conceptual design stage.

Common problems

During early stages of the project clients are exploring and testing a number of alternatives. The project environment tends to be relatively fluid and dynamic with high levels of uncertainty. Clients are trying to establish how they can best maximise their value and architects and other key project stakeholders are trying to assist the client so that the project moves forward in a positive manner. It is during this phase that the potential for things to go wrong is quite high. There are a number of relatively well-documented difficulties that may be experienced during the briefing phase and the brief-taker and design manager need to be mindful of these potential perils.

- ♦ *Communication difficulties.* In some situations it is not unusual for the client and the brief-taker to experience communication problems. This may simply be a slightly different use of language that has created misunderstanding, but it can also be linked to personality clashes and the holding of conflicting values. Communication difficulties may also be created when, as is common in many large projects, parties other than those charged with developing the design develop the brief. Brief-takers must be sensitive to personalities and the ease, or otherwise, of interaction between clients and brief-taker. Problems should be highlighted and discussed early to avoid the hazards associated with ineffective communication.
- ♦ *Effective client representation.* In the majority of projects the client is an individual or team of individuals representing the interests of the building sponsor. It is imperative that the client's representative is able to represent and articulate client needs and organisational values. Mapping exercises can be effective in establishing the most appropriate client representatives at the start of the briefing process. On large projects this exercise may have to be repeated if staff change jobs and/or organisational changes are made within the organisation.

- *Hidden agendas.* It is not unusual for stakeholders to with-hold their views until later in the project, when the revelation of hidden agendas can be highly disruptive. The brief-taker must try and tease these out via workshops and facilitated group exercises.
- *Too little time.* Clients have a habit of trying to rush the early phases of projects, and the temptation to move forward without adequate information or approval of the project brief must be resisted. Explaining the timescale to key stakeholders and disseminating a clear programme of activities can help to reassure clients that the time is being used wisely. Conversely, if too much time is dedicated to the briefing activity people may become tired and jaded. Experience of different types of clients may help to inform the programming activities, with regard to the amount of time required. All activities must be justified and conducted in a timely manner.
- *Assuming too much.* The brief-taker should not assume that the client requires exactly what he or she has initially stated. Good briefing exercises can reveal needs that were not evident at the outset.
- *Briefing guides and 'standard' briefs.* These can be useful tools, but may be out of date or simply inappropriate to the task in hand. The brief-taker should be prepared to question the use of such tools and explore issues relevant to the client context. Brief-takers should also beware of falling into the 'tick-box' mentality of briefing checklists.
- *Poor coordination of data collection activities.* This can lead to missed opportunities and ineffective use of resources as well as an ineffective written brief.

The project to office interface

During the development of the brief there will be an opportunity to assess the likelihood of the project progressing to the feasibility stage and beyond. At this juncture it will be necessary to reassess the resources required for the project and assess the design firm's exposure to risk. The design manager's role is to prepare an outline plan of the resources required, together with a number of contingency plans. These will be determined by the fee income and the project timescale. Consideration must be given to the current and future availability of office resources, especially resources already committed or about to be committed to other projects. Funds and time may be limited, thus the firm must utilise its skills to best effect. This is a delicate balancing act because the design manager will be trying to maximise resources, limiting over- and undercapacity within relatively tight parameters. The better the briefing process, the easier it will be to plan office resources for the following phases. Poorly defined, rushed project briefs will cause a high degree of uncertainty for the design manager, and the temptation to progress the project without going through appropriate control gateways should be resisted. Adequate time must be allowed for this phase and this must be reflected in the fee agreement with the client. This is a challenging time in terms of trying to allocate resources to the project when many factors are ill-defined, uncertainty is high and the risk of the project not proceeding or being delayed is foremost. The design manager will need to manage the external relationships with the client, users and community representatives. Additional external relationships with key project actors will also need attention during the briefing phase. The external lines of communication will need to be balanced against the requirements of the design office in such a way as to enhance the creative input to the briefing process.

Continual iteration of the brief involves close contact with the client and client's representatives. This is a period of learning for everyone involved and a period when trust and mutual understanding are developed between the design office and the client. Time spent in getting the brief right before design work proceeds and assembling the most appropriate organisations and people to work on the project tends to be a good investment, reducing uncertainty and the risk of major problems later in the project. Some clients may need convincing of this and architectural offices must be prepared to argue for adequate fees to carry out the briefing functions effectively and professionally. The link between the client and the design office is crucial for the development of an effective brief and working relationship, through which new business may follow. Thus the client/office interface is also concerned with the marketing and development of new business opportunities.

Chapter Five
Developing the Design

Once the design agenda has been established via a thorough briefing process, the focus turns to the development of creative design proposals. Architects are the most prominent actors at this early stage, although they will be working very closely with others, such as structural and service engineers, in a cross-functional project team. It is also common for craftsmen, specialist trade contractors and manufacturers to be involved at this early stage to provide information and advice on major technical issues to improve design integration and cost control. Depending on the procurement route chosen, main contractors may also be invited to contribute to the design team's deliberations. This is a highly creative, and to the casual observer rather chaotic, process that must be carefully choreographed to provide enough space for creativity to flourish within the established time and resource parameters. Many aspects of the design are being developed concurrently, collaboratively and competitively, involving trade-offs, compromise and the ability to appreciate the contribution of others. This is a period in which the most value can be generated and conversely when waste may manifest itself if not recognised and dealt with systematically, for example through the use of value management techniques. The ease and efficiency of communication between key actors will have an influence on the quality of the design and the effectiveness of the project. Success of this phase is also related to the ability of the brief-taker to transfer the client's requirements to the design team and the ability of the design team to interpret the briefing documents.

Design decision-making is one of the most heavily researched and written about areas of architectural design, and is outside the scope of this book. Less frequently researched is the influence of the office culture and the emergent project culture on the designers' actions. Architecture is a work of collaboration and it is crucial to understand that the environment in which the design team work will be heavily influenced by the attitude of managers and managerial frameworks. The way in which design work is resourced, scheduled and controlled at both office and project levels will influence the design team, hopefully in a positive manner. This applies equally to the conceptual design and detailed design phases, both of which need to be managed effectively in order to utilise resources efficiently and maximise value for the client.

Integral designing

The design process can be characterised as a continuous process of change in which design information has to be well documented, clearly structured and continually updated if mistakes are to be prevented. Knowledge about the design exists on a cognitive level of each team member, on the level of collaborating design organisations, and on an external level via the client, users and other stakeholders. Designers repeatedly generate new knowledge about the design by collecting, sharing and transforming information. Team communication in terms of face-to-face communication is essential to facilitate these processes. From the perspective of the design team the specialist design knowledge is usually embedded in the team and needs to be communicated to become useful knowledge for the design to be produced. To exchange design knowledge, participants need to communicate synchronously and asynchronously using all the available means of communication. Not all designers participate in the same way at the same time. There are many who participate as individuals, working alone for crucial periods and then returning to the project network. Design team members greatly depend on the most current design information to work out their own design tasks.

Collaboration between design team members and integration of design work may be very fluid at the conceptual stage and controls should be as liberal as possible so that creative design may be encouraged, yet tight enough to assure design development is supported and delivered to agreed project milestones. Because of the fluid nature of the project there is a tendency for design work to consume more time than estimated and budgeted. Managerial control and the support of the design and project managers will be necessary to ensure efficient coordination of work packages and the completion of work to agreed quality standards.

It is necessary to recognise that the various contributors to design activities may hold different views as to their perceived amount of risk in relation to design liability, and this may well influence how they behave during the development of the design. The design team will be developing working relationships and effective communication structures, and this requires leadership to allow the designers to quickly develop into a creative and efficient team. Adopting a position or attitude towards architectural design and making sure other project stakeholders are aware of designers' values and ideals is an important first step in setting the culture for the project. Architects must take responsibility for leading design activities and ensure that the values set out in the project brief are developed to their maximum potential. Attention should be given to:

- *Total scheduling.* From the beginning of projects the design and project managers should develop a comprehensive schedule of work that includes all design and realisation phases. This schedule should be revisited at regular stages in the development of the design and revised to suit the evolution of the design. Including the practicalities of realisation at an early stage can help the design team to stay focused on developing design proposals that can be realised efficiently and safely. Consideration of the sequence of work packages can help with the detailing and subsequently the safe and efficient realisation of the building.
- *Total costing.* Early design decisions have a significant impact on the cost of the project, thus it is necessary to develop the project costs as the design develops rather than at the end of the conceptual design phase. Techniques such as design to target cost may help with the development of realistic costs through various design iterations.
- *Total evaluation.* A comprehensive programme of review activities will provide opportunities for key stakeholders to discuss the development of the design and how it will be detailed and subsequently realised within the agreed programme and budget.

To develop and implement these activities effectively requires a continual dialogue between the design team members and those best able to transform the design into a building. This will help to identify problems early and action can be taken to design out waste and hence maximise value. Focusing on how the building is to be realised from the start of the design process will help to mitigate problems with constructability and manufacturability at a later stage, and hence help to reduce project costs and time overruns, as well as helping to improve safety and the quality of the finished building.

Lean design management

Given that approximately 40% of building defects can be traced back to decisions made at the conceptual and detailed design phases, it is important that this waste stream is tackled early. There are a wide range of causes, which often relate to inadequate communication between the actors, failings in the coordination of works packages, use of incomplete and erroneous information and poor understanding of constructability and realisation issues. Waste can be reduced and efficiency improved through good design and management practices. This means starting the project with the right attitude to waste reduction and value creation. Too much emphasis on aesthetics, spatial configurations and styling and too little attention to production aspects is often the cause of design solutions that are unnecessarily difficult and expensive to realise. Creative and innovative designs can be enhanced by knowledge of realisation processes, and when designers are short on construction and production knowledge this can be brought in by involving specialist trades, manufacturers and contractors as early as practicably possible. Greater emphasis on constructability at the conceptual stage will usually bring about savings in labour, materials, time and cost, thus helping to improve design value.

The terms 'lean design' and 'lean design management' refer to processes that directly address customer value by confronting waste in the design and promoting efficiency in the management of the design process. Much like lean construction, there is no clear definition of what is meant by the term 'lean design' and advantages depend on the context in which they are applied. Lean thinking and techniques borrowed and adapted from lean manufacturing can provide architects with a useful array of tools through which the value of the design can be enhanced and waste reduced. The five principles of lean thinking are to specify value; identify the value stream; enable value to flow; establish the 'pull' of value; and pursue perfection. Although developed specifically for manufacturing and mass-produced products, the philosophy is relatively robust and can, with some interpretation, be applied to a project environment. Taking our cue from lean thinking, the five principles of lean architectural design management would be:

♦ *Specify value.* Clearly and precisely identify the client's requirements and identify the specific functions required to deliver a solution. Client (and other project stakeholder) requirements are identified through the briefing process and subsequently tested and refined as the design develops. The specific functions required relate to the management of the entire project, from inception to realisation of a beautiful and functional building. Value in an architectural sense will relate to exchange, operational, aesthetic and cultural value.

- *Identify the value stream.* Identify the fastest process to deliver the building through the integration of the functions identified when specifying value. The target should be delivery at the defined (high) quality and (low) cost in a safe, environmentally sustainable and ethical manner. This is linked to the use of the most appropriate procurement route and design management models, which help to determine how value flows within the project. Standard generic approaches may not be applicable to all design projects and contexts.
- *Enable value to flow.* Remove any unnecessary or redundant cost items from the design to get to the optimal solution. Looking out for redundancy (in process and product) while designing can help to mitigate unnecessary costs. Value management and engineering can also help to identify and remove waste during the design and detailed design phases before the design is realised in a physical form. Reducing waste is sometimes misinterpreted as meaning to reduce variety and maximise repetition, which does not accord with many designers' values.
- *Establish the 'pull' of value.* This means frequently listening to the client and other key stakeholders during the project and responding iteratively. This task is made easier by including the client in the process, for example through formal design reviews and value management workshops. Project and post-project reviews are an additional tool for establishing the pull of value.
- *Pursue perfection.* Incorporate cost-reduction methods and tools into the office culture and practices to enable continual cost reduction for the architectural office and for all clients via their projects. To do this effectively it is necessary to understand workflow within the design office and the interface with the project portfolio. This brings us full circle to understanding the symbiosis between projects and design office.

Lean thinking can be applied at different levels in the transformation process, from the whole project to distinct phases and sub-stages. This helps to provide a picture of the whole project and can assist in the planning and scheduling of the various work packages. Approaching design from a lean thinking perspective also helps to emphasise the need for designers to understand how design value is physically realised and the cost of this transformation process. Depending on the type of project and the approach adopted by the design team, this may involve a greater understanding of craft techniques or manufacturing production techniques, and the associated cost and time parameters. Emphasis should be on the whole life cycle of the building and environmental sustainability. Thus attention should be given to minimising waste, reducing whole life costs and building in flexibility and adaptability for future building users. To do this requires knowledge of the entire design and realisation process, including demolition, recycling and recovery management techniques.

Digital design

Architecture is continually evolving, aided in particular by the use of computer software applications that allow the creation and realisation of organic, fluid and creative structures. This has altered the relationship between the form of the building and its construction. It has also started to alter relationships within the construction team, shifting emphasis towards integral design approaches and concurrent designing. Digital technologies have helped to establish direct links between manufacturers and architects, thus the transition of design information through a prime contractor is, in some cases, no longer necessary. Digital technologies have transformed the way in which we think about buildings and provided the opportunity for new ways of managing the realisation phase. 3D milling machines linked to 3D software packages (such as mesh modellers) allow shapes of all forms to be realised. Digital visualisation techniques (virtual reality) are used throughout the process from initial briefing to manufacturing (and facilities management), allowing all actors to see and experience space much more easily and quickly compared with 2D methods, helping to break down professional languages and the mystique of how to read drawings. Web-based communications allow design teams to work on projects concurrently, helping to promote teamwork and knowledge-sharing. Increased coordination of skills and knowledge can help to make the processes more efficient and productive, helping to facilitate communication between actors. The increasing use of design information models (DIMs) and building information models (BIMs) may also help actors to communicate more effectively and efficiently at this and subsequent stages in the development of the design.

Some designers still prefer the interaction of pen and mind when designing and sketching, transferring ideas to a digital format after the main principles have been worked through. The 3D packages have evolved into integrated building modelling tools that (theoretically) allow actors in different locations to work on the design concurrently. Models that include the time dimension are known as 4D models.

However, there remain a number of challenges in achieving a global information exchange standard, thus making the integration element of the models difficult to attain. The compatibility of computer software is a factor that managers must address early in team composition exercises. Structural modelling has assisted engineers and architects alike in making it very easy to model the behaviour of buildings from the perspective of structure, response to fire and climatic changes, etc. The objective is to test a number of design options against the project brief as the design develops.

Presenting design proposals

The ability to clearly communicate design ideas to clients and other project stakeholders is an important skill. Presentation requires the use of a wide range of communication media, from written reports and drawings to verbal presentations supported with graphics. The way in which the design team presents their design proposals will provide a client with a lot of information about how the designers are likely to manage the project. Similarly, the ability of architects to answer questions related to the design and matters of cost and time will tend to be rather revealing about the ability to deliver a high quality design on time and within budget. Complete and comprehensive coverage of the following will be expected:

- Terms of reference and responsibilities
- Analysis of the site, brief and related parameters
- Approach to the problem represented in design drawings and supporting information, which may include alternative design solutions
- Estimation of cost (including all professional fees)
- Estimation of the programme (including the identification of uncertainty)
- Recommendations
- Discussion with the client and project stakeholders
- Approval from the client to proceed.

Design dialogues

Including the client and all key stakeholders in the design process is an essential feature of good design solutions. Design dialogues and face-to-face meetings are useful vehicles through which to discuss and explore possibilities and preferences as well as allowing exchange of knowledge between the interested parties. Interpersonal communication provides the opportunity for actors to develop mutual understanding of others' knowledge and attitudes and hence work more closely in sharing information and coordinating the various works packages. Face-to-face communication is a rich instrument to communicate design especially in early design stages when much design knowledge is implicit and still held in the minds of the design team.

Design dialogue is a means of communication that offers the highest possible exchange of signals, clues and messages, and thus the best opportunity for understanding the characteristics of the design project. Both sender and receiver are able to communicate directly by use of body language, their voices and also by making sketches. Dialogues are a very effective tool for discussing design problems related to the design tasks of other contributors, by visualising the design using sketches and explanatory stories. They can also be used to develop a better understanding of others' roles in the design process and to fine-tune each other's design tasks.

Meetings and workshops

It is during the conceptual design phases that meetings tend to be most fluid and often called at short notice to discuss, present and resolve issues that have arisen in trying to meet the project brief. Face-to-face meetings are crucial to the development of the design in an integral manner, although they also serve an important function for getting to know the other team members better and contributing to team development. Meetings tend to fall into two types: those to discuss design development and those in which the progress of the project is discussed. Facilitated workshops are also used as a means of exploring creative responses to the project brief. In the early phases of the project the design development meetings and workshops serve a dual function. Actors with different backgrounds and levels of education are often brought together for the first time, thus workshops are about exploring appropriate means of communication and developing working relationships, which evolve alongside the development of the design. Team meetings can be used for several reasons:

- ♦ To understand and explore the design team's interpretation of the brief and to reach consensus about the design (at specific junctures in the programme)
- ♦ To resolve conflicts and discrepancies between various design work packages, thus allowing the design to develop
- ♦ To exchange experiences and knowledge about design possibilities and realisation processes

- To develop a team ethos by bringing people together to discuss often difficult issues face to face
- To evaluate and review the development of the design
- To review the progress of specific design packages against the master programme.

A kick-off meeting is planned at the start of the design process to introduce team members and clarify their role and tasks. It is common to involve the client in this meeting also.

Design development meetings

Design development meetings may include the members of the design organisation only or more likely a number of other specialists comprising the core design team. The purpose of these meetings is to discuss the development of the design. The opportunity to discuss the design face to face helps to establish options and preferences for particular solutions. It also helps to reveal individual attitudes and values. Bringing various actors with complementary skills together in the same place to discuss the design is a key feature of a more integral design approach. Brainstorming sessions may also be used to develop specific aspects of the design.

Progress meetings

Discussing progress and proper closure of design tasks is important and progress meetings need to be scheduled on a regular basis to review progress in accordance with the overall programme. The client, along with key actors, should be invited so that they can be informed of progress and have the opportunity to contribute to the development of the design as part of the project team. Although it is inevitable that issues relating to the development of the design will be discussed in these meetings, the primary purpose is to discuss progress in accordance with agreed time, cost and quality parameters. A typical agenda would include progress reports on the following:

- Design development
- Programme
- Costs. Progressive development of cost information concurrent with developments in the design
- Contractual and legal issues.

These meetings are a good opportunity to agree and sign off the work. They are also an opportunity to reassess provisional programmes and revisit cost estimates.

Facilitated workshops

Facilitated workshops may be used at this phase to explore how the basic project values may be fulfilled and risks and uncertainty managed. A number of design options are presented, reflecting how they meet the project brief while at the same time addressing the contractual project framework. Project economy can be discussed along with restraints imposed by, for example, authorities and relevant codes. Proposals can be considered and ranked or prioritised according to value. At least two or three workshops may be required because there will be a lot of information to work through. The outcome of the facilitated workshop is the selection and agreement of the proposal best suited to the values expressed in the briefing documents. This proposal will be subsequently tested as the design is detailed.

Design critiques and reviews

Closely linked to the need for meetings is the requirement to review designs and exercise a degree of control over changes to the design. One of the great strengths of a formal quality management system is the design review. This is a formal assessment of the design against the project brief. The aim is to check that the design proposal(s) meets the client's requirements, is in line with the design organisation's own standards and conforms to the relevant regulatory requirements. The concept of the design review is not new to architects since design critiques are a familiar part of an architect's training and are used in practice to control design quality. Care is needed not to confuse the two since there are important differences between the informal critique and the formal design review.

Design critiques

Design critiques tend to be relatively informal events conducted within the sanctum of the office. Designs can be discussed openly and critically with a view to improving the value of the design before drawings and associated information are released to the client and/or other project participants. Some offices conduct design critiques on a relatively ad hoc basis, reacting to the speed of development of the design. Other offices have a more systematic approach, programming the design critique for a particular day and time and inviting staff working on other projects to contribute their views and share their knowledge.

Design reviews

Design reviews are planned events, forming an important part of the programme and the project quality plan. Reviews form control gateways at predetermined key stages in the life of the project. To work effectively design reviews should include the project team, consultants, the quality manager, the planning supervisor and the client or the client's representative. Design reviews should include the presence of the client and consultants working on the project so that the project team reviews the design and any alterations agreed by the team and recorded in the office plan. The review system is essentially a series of gates in the design process through which the project cannot pass without a thorough check from the quality manager and the approval of the client and participating consultants. These meetings provide an opportunity to discuss and agree the design before proceeding further; more specifically they should address:

- Design verification
- Design changes
- Statutory consents
- Constructability
- Health and safety
- Environmental impact
- Budget
- Programme.

The design review is a very good tool for detecting errors and omissions. It also provides a checkpoint for ensuring that the design meets the client's requirements and the architectural practice's quality standards. It also gives the planning supervisor an opportunity to check the scheme for compliance under the Construction (Design and Management) Regulations 1994 (CDM). More importantly it provides a window for debate and feedback. It is important to keep these meetings organised but as informal as possible so that ideas can be discussed freely and all members of the project can participate in the process. Planned design reviews where client, external consultants, designer, design manager, project manager and the planning supervisor can review and discuss potential problem areas, and take appropriate decisions, should form an essential part of a health and safety strategy. The design review has another purpose: the check for compliance with environmental/sustainable polices and practices. These may be a combination of the client's requirements and the firm's own pursuit of environmentally responsible policies and will have been discussed and agreed at the briefing stage. As the project proceeds, many situations arise and change; therefore it is important

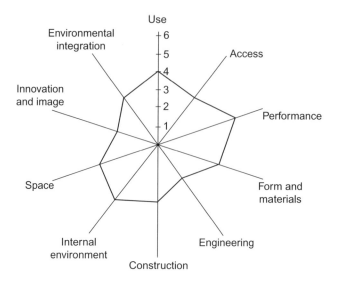

Figure 5.1 Design quality indicator.

to constantly review the project's environmental impact against the predetermined criteria.

Design quality indicator

The design quality indicator (DQI) has been developed as a tool for assessing the design quality of buildings. The tool may be used at key stages in the development, realisation and use of the building and is well suited for use in conjunction with value management and risk management techniques. The four key stages are briefing, mid-design, at occupation and during use. The tool relies on participants completing a questionnaire that addresses the three fields of build quality, impact and functionality. The results are then expressed illustratively as a design quality indicator spider diagram (Figure 5.1). By using the tool at key points in the project it is possible to track the importance given to all ten factors and this helps to focus attention on areas that have not been adequately addressed. The tool is useful for developing and maintaining a clear vision for the building design. It also helps to capture knowledge for guiding future projects and the ongoing management of the building.

Programming and coordinating design work

A number of tools can be used to help design and project managers schedule the multitude of tasks required to realise a design project. Clear goals, timescales and value parameters will have been established and agreed via the briefing process. This global project view then needs to be broken down into manageable work packages using the work breakdown structure. This helps to identify the tasks required, identify and allocate responsibility for specific works packages and also identify interdependencies between work packages. Risk and uncertainty may also be revealed during this process. The challenge is then to estimate how much effort will be required to complete these tasks (see also Chapter 11). Various programming techniques are available to map activities, ranging from Gantt (bar) charts to network analysis, precedence diagrams, line of balance (elemental trend analysis) and time chainage diagrams. These are explained in project management books, so only a brief overview is provided here.

Work breakdown structure (WBS)

The aim of the work breakdown structure is to partition the project into smaller, manageable parts. This is usually broken down as a series of tasks, sub-tasks, individual work packages and levels of responsibility and effort. This is a common technique in project management and has been proven to be an effective way of helping to organise and manage projects. The technique can be applied to design projects although it should be noted that it does not deal with the complexity of interrelated design effort and coordination of design activities. However, at a simple level it can help managers to picture the process as a series of activities and hence help to develop schedules of work and work programmes.

Gantt (bar) charts

Gantt charts are a very useful way of representing tasks from the start of the project to its completion (Figure 5.2). Individual tasks are illustrated as a bar on the chart, showing start and completion dates and project milestones. This helps to provide a visual overview of the tasks and may help to identify the more obvious coordination problems. Project milestones are clearly identified on the bar chart. Computer software packages allow for some highly sophisticated breakdown of tasks to be performed, although for many design projects a relatively simple representation is usually sufficient to help picture the sequence of design activities required. Gantt charts do not show dependency and so it is difficult to see which work packages may significantly affect the successful completion of the project. Programmes form a benchmark to check progress of the various tasks at a given time. A number of different techniques can be used, but one of the most common is

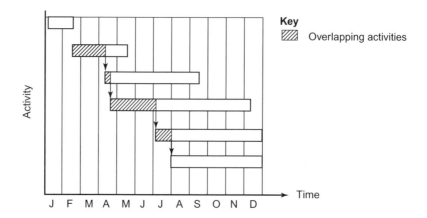

Figure 5.2 Simple Gantt chart.

to use coloured traffic lights (green, amber, red) or faces (happy, sad) to represent progress. Alternatively the completion of the task can be represented as a percentage, for example 75% complete.

Network analysis

The critical path method is a graphical representation of work packages represented as an arrow diagram (Figure 5.3). The arrows represent the tasks and the circles the events (which are numbered in sequence to completion). To undertake network analysis the planner has to first estimate the overall period for completing the (design) project. Individual operations are then identified and the duration assigned to each activity. The next stage is to establish the sequence of work, which is usually done by starting to sketch out the arrow diagram. This helps to identify which tasks are critical, i.e. need to be completed, before other tasks can commence. This can be done manually and/or assisted with computer software packages. Thus network analysis can help to identify dependencies and is often used in conjunction with a bar chart. It is difficult to show concurrent activities clearly on arrow diagrams without the diagrams becoming overloaded with information. Precedence diagrams follow a similar rationale to arrow diagrams, but the dependencies and activities are represented differently. An activity box is used instead of arrows, which allows a number of different relationships to be expressed on the diagram. This makes the technique more useful than arrow diagrams for complex and concurrent activities. The important point to make is that by mapping activities graphically and identifying critical

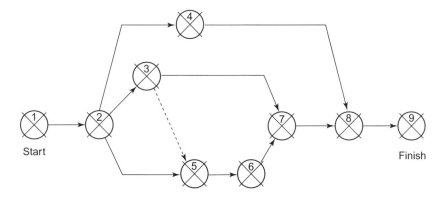

Figure 5.3 Simple critical path chart.

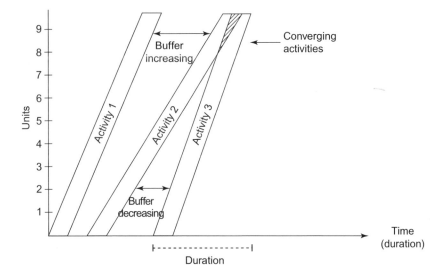

Figure 5.4 Simple line of balance chart.

activities the design manager will gain a much richer picture of the design tasks, thus helping to achieve accurate programming.

Line of balance (elemental trend analysis)

The line of balance technique allows a graphical representation of the rate of work on different activities, represented by the inclined lines on Figure 5.4. If all activities developed at the same speed, the lines on the diagram would be parallel; however, the reality is that some tasks proceed much more quickly than others. Time buffers are represented as spaces between activities. As lines diverge the buffer increases and as lines converge the buffer decreases. Converging lines represent the potential for one activity adversely to affect the other. Line of balance was originally developed for highly repetitive tasks, although the technique may be useful for mapping one-off projects if the activities are well defined. Time chainage diagrams (or location-time charts) are essentially a combination of line of balance and bar chart scheduling techniques.

Coordination

In addition to encouraging and stimulating creative design proposals the design manager will be concerned with coordination of work within the office and between design team members. This involves careful monitoring of staff performance and allocation of the most appropriate staff to the task (see also Part Two). If architectural firms are to be competitive the amount of time spent at this stage needs very careful monitoring and control. Individual designers must be capable of designing within time constraints and must not exceed these limits, even when the temptation to do so is strong. It is not uncommon for firms to lose money at this stage, necessitating (often expensive) short-cuts further along the process. Good design does not necessarily take a long time if the management structure is in place to support the designers. The design manager has an important role here, acting as a motivator to staff while also monitoring the progress of the design in accordance with the programme and intervening if and when required. Coordination activities are rather extensive, but tend to include the coordination of:

- Design works packages (and information flow)
- Costs
- Value parameters
- Quality of information (signing off).

Town planning approvals

Towards the end of the conceptual design stage comes the preparation of drawings and associated documentation to make a submission to the local authority planning department. Development cannot commence without first receiving planning consent. In the UK the town planning process is a democratic exercise and there is always a degree of uncertainty and risk that the decision could be delayed (e.g. to allow the planning committee to visit the site) or refused (e.g. because the proposal is contrary to the local plan). Such decisions will have a detrimental effect on the progress of the project and therefore it is crucial that all the documentation is complete before the application is submitted. This helps the town planning officers to do their job efficiently and helps mitigate the potential of delays due to missing or incomplete information. Few development proposals are straightforward and the interaction with town planning officers, the planning committee and local user groups must be handled with tact and diplomacy.

Strategies

The planning system in the UK is primarily concerned with preventing unwanted development and developers often want to build in areas deemed to be unsuitable by planning departments. The approach taken to trying to achieve planning consent, and hence the pattern of interaction with the town planning department, will determine the nature of the relationship between the design office and the planning department. Although the architectural press likes to publicise the cultural differences between developers and architects (trying to get approval) and the planning department (trying to control development), the reality is that the cultural differences are manifest in the attitudes adopted by both sides. A variety of strategies may be used to suit different clients and contexts:

- *Passive.* The scheme is developed, the application prepared and then submitted with little or no interaction with town planning officers. The design team then waits to hear the outcome of the planning committee's deliberations. There is no attempt to manage the application process.
- *Open.* The scheme is developed in conjunction with discussions with the town planning officer and other stakeholders representing the interests of the community, such as local authority highways engineers, environmental officers, etc. Discussions tend to be open and the design team is seen to be responsive and sensitive to the requirements and wishes of the local authority and other stakeholders. This approach can consume considerable staff time, but tends to be beneficial in achieving planning consent with few, usually reasonable and expected, conditions. This makes the subsequent detailing and programming of the scheme a relatively smooth process.
- *Defensive.* Interaction between the planning department and the design team is conducted with closed and defensive communication, with no attempt to build a relationship. The defensive attitude tends to reveal cultural differences

between the parties very quickly and it is not uncommon for personality clashes to develop as a result. Because of the defensive attitude it may be difficult to predict the outcome of the application process, which will involve uncertainty for the programme.

♦ *Aggressive.* In situations where it is clear that the proposed development is contrary to the development plans of the local authority (and approval is highly unlikely), it is common for the design team to take what many planning officers would perceive as an aggressive approach. Interaction is likely to be very limited and possibly adversarial. The approach is to submit two or even three different schemes to try and cause the planning department as much difficulty as possible. The intention is to appeal the expected refusal. Double-tracking and even triple-tracking (with slightly different proposals), with a view to appealing, is not liked and is perceived as aggressive behaviour by town planners; clients on the other hand may have a quite different view.

Implications

Obtaining planning consent can be a time-consuming process and one fraught with uncertainty about the timing of decisions and the outcome of the decisions. For a variety of reasons schemes do not always progress smoothly through the planning system and delays in receiving an approval (or refusal) can upset carefully made programmes. A democratically elected planning committee decides planning consent, and the decision of the committee is outside the control of the applicant and their agents. However, that is not to imply that the application should be submitted then forgotten about. Without approval there is no building project and it should come as no surprise to know that successful architectural firms pay a lot of attention to the application process and take a proactive approach in managing the application procedure. Monitoring the progress of the application and being ready to take action if further information is requested or a delay is suspected can help to speed up the process. Approvals can have a significant influence on the project programme and hence resourcing within the design office. Some approvals may be forthcoming sooner than expected and some may be delayed. Therefore the programme will need to accommodate some uncertainty and hence flexibility at this juncture.

It is not uncommon for the client to agree to the development of the detailed design drawings and the preparation of the documentation for Building Regulations submission while the planning application is being considered. The risk is that the planning application is delayed or refused, leading to abortive work. A less serious risk is the requirement for changes to the design before approval is granted and/or the imposition of conditions that affect the detailing phase. It is important that the consequences of proceeding without the necessary approvals are discussed with the client and that the client is aware of the cost and time implications if things do not unfold as anticipated.

Approvals and common problems

Although the transition from conceptual design to detail design appears to be relatively clear-cut in process models, the reality is that there is considerable overlap between the conceptual design stage and the detail stage. The use of control gateways will make the transition more transparent; however, it is unlikely that the conceptual design has finished evolving and it is highly probable that many detailed design decisions have already been made. Design iteration tends to make this boundary rather superficial, although it is usually necessary to make a distinction between phases for a variety of reasons. First, the act of achieving full planning approval will 'fix' the design layout and appearance of the building and associated site works. Changes to the approved design, for example the layout, appearance and external facing materials, will need to be referred back to the planning department for approval. This can prove to be time-consuming and there is no certainty that the revisions will be accepted. Second, the granting of full planning approval is usually the trigger for clients to decide to proceed with the detail design work, building regulation submission and contract documentation based on the approved planning application. Third, this juncture is a convenient one at which to bring the team members together to reappraise the programme, budget and design before proceeding further. Fourth, this transition is often a trigger for payment of professional fees.

Common problems

Given the relatively creative and fluid nature of the conceptual design phase it is necessary to have an underlying framework that stimulates creativity, yet also provides definitive milestones for delivery of design work packages. Without a framework the development of the design will be virtually impossible to manage. Assuming that the design team has been assembled with care, and that efforts have been made to maintain the team spirit during the conceptual stages, any problems that develop are likely to be minor and easily resolved. Communication between individuals and groups should be relatively open and coordination of work should be a relatively smooth undertaking, requiring minimal managerial interference. In situations where the design team has been put together hastily and people are unfamiliar with fellow actors' working habits, there may be problems with communication and coordination in the early stages, which may hinder design development until the participants have found how best to work together. There are other common problems that may be avoided with a little thought and forward planning:

- *Failure to respect the briefing documents.* It is not uncommon for the design team to 'forget' the aims and objectives as stated in the briefing documents as the design develops, only to revisit them too late in the programme. Formal design reviews should help to identify discrepancies between the design and the brief and provide a forum to discuss how to proceed.
- *Programme overrun.* There should not be any excuses for project overruns at this stage, assuming an accurate estimation of design effort and an effective briefing process.
- *Cost uncertainty and poor estimates of cost* are a common cause of dispute. The better the cost certainty at the design phase, the less uncertainty in the detailing phase.
- *Incomplete design work* may occur for a number of reasons and may delay the progression of the project. All uncertainties and missing information should be discussed at design reviews and the consequences discussed and recorded.
- *Communication difficulties* are often caused by the inability of team members to meet and discuss their differences.

The project to office interface

Design quality is central to the health of the architectural office. Being able to deliver design proposals on time and to budget is a fundamental aim of every project that passes through the office. The relationship between independent projects and the office project portfolio is particularly important during the conceptual design development phase. The amount of design effort required must be estimated as accurately as possible and resourced in relation to the office project portfolio. Similarly, the interface between the office and other project participants must be managed sensitively. Failure to deal with these factors will most likely result in poor programming and coordination of design effort, and deadlines may be missed. Boundaries in project management models are, especially in the early stages, rather superficial. For example, working on the conceptual design involves some thought and work related to detailing and realisation. Additional time spent in the design phase to resolve a specific design issue may be recouped in the detailing phase because important decisions relating to the detailing have already been made. Such fluidity makes scheduling resources a challenge unless the design manager allows for some flexibility within individual work programmes. The design manager's role is to encourage creativity, while ensuring that deadlines are met and the quality of the design is acceptable to the office.

Chapter Six
Detailing the Design

In the majority of projects there is a clear cut-off between the conceptual and detail design phases. It is here that the culture changes from the abstract to the concrete and different people become involved as the scheme enters production and codified information is materialised. Conceptual architects give way to constructing architects, architectural technologists and architectural engineers aided by a variety of technicians and associated support staff. Specialist contractors may become more involved in the process and contractors and workers may be keen to offer feedback from their direct site experience to help the detailing process. Design work continues as the concept is detailed and engineered for manufacture. Much of this is highly specialised design work and is provided by specialist trade contractors. Manufacturers of building products and components also have an active role, often assisting with technical input and the provision of detailed drawings and specifications for their building components and products. Emphasis tends to turn away from aesthetics towards practical issues concerning time and cost and ease of manufacturing and assembly. There is, however, a need to retain a high degree of creativity at the detailing stage. Client values codified in the conceptual drawings need to be translated seamlessly into production drawings and subsequently into manufactured products and components. Thus synergy between the conceptual design and the detailed design is important. On very small projects it may be possible for the architect to do the detailing also, and here the flow of conceptual design thinking into the detailing stage should be relatively straightforward. In the majority of projects, where detailing is carried out by individuals not party to the earlier creative design thinking phases, effort is required to ensure that the transfer of design intent is done efficiently.

Detailing (or engineering) the design is one of the most neglected areas in the research literature, yet one of the most important stages in the lifeline of a project for determining the quality of the finished building. During this period numerous decisions concerning how the building is to be realised are made, confirmed in the contract documentation. How the detailing is managed, who contributes to the detailing phase and when the detailing is carried out continues to be a matter of some debate with the constructor sector and varies widely between projects. However, at some juncture in the life of a project the scheme has to be detailed, and this involves the input from a wide variety of actors. In contractor-led projects the contractor will usually deal with the detail design, encompassed in the production function. In architect- and management-led projects it is not uncommon to complete all, or substantial parts, of this work before the main contractor takes over. To what extent the main contractor, specialist contractors and manufacturers are involved at this stage tends to be determined by the needs of the client, the approach of the design office and the procurement route.

From a management perspective the detailing phase is concerned with interfaces, boundaries and joints. Coordination of many different works packages and production information takes high priority. Different values, goals and attitudes of the actors need to be recognised and accommodated in the planning process. A seamless transition between design and detail phases is an ideal. The degree of difficulty in detailing the design will relate to the complexity of the conceptual design. Some estimation of perceived difficulty is required in order to adequately resource and programme detailing activities.

Integral detailing

Detailing is a crucial phase during which the value of the design can be enhanced and waste of materials and resources minimised. Many of the decisions made during the detailing of the design will have been determined to lesser or greater extents by the approved conceptual design. This does not mean, however, that this phase is simply a case of applying standard details and specifications; rather it is a creative phase in which many details are explored from first principles and well-worn approaches to detailing constantly questioned. This phase is a challenging one for all actors as various works packages are coordinated and eventually brought together as a final set of information which informs the physical manufacturing and assembly stages. It is about processing and producing information, coordination of interdependent elements of work, timely transfer and easy access (see also Chapter 12). It is a phase in which close working relationships underpin efficient information-sharing and effective decision-making.

Utilising the knowledge of other actors is fundamental to delivering value. Crucial areas are:

♦ Close working relationship between conceptual designers and the detailers
♦ Understanding of production/assembly constraints and opportunities
♦ Appreciation of production costs.

Constructability

Buildability and constructability are interchangeable terms used to describe the ease of producing (manufacturing and assembling) the building efficiently and safely. Similar principles underscore the building's disassembly strategy at some future date. Core themes are greater simplicity, more use of standard components and better communication between the designers and the producers. To many architects buildability is synonymous with good design and good detailing, and something that architectural firms have always taken seriously. A large proportion of failures in building can be traced back to problems with production information and a lack of understanding by detailers about how different components interact. For constructability to improve, designers and detailers need to be better connected to production activities, for example through greater involvement with contractors and specialist sub-contractors and use of off-site production techniques.

♦ *Greater simplicity*. The argument for greater simplicity is a persuasive one. Buildings are extremely complex products and the way in which they are designed and constructed is often complex. Some architects tend to use a limited range of solutions to suit a particular design style or architectural language. Contractors have started to use a small number of 'solutions' for discrete elements of buildings, such as walls, roofs and windows, exploiting lean production and management techniques to reduce variability, improve quality and deliver greater value.
♦ *Greater use of standard components*. Standard components have been used in construction for a long time. More recently the decline in the number of skilled operatives, combined with the drive for better quality at a lower cost, has led to greater use of prefabricated components. As off-site production becomes more sophisticated and more widely available, so the opportunity to realise creative and innovative designs efficiently, safely and cost-effectively becomes a realistic option.

♦ *Better communication.* If better quality is to be achieved, waste reduced and value maximised, then it is necessary to improve the manner in which design and realisation teams communicate. Procurement routes that rely on collaborative and integrated working can help to bring construction knowledge into the team and hence help with improving constructability. Close cooperation between designers and tradesmen is also possible in competitive tendering forms of procurement, although the relationships are developed on a different level of trust. Introducing construction knowledge into the design phase must also be balanced with the need to maintain design expertise in the realisation phase so that decisions are made that continue to respect design intent.

Manufacturability

With developments in off-site production processes and the adoption of lean production techniques has come the notion of designing for manufacturability. In some respects the underlying principles of constructability remain central tenets of the approach; however, to design for manufacturability requires an understanding of manufacturing processes, especially the restraints and possibilities associated with specific processes. This means working closely with manufacturers so that the design can be realised economically and as intended. Dialogue between manufacturers and the design team can help to identify any problems with the design that need to be resolved before the manufacturing process can be commenced. Dialogue also allows the design team and manufacturer to agree the amount of design information required to inform the production process. In the majority of cases the manufacturers like to be involved early, when the design is still in a conceptual stage, so that they can advise on what is, what may be and what is not possible within a defined budget and timescale. Once the conceptual design is complete and approved by the client, then the manufacturers, usually working alongside the conceptual designers, start to detail the design for manufacturability. Lean thinking and lean production techniques can greatly assist in achieving high quality buildings that represent good value to the client.

The ability to physically and/or digitally model the design and its details quickly and efficiently forms an integral part of the design process. Physical modelling has for a long time been one way of helping the design team to express their design concepts and hence communicate their thoughts to others. Model making, including full scale mock-ups of details, is still used by many design studios keen to resolve constructability issues before the design details are finalised.

Designing with digital tools, such as DIMs and BIMs, allows designers the opportunity to model, detail and realise highly complex three-dimensional shapes through rapid prototyping and digital fabrication. Computer modelling provides an interface between mental concepts and physical realisation. Rapid prototyping (RP) methods can help to save time that may otherwise be wasted in the building/manufacturing of mock-up simulations. Digital fabrication (digital printing and laser cutting) creates high quality, highly accurate artefacts much faster than is possible with physical model-making techniques. These can be fabricated to scale, e.g. 1:2, and in some cases at full scale. Detailed designs, for example component designs and joint interfaces, can be produced as part of the design development process, and advances in software and rapid prototyping devices make it easier for designers to approach design and realisation as a continuous and integrated process. More specifically in relation to the detailing phase:

◆ *Component design.* Component design can be developed and tested and digitally fabricated before design information is finalised for realisation.
◆ *Assembly description.* Building the digital model from virtual components allows the sequence of assembly to be tested and refined, thus helping to avoid problems with geometric configurations and work sequencing during the real-world realisation phase.
◆ *Manufacturing descriptions.* Developing component designs and assembly descriptions virtually also creates information to assist with manufacturing the real objects.

Integral working

The fundamental requirement for collaboration and better integration is open and effective communication between the actors involved in the project. Integrated supply chains and integrated project teams allow actors to become familiar with other actors and thus able to work together more effectively than if they were meeting for the first time. This is particularly pertinent for the detailing phase in which integrated design solutions are developed with a multitude of interested actors. One result of better integration is increased likelihood of repeat work for the same client. Care is required, however, to ensure that the rules on free competition are not compromised. For integral working to be effective it is necessary to ensure the following:

◆ *Early involvement.* This will vary between professionals and trades and be dependent on the scope of the project, but involvement should be no later than the detailing phases or conceptual phase for major trades. Early involvement provides all actors with the opportunity to contribute to the design, detailing and planning stages before decisions are finalised. This can help to realise additional value and eliminate waste from later stages of the project. Early involvement can also provide the opportunity to negotiate payment terms and contract conditions.

♦ *Shared tools*. To work collaboratively and concurrently on design projects requires all team members to use the same IT and ICTs. Rivalry between tools will result in inefficient communication and disjointed working methods. DIMs and BIMs must first and foremost facilitate the development of the project if integral working is to be attained and maintained.

♦ *Shared benefits*. The aim is to provide benefits for the entire project team, including shorter programme time, easier identification and resolution of problems (and fewer disputes), better integration of building components, increased efficiency and better working relationships; and financial benefits should be commensurate to the level of commitment to the project.

♦ *Shared values*. Emphasis should be on value-adding activities and innovative solutions. Team members need to agree their collective values and goals.

♦ *Shared risk*. Risks should be identified, quantified and minimised. Remaining risk should be shared and/or an agreement made to allocate risks to the actors best able to manage them.

Relationships with manufacturers and suppliers

It would be misleading to give the impression that designers develop their detail designs and specifications in isolation. Successful design relies on cooperation between manufacturers and suppliers of materials and components and designers. Manufacturers have a vital role to play in helping the designer to detail particular aspects of buildings, especially in circumstances where the detailing may be unfamiliar to the designer or to the design office. On large projects and projects with unusual details, many manufacturers will offer to provide the technical drawings and written specification clauses for the designers; for example, cladding companies will provide a complete package. This saves the design team a lot of production work, shifting their emphasis to coordination and checking information from other sources.

Manufacturers (many of whom have their own detailing/technical departments) have a much better understanding of their materials and building components than the majority of designers and technologists could ever hope to achieve. For many designers the service provided by the manufacturing company and/or supplier is equally as important as the characteristics of the product. Help with detailing difficult junctions and writing the specification will be welcomed by busy designers with tight deadlines. Technical helplines and the prompt visit to the office by a technical representative to assist and provide product-specific knowledge are important services that can give manufacturers competitive advantage over their immediate rivals. Efforts to develop a working relationship between manufacturer, designer and contractor are a small investment for all parties to ensure a relatively trouble-free partnership.

By making it easy and quick for the designer to import standard details and standard specifications into project information, manufacturers can find their products specified without even being contacted by the designer. This 'free' information has been carefully designed so that by selecting a particular manufacturer's detail, the designer is also confirming his or her choice of product. The situation is a little more complex where performance-related specifications are being used, but manufacturers do provide performance specifications for their products that are written so as to confine the choice to their product only. Manufacturers hope that the designer, and hence the design office, will adopt their particular detail and their product as a standard detail. Many manufacturers will also employ technical staff that will provide bespoke details for a particular project.

Relationships with contractors and trades people

Relationships with main or prime contractors will vary between projects depending on the type of contractual arrangement. Even when competitive tendering is used there may be informal links between designers and trades people, who may be contacted for 'informal' advice on detailing and technical issues. Working with specialist contractors and trades people can help architects to develop their knowledge about constructability and hence inform the design process.

Creative clusters

The concept of creative clusters has been explored by some architectural design teams, keen to improve working methods and knowledge creation. The idea behind the concept is to bring together experts to discuss specific details and explore different ways of resolving the interface between materials compared with well-known solutions. Typical members would include architects, engineers, manufacturers, specialist contractors and site/factors workers. Various creative techniques such as brainstorming, synetics, lateral thinking, gaming and simulation may be used to try and tease out better-value solutions. Such activities need to be managed and the meetings tend to work at their best if they are facilitated by someone qualified in exploring creative solutions (which leaves the members of the creative cluster to concentrate on the problem rather than the process). Time is also required which needs to be included in the master programme and included within professional fee agreements.

Meetings and workshops

In order to achieve optimal communication between the actors it will be necessary to meet and discuss the project on a regular basis. Some of these meetings, for example between specifier and manufacturer, may be arranged at short notice and be relatively informal, arranged to suit a particular need. More structured meetings will be required to discuss the development of the detailed design and the manner in which it will be realised. Here the focus is on improving the constructability of the project, while trying to reduce waste in the later stages. Although the primary concern may be to resolve a particular detail, factors concerning cost and availability to suit the project programme will also feature strongly. Value management workshops may be used during this phase to help identify waste and improve the value of the design before it is confirmed in the contract documentation. Workshops will involve interaction between the main contractor and the specialist contractors.

Coordination of production information

During the detailing phase the design manager has a number of responsibilities. Not only has he or she to ensure that target dates are met for the production of relevant information, but also the quality of the information must be constantly monitored and checked for compliance with both the firm's standards and those of the client, as set out in the project quality plan. More specifically:

♦ Drawings should constantly be monitored for accuracy. It would be reckless to issues drawings to parties outside the office without checking them for accuracy. Surprising then, how many drawings do get issued without going through any formal checking procedure. The control of drawings in architectural offices often leaves something to be desired, especially where jobs are being run to tight time constraints. Good control can reduce potential claims and avoid the need for additional work at a later stage.

♦ All project information should be coordinated through the use of drawing registers; this is equally important for electronically generated/stored images as for information on paper. While individuals may create great ideas, buildings are complex products requiring the input from many different individuals with different skills. Coordination is a fundamental element of design management – not just coordination within the firm but the coordination of consultants (other designers) from other firms. Within the temporary structure of the project team people need to have a certain degree of empathy and respect for one another if communication is to flow. Coordinating communication within the office and with outside consultants is problematic and calls for particular skills.

♦ Design changes should always be referred back to the client for approval, a fundamental aspect of any quality assurance system.

Coordination

Design detailing involves the production of a large number of detailed drawings, schedules and specification of materials and workmanship. This information serves two functions. It is used to generate the bills of quantities and to realise the building. Quality control should be foremost in the design manager's mind and coordination of information foremost in the project manager's mind. This stage is often viewed as being concerned with implementing the design quickly, accurately and as cheaply as possible. Although poorly researched compared with the conceptual design stage, it is arguably the most important stage from the viewpoint of the future durability of the completed building.

The construction process relies on a vast quantity of information to enable a project to be built, used, maintained, reused and eventually recycled. All contributors to the building process have a role as information and knowledge brokers, applying their knowledge to individual projects in the form of codified information. Communication is an act during which participants create and share information in order to reach mutual understanding. Building projects require information in the form of drawings, specifications, schedules, calculations and written instructions. Not only do they have different purposes but they are usually prepared by individuals from different backgrounds, such as architects, engineers, sub-contractors and specialist suppliers, often using different terms and graphical representation. This codified language is, in effect, a professional dialect, a dialect that not all actors fully understand. Indeed, many actors may not need to understand all of the languages used due to their high degree of specialisation. Interpersonal communication between two or more individuals is often concerned with resolving queries over the interpretation of the information provided.

Drawings are used to transmit the designer's intent to other actors during the development of the conceptual and detail designs and to the contractor/production facility as a set of contract drawings. It is widely known that the format and intent of the drawing is far more apparent to the originator than it is to the receiver; as such it is not uncommon for the receiver to request clarification or even misread the originator's intentions, sometimes with costly consequences. The effect is magnified when several drawings from different originators are being referred to at the same time; it is rare, even with the use of electronically generated drawing systems, for architects, structural engineers and electrical and mechanical engineers to use the same symbols and terminology. Coordination is a challenge for the user and especially the project manager. The generation of drawings within the design office is a process that relies on the use of information and knowledge, much of which will not be included in the finished drawing. Such information must be managed within the office and the quality of the resultant documents checked and controlled before they are issued.

Programming implications

As the production drawings, and especially the specification writing, are at the end of the process they are the two stages that frequently lose allocated time, resulting in rushed work that is inadequately thought through or checked. The result can be documentation with too many omissions and errors that inevitably provide the contractor with opportunities for claims and/or inadequate work. Time and cost are closely related, and the manner in which these two valuable resources are managed will affect the quality of the service provision and of the finished building. Clients want a quality building for as little financial outlay as possible, and (of course) they want it delivered in a short time period. From the designer's perspective, the budget is never quite generous enough to allow good-quality materials, and the timeframe to achieve a good design is always too tight. Builders are then on the receiving end of cost-cutting exercises and tight programmes.

The design manager must allow adequate time for writing and checking the specification prior to issue. The task of specification writing should be clearly separated from the task of producing the production drawings. In practice, the tasks of detailing and specifying are often difficult to separate, but they are quite different tasks and must be costed accordingly. To produce a set of comprehensive, error-free drawings takes time; so does the writing of a comprehensive, error-free specification. They are interrelated but separate tasks and must be resourced accordingly even when draft specification clauses are written as the design proceeds.

Time and cost

It may be an obvious statement, but the time taken, and hence the effective programming of the production information, is influenced by the manner in which the design organisation is managed, and this varies widely from the exemplary to the chaotic. Time is required to research possible solutions, to think about the consequences of design decisions, to produce and check the drawings and schedules and to coordinate these with each other. Time is also required for other consultants to integrate information with their own. Time will also be needed to make changes, because there will be some. Apart from all that, time is also needed to record and manage the process. It is necessary for the design manager to set targets and monitor the time taken so that future programmes can be planned with more accuracy. Use of data collected on timesheets, feedback meetings and monitoring can provide the information to allow some very accurate planning and improved quality of work. This holds true for new build and work to existing buildings. The cost of producing information is often underestimated and is not particularly well controlled in many design practices. Given the quantity of drawings that have to be produced during the detail design stage, the careful management of their production and especially of the time spent in producing them is critical to the profitability of individual jobs and will influence the long-term viability of the business. Each and every drawing, schedule and specification should be costed as a percentage of the job and allowances made for unforeseen changes, which can easily affect a job's profitability.

Design reviews and coordination

No matter how good the members of the design team and no matter how effective the quality-control and quality-management system, discrepancies, errors and omissions do occur. Such errors are frequently related to time pressures and changes made on site without adequate thought for the consequences for other information. Many faults in buildings can be traced back to incomplete and inaccurate information and also the inability to use the information that has been provided. Discrepancies between drawings, specifications and bills of quantities can, and do, lead to conflict. Some of these can be avoided, but some slip through the net. Regardless of the sophistication of the technologies employed to minimise mistakes and ensure coordination, it should be remembered that people make the decisions and input the information. Thus, errors may occur.

Accommodating design changes

The fluidity of the conceptual design is being transformed into fixed information in the detailing phase. Because of the number of people involved and the amount of work required to detail building designs the majority of changes to the design tend to have serious consequences as the project moves towards physical realisation. With a large number of people working on the detailing of the building it is inevitable that detailing problems will arise and some rework may be necessary to resolve the problem. All contributors should expect a certain amount of uncertainty and thus allow time in the programme for such eventualities to be resolved. In an ideal world, the process of producing the production information would be a smooth affair with everyone contributing their information on time, with the information received being complete, cogent, error-free and sympathetic to other contributors' aims, objectives and constraints. In reality, this is rarely the case, regardless of how good the managerial systems and the effectiveness of information coordination. Project teams are often assembled for one job and the participants may not have worked together previously; it is only towards the end of the project that teams start to communicate effectively. In the meantime, there is the potential for errors to occur simply because no empathy has been achieved. Because of this, the possibility of design changes occurring needs to be allowed for in all programmes. Changes to the design can come from a variety of sources and not simply be generated internally within the design team. They can come from the client or from the contractor if the latter is involved early in the process. All changes need to be approved by the client before they are implemented, costed, their consequences fully considered and the change recorded.

Selection and specification decisions

Specification of materials and workmanship is usually a labour-intensive job and too often seen as a relatively mundane process in which the main decisions are confirmed in the written specification. The reality is that the detailing, selection and specification of materials and components form a dynamic and creative process that relies on the input from other consultants, manufacturers and specialist trade contractors. The specification process is first and foremost concerned with decision-making, dependent upon the development of detailed drawings and schedules and dependent upon the actions of others. Project specifications will be required to support drawings from the architects, structural engineers, services engineers and landscape consultants (as a minimum). Coordination of the project specifications is therefore a crucial function. Designers can define the quality of materials they require through their choice of proprietary products or through the use of performance parameters.

Prescriptive specifications

A prescriptive specification describes a product by its brand name, which sets the performance as defined in the manufacturer's technical specification. This method of specification is usually quicker for the specifier than using the performance method and is favoured by designers for materials that will be visible when the building is completed. One of the inherent problems with prescriptive specification is that of anticompetition. For public works, the practice is not to use proprietary specifications, the principle being that all relevant manufacturers must be able to compete for the work should they wish to do so. Some large organisations follow similar principles by adding the words 'or equal approved' to allow some choice and competition between suppliers.

In specifying proprietary products and not allowing substitution, the designer has made a choice and given the contractor precise instructions as to what to use. Responsibility for the specification rests with the design organisation and the implication of not allowing any substitutions is an implied guarantee that the product is fit for purpose and represents good value for money. Warranties, guarantees and insurances should be sought from the manufacturer to transfer the implied liability from the designer's office. The clause 'or equal approved' may be added (see below) to provide some latitude for change. Under traditional forms of contract, the contractor cannot make changes without the permission of the contract administrator. Given that a lot of time and effort will have gone into choosing a particular product in the first place, many specifiers are reluctant to change their specification without a very good reason, for example a problem with delivery or an unforeseen technical difficulty on site. When changes are unavoidable, care should be taken to acquire and check the manufacturer's warranty before issuing the necessary instruction to the contractor in accordance with the contract. Because many changes are made under time pressures, this is not always done in practice but sought after the event; this is not good practice and should be resisted.

By adding the clause 'or equal approved', the contractor has some latitude in changing specified products as long as they are 'equal', and approval is sought from the contract administrator before the change is implemented. The design organisation remains responsible for the final choice of product and has a responsibility to check that any alternatives suggested by the contractor are fit for purpose and equal to that originally specified. Requests for changes must, under the contract, allow the contract administrator sufficient time to consider the proposed alternative. There is also a requirement for the contractor to provide the contract administrator with sufficient information (i.e. the relevant technical details and cost) from which a considered decision can be made. Too often, the contractor merely submits a list of products assuming (or hoping) that the design office has the relevant information. If products are unfamiliar to the office, then literature and samples will need to be sought, which takes time and can be arduous. Care should be taken to ensure that any cost savings are fully documented and passed on to the client (not the contractor). The use of 'or equal approved' can lead to arguments as to whether or not the product is 'equal' (some characteristics will be, others may not). Some designers specify proprietary products and then add the wording 'or equal'. This is an open invitation to the contractor to use alternatives without asking for approval and is not considered to be good practice.

Performance specifications

Performance specifications do not identify particular products by brand name; instead, a series of performance characteristics are listed (essentially a technical brief), which must be met. Performance-based specifications vary in their scope. They can be used to describe a complete project, one or more systems or individual components. For example, clients may produce a performance specification for a design and construct project, engineers may produce a performance specification for the mechanical and electrical specification, and designers may specify such items as fire resistance and thermal insulation by the performance required (which is quantified). This leaves the choice of product to the contractor and is popular in contractor-led procurement routes, such as design and construct, because it gives the contractor greater flexibility over product selection. Performance specifications are best suited to large projects, while on small to medium-sized ventures it is common to use descriptive specifications for the majority of the work, with performance specifications for items such as the heating, ventilation and air conditioning (HVAC) system. Recently there has been increased interest in performance specifying, the argument being that it encourages innovation and reduces cost, although there is little research to back such an argument.

Passing the choice of product to the contractor means the contractor is given a design function and is expected to exercise reasonable care and skill in the same way as a designer. With performance specifications, it is not uncommon for the contractor to make last-minute changes to products in order to save money or meet programme deadlines. Care should be taken to record the final product choice, both as evidence in the event of a claim and for reference when alterations are made to the building. It is also important to check that the product selected complies with the performance specification required; sometimes they do not, the contractor hoping that the specifier does not have time to check thoroughly.

Performance specifications are generally regarded as being more difficult and time-consuming to write than prescriptive specifications, but they are used for complete buildings (e.g. design and build contracts) and for sub-systems (especially building services and prefabricated building systems). One of the main challenges for the designer is deciding on the level of performance required: too narrow, and the bidder is given little latitude; too wide, and the scope becomes too great to make sensible comparisons from the solutions presented by competing contractors. Care is needed to establish levels of performance that suit the project and the client. Performance specifications tend to be used by client organisations keen to leave the choice open (in the hope of getting the same performance cheaper than if a proprietary product were used). One argument put forward is that performance specifications are more effective in ensuring constructability and hence value for money on behalf of the client. There is little evidence to support this claim; indeed it could be argued that a good design team could ensure constructability and value for money through the use of prescriptive specifications. It would be misleading to suggest that one method is better than another; it is rather that different situations require different approaches.

Project specifications

The degree to which individual projects draw on the office master specification will be determined by a project's characteristics and its compatibility with the master. Problems may be experienced in situations where a design office concentrates on, for example, residential work, and then acquires a commission for an industrial unit. In such situations, the master specification will be of less use than with the normal housing projects, and greater care is needed in its application to this unfamiliar situation. Decisions about product selection may be referred back to the office manager for approval.

- Individual projects will require their own bespoke specifications. Just as every site is different from the next, so too are buildings and the specification.
- The quality of the written project specification will be determined by office policy and the abilities of the individual doing the writing. In offices where different designers write their own specifications, there may be a wide variety in quality.
- The use of quality management systems and reliance on the office master (and/or a national standard format) can help to make the specifications more consistent within the office.
- Rolling specifications should be avoided because of the dangers of erroneous or irrelevant clauses.
- Specifiers should be able to use a master specification as their starting point, in the confidence that it is up to date and free of errors.
- The establishment and, as importantly, maintenance of a master specification require investment by the office.

Designers have different ways of working, but it is regarded as good practice to develop and build up the specification as the detail design proceeds. Once the first draft has been completed, it is then a case of editing the document to suit final design decisions. As with the master specification, someone other than the specification writer should check the project specification. Sometimes the design manager, sometimes the chief specification writer, does this job. It is poor managerial control to issue specifications and drawings without a comprehensive check for errors and coordination. If the master specification is kept up to date as changes to materials and codes occur, then there should be no need for feedback from individual specifications. However, good and bad experience of materials, products and working practices gained from individual jobs should be considered and the master document revised to accommodate new knowledge.

Preferences and habits

Designers and detailers will develop a repertoire of well-rehearsed solutions that work, based on experience acquired through education and practice. Research has shown that specifiers draw quite heavily on building materials and products that they know from previous projects. This information source also operates at the office level, with a collective range of preferred materials and products that happen to suit a particular design approach and are known to perform, or more accurately not fail, in use.

The advantages are:

- It saves time looking for information.
- The product is familiar so that uncertainty is reduced.
- Details and specification clauses can be imported from a previous job.

The disadvantages are:

- It reduces the likelihood of specifiers looking for alternatives and so might hinder innovation.
- There is a greater chance of superseded information being used.
- There is a greater chance of error through the use of rolling specifications.

Quality management systems prohibit the use of individual files of product information because of the danger of it being out of date; however, many specifiers maintain their own favourite products and sources of information based on their individual experience. Use of products from this personal collection reduces the amount of time spent searching for products to suit a particular situation, and because they are known to perform well (or more to the point known not to fail), their selection poses little risk to the specifier. This palette of product information is essentially a knowledge base that is used to aid the specification process. It may be maintained as a file of paper literature or in a digital file that can be quickly imported into drawings and specifications. Design managers need to ensure regular audits to either eradicate the use of personal sources or ensure that the information contained in personalised files is current and in accordance with office standards; the former is easier to manage than the latter. Similarly, the majority of design offices build up some experience of successful and unsuccessful products and details over time. This experience may be disseminated through internal memoranda or office standards leading to the development of an office palette of favourite products, possibly incorporated into standard details and the master specification. Such practice reinforces established patterns of behaviour and helps to make the office more efficient; however, it tends to discourage independent thought or action, in some cases forming a barrier to the use of innovative products.

Building regulations submission

Detailed information describing the construction of the proposed building must be submitted for approval to the local authority building control department. Architectural details must demonstrate compliance with the Approved Documents (England and Wales, Northern Ireland) or Guidance Documents (Scotland), which set performance requirements to be met or bettered by the proposed design solution. The Approved Documents are intended to provide guidance for some of the common forms of construction while encouraging alternative ways of demonstrating compliance under the 'deemed to satisfy' standards. Designers and builders have a choice: they can accept the suggested method in full, in part or not at all if they can demonstrate an alternative method of compliance. In reality, many designers and builders find it quicker, easier and more convenient to work to the solutions suggested and illustrated. Alternatives are more time-consuming to develop and may take longer to be approved compared with a more conservative, 'safer' approach. The performance approach provides a route to greater levels of creativity and innovation and may provide the opportunity to design using less material and resources than might otherwise be required. Adequate time must be allowed to suit the approach taken and some flexibility may need to be built into the project master programme to allow the design team to respond to questions and provide additional information if requested.

For small and relatively routine projects the application procedure should be relatively straightforward with a high degree of certainty over the decision. For larger and more complex buildings the process will involve a greater degree of consultation and is likely to be time-consuming. It is a sensible strategy to work closely with the local authority officers to ensure any areas of uncertainty can be discussed and dealt with before the application is submitted, thus helping to avoid unnecessary delays because of insufficient information. Appropriate permissions must be in place before demolition and construction work commence, and this may have implications for the commencement of the realisation phase of the project.

Costing the project

Detailing the design results in a greater degree of certainty and as a direct result the cost of realising the design also becomes more clearly defined as the detailing progresses. Costing the detailed design will be influenced by the approach taken. Off-site assembly is very tightly controlled and the producer will provide a total production cost that is very accurate. Repeat building types should also provide a high degree of cost certainty, since the building costs are known from past projects, the main uncertainty being the ground conditions and factors relating to the site, such as boundaries and roads and conditions attached to town planning approvals. Non-repeat building designs may be more difficult to cost with as much certainty as the repetitive designs and may be influenced by the amount of off-site manufacturing to be used. Working closely with manufacturers, suppliers and specialist contractors can also help in the development of relatively accurate cost information.

The detail design stage is primarily concerned with transmitting the design intent to the people who are going to assemble the building on site, via the contract documentation. However, the first use of the documentation is to prepare the bills of quantities for the tender stage. It is important to remember, therefore, that the contract documentation will be analysed for the purposes of assembling a contract sum and used to realise the building, i.e. the contract documentation has two functions.

Bills of quantities

It has been common practice for the client-approved drawings, schedules and specifications to be translated by a quantity surveyor into quantities of materials and work, a process known as 'taking off'. The resulting documentation, the bills of quantities, are then used by the contractor for costing the project. This means that in a competitive tender the invited bidders are making their bid based on the same information. In some countries it is the contractors who 'take off' their own quantities for the purpose of estimating the quantity and cost of the work. This increases the amount of work for each contractor and also makes it difficult to compare bids since each contractor may interpret the information slightly differently. In the UK system the process of translation by the quantity surveyor is useful in helping to identify errors, omissions and discrepancies in the drawings, specifications and specifications. Thus the quantity surveyor has an informal role as checker of the information, a role many would argue should be done before the information is released from the design office. This also means that detailed cost information is held outside the design office, with the architect's office having little knowledge of costs other than that provided to them by the quantity surveyor and contractor (via the priced bills of quantities). With the development of more sophisticated computer software packages it is now possible to generate the bills of quantities from the drawings, schedules and specifications.

This may render the quantity surveyor surplus to requirements in some circumstances, although it should be remembered that the quantity surveyor's ability to spot discrepancies may be lost.

Competitive tendering and negotiation

The success of tendering and negotiation depends on first narrowing down the potential organisations and individuals to those who are known to be respectable and trustworthy. This may be a time-consuming task, requiring the analysis of a considerable amount of information relating to the organisations in question. It is becoming common for the project team to invite prime contractors and specialist contractors to discuss the project and try and establish a working relationship based on shared project values. Organisations that hold different values to the project team should be rejected at this stage. There are essentially two approaches to realising the design in a physical manner: to competitively tender the work or to enter into negotiations to agree a contract sum. The choice of one method over the other will relate to the type and size of the project and various conditions relating, for example, to the competitive tendering of public projects.

- *Competitive tendering.* A select list of contractors is invited to price the work and submit a tender price. In the UK it is common to appoint the lowest tender, although there is plenty of evidence to suggest that this is not always the wisest thing to do. The policy is often to get the job at any cost and then make numerous claims for extras. In some countries the practice is to find the average tender price and appoint the tenderer closest to the average. The argument here is that the tender price is likely to be more representative of the final cost and there will be less likelihood of claims for extras.
- *Negotiation.* It is becoming more common to use negotiation since it is considered to be a less wasteful process and is widely promoted as offering more value to all parties. The project manager will invite the contractor to discuss the project and to prepare a priced bill. Working closely can provide several advantages, although the price can never be shown to be the cheapest.

Pre-contract issues and common problems

Before starting to realise the building in a physical form it is critical that the design is approved by the client and that it is as 'perfect' as possible given the project constraints, i.e. the design should be fit for purpose and satisfy the client's value parameters set out in the briefing phase. The final gateway review provides an opportunity to discuss and confirm the design, budget and programme before physical realisation commences. Any changes after this event are likely to be expensive. The process of tendering and/or negotiating the contract sum may well have identified some errors in the contract documentation that should be corrected and reissued to the contractor prior to the work commencing. A process plan is produced that helps to map the various production activities and help identify missing information. Information flow is an important consideration at this stage. On completion of the construction schedule, in an ideal world, the information should be complete and there should be 'no scope' for uncertainty of the delivered value at the production phases.

Pre-contract meeting

The pre-contract meeting is an important event in which the key participants can discuss the project before work commences. Although much of the emphasis may be on contractual and legal matters and the resolution of any outstanding questions, the pre-contract meeting serves to establish the culture of interaction between the design team and the realisation team. It is during this meeting that the design team should clearly set out the philosophy and values behind the project, something sometimes difficult to do in words and pictures alone. This helps to emphasise important issues and helps to set out the rules of engagement for making changes to the project should they be necessary.

Common problems

It is very common for construction work to commence on site before the detailed design work is complete. In some cases this is part of a well-thought-through strategy of concurrent design and/or fast tracking techniques. Alternatively, work starts because the design team has not managed to produce the appropriate work on time, and given commercial pressures clients are understandably keen to start work as fast as possible. In both cases it is necessary for the design manager and the construction managers to quickly develop an effective means of communicating about the outstanding work, its impact and scheduled date for completion and issue to the construction site. Failure to do this will inevitably lead to some (unnecessary) rework, which will have time and cost implications. Many of the problems that arise during the detailing phase relate to the following:

- Poor estimation of the time required to complete the various works packages may cause coordination problems and delays to the overall programme.
- Failure to check the development of the details against the parameters set out in the project brief will result in wasted effort and expensive rework.
- A high degree of synergy is required between the conceptual and detail design teams to ensure that design intent is transformed from the conceptual design into a complete set of production information. Drifting away from the ideals contained in the conceptual design must be prevented to avoid rework and programme delays.
- Failure to develop the project costs as the detailing develops may lead to a design that is too expensive to realise.
- Quality of the information produced may suffer if the tasks have not been adequately resourced and coordinated.

The project to office interface

The attitude of the design office to engaging with physical production will influence the manner in which the detailing is managed and the amount of interaction between project and office at this stage. Similarly, the contractual arrangement will determine the amount of input to detailing and control over detailing decisions and the manner in which the building is realised. Assuming that architects are concerned about the quality of the completed building, it is important that the designers retain influence (control) of the client values and design intentions at this stage. Many good conceptual designs fail to be realised as intended because of poor detailing decisions.

The design manager's role is to ensure that design intent (client value) is implemented and enhanced in the detailing phase. The amount of influence the design office has during this stage will have been determined by the procurement route chosen and the contract entered into. Similarly, contractual issues will also determine the level and extent of integral working. This involves sensitive coordination of information produced within the office with that from external suppliers, i.e. consultants and specialist suppliers and manufacturers.

Careful allocation of staff to detailing work is required if this is to be a profitable stage for the design office. Too many architectural offices complain that they cannot make any profit or often lose money during the detailing phases. This tends to be related to poor allocation of staff to specific packages of work, inadequate coordination of activities and information, and failure to manage design changes.

Chapter Seven
Realising the Design

It is at the realisation phase when the client's values, codified in drawings, specifications, schedules and bills of quantities, are translated and converted into a physical artefact. This is generally known as the assembly, construction, production, implementation or realisation phase and is covered extensively by the large body of construction management literature. It is here that the culture of the project changes significantly, with emphasis shifting from the design team to the production team. The focus is on realising the project to budget, within programme, safely and to agreed quality parameters. The manner in which this process, or more specifically series of processes, is managed will depend on the type of project, the procurement route and the way in which the design was detailed for realisation, be it an emphasis on craft-based technologies, fast-track construction or off-site prefabrication. The building sponsor will be concerned with the delivery of the building to agreed parameters and the design team will be concerned with maintaining the design vision and enhancing value. It is the detailing that informs the realisation processes. Designers specify the position, quantity and quality of the building work; they do not tell the builder 'how' to construct it. This is the contractor's or manufacturer's responsibility (hence the need for method statements). The quality of the completed building depends on the ability of those carrying out the physical work and the management of the work.

Architects and technologists often talk of 'making buildings' but very few build in a physical manner. Detail design decisions are codified in drawings, schedules, models and associated written contract information. Factory workers and site-based operatives then translate this information into physical activities and physical objects. This work is, with the exception of very small building works, sub-contracted by a prime contractor to specialist sub-contractors and suppliers, i.e. it is the contractor that usually manages the realisation phase. Detachment from construction activities may be a sensible business strategy for some design offices, but the dislocation from the physical act of building is a little disconcerting. Good architecture requires a thorough understanding of the technologies being applied, regardless of the construction methods employed. Experience of construction and reflective feedback into earlier conceptual and detailed design stages is crucial in the drive for continual improvement and crucial to ensuring safe and efficient constructability. Understanding the complexities of production, especially the interface of design, technology and management, will help designers and engineers to better realise their detailed designs. It may also help architects to contribute in a positive manner to the management of the realisation phase and to be better equipped to advise clients. A related factor is the amount of influence a design office has over the realisation process and hence the quality of the final product.

Getting involved

Before the drive for professional status architects were directors of the work, and were in direct contact with the workers and the work they produced. There was no intermediary in the form of a main contractor or project manager. Drawings were rarely needed because of the empathy that existed between designer, craftsmen and materials. A combination of more complex technologies, an ever-increasing choice of building products and a growth in the number of intermediaries has resulted in architects becoming disengaged from the physical act of building. More recently, with the revised interest in prefabrication, off-site production and supporting digital technologies, architects have started to become more involved in the realisation of buildings, working more closely with manufacturers and specialist sub-contractors, and (in some cases) have become better positioned to influence the implementation of client values. Collaborative and integrated working has helped to close the gap between the design and realisation cultures, and design and management procurement has put architects back in direct contact with the workers and the physical artefact.

A small number of architects and engineers have seized the opportunities presented by off-site manufacturing and have started to offer a complete design and production service to clients. The return to the site has been made possible by sophisticated computer software and computer-aided manufacturing. The architect's role is one of managing a small number of works packages for the groundworks, foundations and services. The building is manufactured off-site, transported to site and bolted into position using cranes and a small number of personnel. The architect becomes the manager of an assembly process, coordinating fixing and fitting operations as discrete works packages. The arguments for a design-led form of contractual arrangement are not new. In the 1980s there was a proposal for an Alternative Method of Management (AMM) from the architectural profession. This recognised the growing importance of sub-contracting and removed the main contractor from the process. Such a system is, theoretically, well suited to architectural firms since the ability to communicate their ideas directly to the sub-contractors and the ability to learn directly from them on site can go a long way in improving the quality of the finished product. The problem comes from the environment in which construction takes place, an adversarial, fiercely competitive environment, in which main contractors will not relinquish control to architectural firms readily. AMM was not adopted widely, partly due to the architect's weak position, but mainly because the system relied on cooperation and contractors were not prepared to accept this. Since this period there have been a small number of architects who have continued to build using a design-led procurement method. Now, with increased sophistication of IT and evolution of prefabricated building technology, it has become a realistic option for architects to manage the realisation process.

The term design and manage is sometimes used to describe an architectural practice that also manages the physical realisation of the design. The use of discrete works packages allows the architect to communicate directly with trade contractors and eliminates the need for a main contractor. Through the employment of an individual with contracting and management skills (a contracts manager), the architectural firm is in a position to manage, administer and coordinate the sub-contractors, taking advantage of the minimal capital outlay required. Architectural firms can control the whole construction process, thus ensuring continuity in the product quality chain, while also charging a management fee. The client has single-point responsibility while the independent selection and control of sub-contractors provides the opportunity (theoretically) for improved completion times, improved quality, reduced costs and improved communication within the project team. Communication routes are more direct (with sub-contractors being in contact with both client and architect). Another advantage is that the designer is in direct contact with the sub-contractors so problems can be solved more quickly (reducing claims and variation orders). Communication may also be improved through the simplification and removal of unnecessary managers, in line with lean thinking. This procurement method has many similarities with design and build but the difference is that the team is led by a design-conscious professional rather than a cost-conscious one.

Advantages

Design and manage is possible to implement and a few design organisations have adopted management contracting and/or construction management techniques in pursuit of better building quality. With the increased emphasis on prefabrication and off-site assembly the degree of complexity being managed on the construction site is much reduced, thus making activities much easier to coordinate. Improving communication through the reduction in the number of (competing) intermediaries is difficult to achieve unless the designer is in a position to influence procurement decisions. Construction management by architectural firms, based on the integration of client, architect and tradesmen, may go some way to improving the transfer of information within the temporary project team. From the client's perspective the concept of single-point responsibility is appealing since the client has to deal only with one firm, regardless of when queries or problems occur. From the architectural firm's perspective such an approach represents a large increase in both responsibility and the exposure to risk that accompanies it, although the approach usually relies on client involvement and the client's willingness to share risks. This approach may be best suited to small and/or repeat building types, which will allow the design office the chance to build up knowledge and experience to move into larger and more complex undertakings.

Disadvantages

On first impression, the thought of architects dirtying their hands with building may be, perhaps, a little unusual. Architectural education does not teach architects to build; it teaches them to design and some architectural practices are content to stay away from physical production and assembly. Even for the architects that work closely with construction activities the idea of getting involved in construction management may be unsuitable because it introduces overheads (management staff) that may be financially difficult to justify across the whole project portfolio. Appropriate experience, skills and aptitude may have to be bought and brought into the office, which is not without an element of risk. Alternatively, some practices may set up a separate legal enterprise to deal with the realisation phase. There may be some resistance. For example, clients may take some convincing that architects can look after their interests at this stage, and may be reluctant to engage in design- and management-type arrangements. Also, by entering the contractor's territory they will meet resistance to the new competition and some contractors have been known to respond by removing architects from their list of approved suppliers for design services. Another disadvantage, in the short term, is associated with the learning curve. Time and projects will be required to develop the experience and knowledge to offer these services competitively. As a general rule of thumb it may take two to three small projects before the architectural firm is able to make a profit.

Resourcing and cost control

The managers' prime function is to coordinate information and to allocate, manage and coordinate resources (e.g. the actions of specialist sub-contractors and numerous other actors). The construction costs comprise labour, materials, plant and equipment and associated costs, discussed below. The term 'total project cost' represents the client's total expenditure on the project. This includes the cost of the land, legal and professional fees, the cost of construction, interest charges and associated fees.

Labour

The labour cost is the cost of employing people to carry out physical and managerial work on the site, in factories and in workshops. This cost comprises the operative's wage, holiday pay, national insurance contributions and pension scheme. The amount of labour required, the skill level of the labourers and the length of time people are employed will determine the total labour cost. Some of the labour cost can be reduced by outsourcing production 'offshore' to low wage economies if prefabrication is used. As noted earlier, the manner in which the design has been detailed will influence the ease of constructability and this directly determines the length of time required to complete an operation, the number of personnel required and their skill level, and hence the labour cost. With the widespread use of sub-contracted labour the main contractor's concern is with keeping the cost of labour within the estimate. Day-to-day control of labour is the concern of the sub-contractors' managers.

There are very few main contractors who employ direct labour or own plant and machinery. The vast majority of their work is sub-contracted to specialist trade contractors and plant hired when required. Main contractors are no longer builders; they have become administrators of a complex web of sub-contracted relationships and complicated responsibilities for quality. In doing so the main contractor takes on the risk and a considerable amount of design responsibility.

In order to stay competitive contractors have downsized their labour to reduce their overheads. Instead they employ labour-only sub-contractors when required, by sub-letting the main labour content of the work, sometimes described as a 'hire and fire' policy. Work is also sub-contracted to trade contractors and specialist contractors. The trade contractors are skilled workers (e.g. plasterers and painters) and are largely responsible for the building's finishes. Trade contractors have a significant impact on the overall quality of the finished building and need to be selected with care. Main contractors tend to develop informal relationships with good trade contractors to help ensure a high quality of work. Specialist sub-contractors (sometimes called technical specialist contractors) also play an increasingly important role by designing, manufacturing and installing (and maintaining) materials and system solutions. The increasing use of prefabricated components and off-site production of building elements has helped to emphasise the importance of the specialist contractors and their design input. Thus successful completion of the project is influenced to a large degree by effective selection and management of sub-contractors. From the architect's perspective it raises a number of questions about the control of the design, especially the detailed design. Leaving the selection of specialist sub-contractors to contractors means that the architects have effectively abrogated responsibility for the design to others, and under many contractual arrangements there is very little they can do to influence the quality. Appointment of sub-contractors can be 'nominated' by architects. This gives the architect greater control over the work and tends to be used when the work is of a specialist nature. Another approach is to 'name' sub-contractors when the architect wishes to restrict the contractor to a limited choice of suppliers. When appointed by the main contractor the term 'domestic' sub-contractor is used.

In some respects the use of sub-contractors has led to increased fragmentation and complexity of relationships within construction teams. Increased specialisation has also been blamed for making the detailing of buildings complicated and a challenge to coordinate. But this appears to be a transitional period as specialist (technical) sub-contractors mature and maximise the potential of new building technologies. By working closely with main contractors, architects and engineers the specialist contractors are transforming the manner in which buildings are assembled. This is starting to lead to less, not more, complexity. System solutions (for example for walls and roofs) considerably simplify the production process and can lead to safer and quicker operations on site. They also make the management of construction much simpler, with fewer sub-contractors to manage and minimal reliance on site operatives and all the ensuing complexities that go with it. Selection of sub-contractors needs to be carried out objectively and consistently. Specific prequalification criteria may include:

- Documented track record/performance
- Appropriate experience of similar types of work
- Financial soundness
- Technical competence
- Appropriate quality management systems
- Shared values (and empowerment).

Some of these requirements can be dealt with through written documents, but to know how and what input a specialist contractor will make to the project requires some face-to-face interaction. Early involvement of sub-contractors and suppliers can help to minimise risks and contribute to more efficient supply chain management. Meetings provide an ideal opportunity for the managers of the construction project and those hoping to contribute to it to explore and exchange values, goals and aspirations. Only if the sub-contractor's culture and values fit those of the project, and the managers are confident that an open and constructive dialogue can be maintained throughout their period of involvement, should they be appointed. Cost should be secondary to the ability to work together (and should be negotiated). Early discussions can help in the pursuit of designing for better constructability and manufacturability.

Materials

Materials expenditure often represents a major proportion of the contract sum. Control of purchasing, scheduling, delivery and material handling on the site will have a major impact on the effectiveness of the construction process. So too will the control of material waste. Many contractors use a central purchasing system, to help control material purchasing and hence also benefit from larger discounts for bulk purchases and reduced transportation costs. The cost of materials relates to the unit cost of the material and associated transportation costs. The unit cost also includes a percentage to allow for materials wastage, which can and should be reduced by good site practices and management.

Materials waste on construction sites is a serious problem, the cost of which is passed on to the client as materials wastage and incorporated into unit cost rates for materials. The contractor's estimator will, typically, allow somewhere between 2 and 5% for wastage, although research has shown that losses tend to be considerably higher than this in practice. With landfill space becoming scarce and the cost of disposing of materials at licensed tips also increasing, the need to address the problem has become paramount. In many cases materials waste poses an unnecessary health and safety hazard and the contractor's safety management procedures should aim to mitigate the problem. Clients are also, quite correctly, starting to question why they should pay for the careless behaviour of others and are starting to look more closely at materials costs and waste. Moving assembly to factory-controlled conditions can help to reduce waste, although this approach may not always be desirable or feasible. A variety of approaches can be taken to reducing materials wastage, for example:

♦ *Design*. Careful detailing to minimise the need for wasteful cutting on site and to ease constructability.
♦ *Specification*. Elimination of overspecification through better specification writing practices.
♦ *Ordering*. Eliminate the tendency of ordering additional materials 'just in case' they are needed.
♦ *Damage*. Damage to materials and components on the site can be significantly reduced through careful storage and temporary protection, just-in-time deliveries (helping to minimise storage and double handling), and sensitive workflow programming to minimise the possibility of workers damaging already completed work.
♦ *Errors and rework*. Errors can be reduced by the supply of good-quality information, a safe and comfortable work environment and support from the managers on site. Careless workmanship can be minimised through careful selection of organisations and staff charged with realising the building.
♦ *Preventing theft*. Theft from sites is a constant problem. This includes theft of materials and equipment by unscrupulous workers and theft when the site is unoccupied. Careful vetting of all workers on the site can help to reduce theft, and active and passive site security can help to deter burglars and vandals.
♦ *Better site management*. Managerial culture has a role to play in establishing a 'get-it-right-first-time' culture and promoting a sense of pride in the work, helping to minimise waste.

Plant and equipment cost

Hand-held tools, machines and equipment may be hired, leased or owned by the specialist and prime contractors. Work should be planned so that expensive plant, for example tower cranes, is utilised effectively and for the minimum period, thus helping to keep costs down. Plant and machinery should not be standing idle.

Preliminaries, overheads and profit

A percentage of the contract sum, typically somewhere between 5 and 15%, covers the preliminaries, office overheads and a reasonable profit.

A leaner approach

The lean philosophy was originally taken from the Japanese production management approach to volume manufacturing and lean has since diffused to become a fashionable concept in many construction sectors around the globe. Lean concepts borrow many tools and techniques from the quality management field, which was also concerned with reducing waste and improving value. The term 'lean construction' tends to be interpreted quite widely, ranging from a term to include design and construction activities to very narrow interpretations related to specific production functions and/or application of tools by contractors. Many buildings are not mass-produced in high volumes but are unique configurations of mass-produced and hand-crafted components, and so some care is required in transferring lean production methods to the construction context. It should also be noted that the lean approach has been heavily criticised in the production management literature for the lack of attention to human resource issues. Although the lean construction literature is very positive about the perceived and observed benefits of such an approach, caution is required before adopting or adapting the principles and tools to all construction projects.

Lean construction

Lean construction aims to eliminate waste in processes by looking at the realisation phase as a complete system. Emphasis is on improving safe working practices and methods to help reduce the amount of time and number of people necessary, and hence reduce costs for the organisations involved and the building sponsor. Lean construction should have a clear set of objectives for the realisation process before work starts. Analysing all work activities and being able to plan ahead to ensure a continuous and uninterrupted flow of work is an essential prerequisite for helping to reduce waste and hence improve value. Typical waste during realisation relates to:

- *Waiting.* Waiting time is not productive. Thus planning and scheduling activities should seek to reduce uncertainty in information, programming and resourcing. For example, providing temporary weather protection can help to eliminate waiting due to inclement weather.
- *Material movement.* Moving materials around on the site is usually unnecessary, wastes time and will almost certainly result in increased damage through additional handling. Just-in-time deliveries can help to reduce material handling, although this requires expert scheduling skills to be effective.
- *Rework.* Correcting work that has been carried out incorrectly is expensive and (with the benefit of hindsight) usually avoidable. Causes include incomplete and erroneous information, rushed and poorly thought-through work and poor coordination and planning of work packages.

These three waste streams should not be left just to the realisation team to address, but should be considered and tackled in the design and detailed design phases. When the contractor is appointed the contract documents should be complete. The reality is that they are not, and much of the interaction is concerned with requesting and providing additional information, i.e. the final development of designs, changes to details and the coordination and integration of components, to ensure that the building can be assembled safely and within agreed parameters of time, cost and quality. The key objective for designers is to ensure that information flow during the realisation phase is timely and the information exchanged is complete and accurate, thus the potential for uncertainty is minimised.

Planning, control and management of work activities is a central theme of lean construction. The aim is to reduce uncertainty and variability to help with the planning, control and management of work packages. Emphasis is on 'pull-based' planning in which the work is planned based on detailed feedback from the current state of the work (percentage of planned work completed). These systems rely on a relatively flexible workforce and good communication between workers and managers. Workflow analysis and workflow scheduling, including mapping construction supply chains (via value stream analysis or value stream mapping) and work structuring, are necessary to ensure safe and efficient work.

Moving work off-site to highly controlled factory environments can help in the desire to improve quality, safety and reliability. Quality is predictable and costs are certain. Deliveries to the site and positioning of the prefabricated units are simple and quick operations that require relatively simple logistical skills. With the exception of the groundwork and foundation work packages, there is very little site-based activity that needs to be managed. Thus the need to manage numerous sub-contractors and the ensuing challenges related to quality and health and safety are largely removed from the site. This has led some architects to question the role of the main contractor and to take on the management role, becoming fully involved with the realisation of the client's values. Whatever the approach adopted by individual design offices it is important that architects and fellow designers have an understanding of how buildings are realised. This will help to inform the design and detailing processes and go some way to reduce waste and maximise value.

Programming

With off-site manufacturing the programming at this phase will be concerned with the preparation of the site to receive the manufactured components (e.g. foundations and services connections) and the safe delivery and assembly of the component parts. The site works can usually be completed, checked and signed off well in advance of the scheduled delivery of the manufactured components, which can help to simplify the programming. In comparison, site-based construction involves considerably more activities to be coordinated. Workflow planning allows different trades and activities to coexist on the site without hindering the work of others. Specialist sub-contractors and trades will supply detailed programmes for their work packages and a method statement that explains how the work will be carried out in a safe and efficient manner. One of the main challenges is deciding how much autonomy is to be given to the workers, i.e. how much control the manager wishes to exert. This depends a little on the personality of the construction manager, whether they are 'hands-off' or 'hands-on' and the management tools employed. The construction project manager's job is to coordinate the different works packages so that work may flow smoothly and safely. To do this it is necessary to use programming techniques. These will vary depending on the type and complexity of the project, but typically will include one or more of the following:

- Gantt (bar) charts
- Network analysis (critical path)
- Precedence diagrams
- Line of balance (elemental trend analysis)
- Location time chart (time-chainage diagrams).

Buffer management

Buffer management is a very simple concept that aims to manage the interface between clearly defined work packages. This is achieved by allowing space (time) between separate activities on the master programme. Buffering allows for some flexibility in the length of time taken by work crews and also allows time to check and sign off the work before the next trade takes possession of a defined space. This helps to prevent conflicts between different trades and sub-contractors trying to work in the same area at the same time and thus hindering one another in the process. Buffering techniques can help to simplify the flow of work and mitigate the knock-on effects of local delays on the work of others. Buffering works packages may also be a safer way of operating on highly complex projects and in areas of buildings where working space is restricted, thus minimising the number of people and activities taking place in that space. Some managers would argue that buffer management techniques add unnecessary time to the programme and hence add waste. Others would argue that buffer management is an essential tool to ensure safe and continuous workflow, and is essential to a well-managed project. Used in conjunction with self-managing work crews, buffer management techniques have proved to be highly effective on large projects (such as hospitals) where a production line approach can be utilised to great effect.

Acceleration

Accelerating the speed of work so that the project, or a phase of the project, can be completed earlier than initially programmed is different to fast-track projects. The decision to accelerate is made when the work is in progress and will involve a certain amount of uncertainty, revised scheduling and planning and reallocation of resources. Acceleration may also have implications for the scheduling of work in a safe and effective manner. When accelerating the work the direct costs (labour, plant and materials) will increase and the indirect costs (supervision and administration, temporary accommodation and associated costs) will decrease because of the earlier completion. Accelerating the work may require work to be carried out during the weekends (for which permission will usually be required) and will usually involve payment for overtime and incentive-based payments to ensure the work is completed on time. Additional supervision may also be required for weekend working and for the supervision of an increased number of work crews. Scenario-planning may help in deciding how best to accelerate the work and the impact in terms of workflow and costs.

Interaction

Interactions during the early stages of a project are usually conducted in a relatively free and open atmosphere because the level of information in the system is relatively low and unstructured. Over time the amount of information increases and informal and formal structures emerge, creating implicit rules of engagement. Goals and targets are set and the pressure to develop and exchange information increases. The number of actors contributing to the process and the amount of information are at their peak during the construction process, and it is here that the possibility for misunderstandings and conflict is highest. Pressures resulting from limited time and increased workload can affect the ability of team members to work together, leading to changes in communication patterns that may either impede or improve performance. Although drawings, specifications and schedules forming the contract documents are often assumed to be complete and free from error, the reality is that they are not. Even where the information package is 'complete' before production begins in factories and on the site, there are likely to be a number of requests for clarification and additional information. Much of the interaction during the construction phase is therefore concerned with the final development of detailed designs, changes to construction details and coordination and integration of the specialised components to ensure that the building can be assembled safely and within agreed parameters of time, cost and quality. A key objective for designers is to ensure that the information flow does not interrupt the construction process, but this is not always achieved in practice. It is probably unrealistic to expect the participants to know everything or be prepared for every eventuality. Thus all actors need the appropriate skills to be able to provide and extract the relevant information to stimulate and influence the behaviour necessary to deliver the project successfully. On fast-track projects the information provision to the contractor is phased and carefully coordinated to ensure a timely flow of information at specific milestones in the project.

Clarification of information and discussion of progress and problems are usually conducted within the forum of formally scheduled progress meetings and ad hoc meetings called to discuss a specific problem. When discussing complicated issues each actor will need to explain the situation in such a way that others (less familiar with the issues) may understand the context and hence be able to differentiate between what is important and what is not. Professionals may use different communication mechanisms, expressions and emotions to ensure that others pay greater attention to their message. Actions that ensure other professionals' attention is focused on their interaction may be very useful in environments where large quantities of information are exchanged. Open and supportive communication is conducive to building trust and facilitating interaction between construction team members. Defensive behaviour tends to develop during problem-solving and this can adversely affect the ability of team members to work together. It is when communication between team members is most needed, during times of uncertainty and crisis, that relationships tend to break down and communication becomes difficult.

Open exchanges of information and sharing task responsibilities are essential for effective teamwork. Interaction that builds and maintains the fragile professional relationships necessary to accomplish tasks is fundamental to the project's success. It is important that research identifies how interaction can be used to strengthen and maintain relationships, enabling participants to work on tasks effectively. Open exchanges may involve both supportive and critical comments. Open communication can be very effective, but if it is not managed in a sensitive and appropriate way for the context it may be destructive to relationships. All actors need to be equipped with the appropriate communication skills to ensure that matters that may cause conflict can be openly discussed while at the same time ensuring that the relationship is maintained and not damaged. Negotiation, influence and persuasion have an important role to play within a business setting. Thus it is necessary to develop communication skills and understand the effectiveness of negotiation approaches so that they can be adapted to suit the business or project context.

Construction progress meetings

Dialogue between management and design professionals is essential if individual aspects of the building are to be successfully integrated and problems resolved quickly and amicably. For certain types of interaction, such as complex negotiation, there is no substitute for face-to-face meetings. In a decentralised structure, such as a meeting, members have more avenues of interaction and may be able to seek assistance from someone considered supportive. A number of different types of meetings routinely take place during the design and construction process. These include the formal progress meetings, sub-contractor meetings, project initiation (start-up meetings) and handover meetings as well as the more informal meetings arranged for a specific function, for example to encourage team building.

Construction progress meetings are fundamental to the smooth running of the construction contract. They are usually held on or adjacent to the construction site in temporary site accommodation and attended by key participants in the project. The site meeting serves as a forum to discuss the technical coordination of the work as well as helping to develop and maintain relationships between the actors who have the most influence and control over the project. The purpose of meetings seems to have changed little over the years: a forum to resolve misunderstandings and reduce friction, while allowing discussion and decisions to be made, to allow the work to proceed. Informed decision-making is an essential part of construction projects, providing the basis for work to proceed.

There are few construction publications that give real guidance on which or how many professionals should be present in progress meetings. General management text suggests that for economic reasons and optimum results the number of people attending meetings should be kept to a minimum. The group should be just large enough to include individuals with all the relevant skills for the problem solution; this is known as 'the principle of least group size'. The optimum size for problem-solving groups is usually five and for discussion groups is six. When groups have fewer than five people, members often complain that groups are too small, although the opportunity increases for individual talk. Similarly, members become dissatisfied with discussions when groups are much larger than six people. In construction projects it is common for the group members to number around ten, or even more, which is less than ideal.

Construction professionals enter and leave the process at different times and contribute to different extents depending on their particular expertise, and so it is likely that different professionals will attend sequential construction meetings. Problems with group development may be experienced when membership of the meeting is not stable. Where people have taken part in a series of meetings on related subjects, and different people are present in each of the previous meetings, the group participation is the same as if the group had met for the first time. This phenomenon is due to the fact that groups need to go through socio-emotional development. As new members enter the group they cautiously interact, testing and checking behaviour and responses, understanding the roles and behaviour of others, and then establishing their position within the group and adopting the group norms. While an individual may be able to influence the group, their influence is dependent on the nature of the group that they have entered and the context that the group has set. Considering the temporary multi-organisational nature of the construction team and the often lengthy time period between projects, it is difficult to perceive a situation where a team on one project would continue to work together on another project without any personnel changes. Equally, depending on demand, professionals may or may not choose to attend meetings. Such instability may affect group development.

Within organisation settings, some people are less willing than others to communicate ideas. The group's norms may also influence individual members to accommodate desired communication behaviour. Some members may have a greater influence on the group interaction and decision-making. Factors such as communication dominance, influence and reluctant communicators may affect the group's interaction. Such attributes are likely to be important in the decision-making process that leads to project success or failure.

Misunderstanding and conflict

Communication problems tend to be most prevalent during the construction phase, when the level of information and the pressure to perform is at its highest. Increases in the amount of information have been linked to increased levels of conflict. This would suggest that the construction phase, where the majority of professionals associated with the process are involved and where the cumulative sum of information reaches its peak, would be prone to conflict. Problems will arise and the design office must be prepared to deal with them quickly and accurately in accordance with the contract conditions. Disagreements between the design and the construction team tend to be related to requests for changes, the quality of the work, time and cost overruns. Many of these problems can be resolved during regular site progress meetings, via an impromptu meeting on site or through discussion over the telephone.

Personal differences between architects and construction managers may result in, or conversely prevent, conflict. The different backgrounds, education and training of actors may lead to different perceptions of what is of greatest importance to the project at any point, and this could result in disputes. Professionals tend to concentrate on their own area of specialist knowledge, yet devote little attention to understanding other aspects of work that may present difficulties when attempting to integrate work packages. Each specialist must have an understanding of how his or her work package is affected by, and affects, the work of others. As actors realise that components, ideas and beliefs do not integrate, conflict inevitably emerges. Dealing with conflicting ideas is an essential component of effective integration. When faced with a situation that requires a multidisciplinary input, two problems emerge: the professionals will concentrate on the detail associated with their specialism and when proposing solutions the actors will attempt to reduce their organisation's resource costs. Professionals tend to use interaction to influence the discussions so that the resulting decisions favour the individual and their organisation. During the construction process, problems both large and small may emerge that will affect individuals and their organisations' ability to perform the tasks with the resources originally allocated to the project. Meetings, negotiations and discussions are held to resolve problems.

Problem-solving often involves a redistribution of resources (possibly meaning that some will benefit and some will not). Similarly, solutions to problems require something to change, and the act of change is not always attractive to all actors. Combined, these factors could lead to a defensive attitude among some actors. Conflict may emerge as organisations defend their allocation of resources. Conflict can be beneficial, leading to improved performance; however, if the level of conflict threatens cooperation, it is much less desirable. The temporary construction organisation is subject to communication problems. The complexity of the construction industry and ineffective communication increases the potential for dysfunctional conflict. When conflict develops, actors must ensure that interaction is managed so that the relationship is not permanently damaged.

Design changes

It is common to employ a clerk of works to monitor and check the quality of the work on behalf of the client. The clerk of works will aim to ensure that the work is carried out in accordance with the contract drawings and specifications and will keep a record of all changes. He or she will need to be present on the site during working hours and has the authority to condemn work if it fails to meet the required standard. The clerk of works has a difficult position, since it can be difficult to retain integrity and not favour one side over another. The clerk of works will be under a lot of pressure from the contractor and the project administrator. This is concerned with trust and fairness, and good clerks of works are able to distance themselves from the work and make rational and fair decisions according to the contract conditions.

Changes during construction are wasteful of resources and in the majority of cases have significant cost implications. In new-build projects the only uncertainty should be the ground conditions, assuming that all of the information was complete and approved before work started. Once the ground works package is complete then there should be no reason for changes to the design or production methods unless the client requests a change. Design quality should be certain and cost forecasting should be accurate. In work to existing buildings there is more uncertainty since it is impossible to predict exactly what may be found when the building is opened up. The amount of work required and hence cost estimation is therefore less certain. Although every effort should be taken to limit the possibility of uncertainty at the production stage, it is likely that some changes may be deemed necessary. Changes to the agreed contract documentation will result in adjustment to the agreed contract sum. Most changes result in revising work and/or additional work as well as disruption to the pro-grammed workflow. The inevitable result is an increase in costs, which someone has to pay for. Therefore it is necessary to track all requests for design changes, and efforts should be taken to minimise the number of changes that occur during the realisation phase. Changes may be required for a variety of reasons, some of the most common related to the following:

- *Unforeseen circumstances.* For example, problems in the ground or surprises when opening up an existing structure. This can be mitigated through extensive surveys prior to work commencing, but the risk of some unforeseen event cannot be completely eliminated. This is normally covered in the contingency sums.
- *Client requests.* These are normally related to clients revising their requirements, i.e. changing their minds, which can be mitigated by involving the client fully in the earlier design phases.
- *Designer request.* This tends to be related to the realisation that something could have been better, and/or to poorly conceived design work.
- *Contractor request.* Requests may be related to construc-tability issues and availability of materials to suit the pro-gramme. It is important to distinguish between those items that are a genuine problem and have to be revised (e.g. clashes of services) and those requests made to suit the contractor (e.g. change of materials to save the contractor some money).
- *Problems related to the information provided*, resulting in requests for additional information and clarification.

Off-site production changes are not possible once manufacturing commences, thus the design team and client must be absolutely certain that the design is correct before production starts. With site-based production there is always a possibility of making changes as the building is erected, assuming someone is willing to pay for the privilege. There may be considerable pressure to change the specified product and/or specified level of performance during the tendering and realisation phase of the contract. Most changes are formally requested and approved before being implemented and are subsequently recorded in the as-built documentation. However, there is evidence that unscrupulous contractors and sub-contractors may change specified materials and components for cheaper alternatives and not inform anyone. A vigilant clerk of works can help to prevent some of these unwelcome habits; so too can the employment of reputable contractors and sub-contractors.

Tracking design changes

Changes, regardless of their origin, need to be referred back to the design manager and checked against critical documents such as planning approvals and the project brief, before they are implemented. Requests to change building products and details have implications for the durability of the building and must be given careful consideration before a decision is made. In many cases this is not a quick process, since the changes may have implications for other interconnected aspects of the building. This means that the manager of the construction contract must make requests for changes in adequate time and be prepared to wait for an informed decision. Contracts stipulate clear rules and timescales for requesting and responding to changes. All approved changes must be recorded and the drawings, specifications and schedules revised. This will ensure the 'as-built' drawings are an accurate record of the completed building. Changes made without the knowledge of the contract administrator will not of course be recorded in the as-built information.

Closing out projects and common problems

Completion of the project and handover to the client is known as closing out the project. This is the stage at which the project has reached its stated aims, i.e. the works have reached practical completion. It is common in large and complex projects to phase the work and release practically complete sections of the work at predetermined dates; thus the project is handed over in stages, usually known as sectional completion. These formal handovers to the client are important events and need to be managed so that the client experience is a good one. The client rarely forgets messy handovers. Closing out the project should be a cause for celebration for all project stakeholders and it is common for architects and/or project managers to arrange an event to mark the successful completion of the project. From the architect's perspective this is a good opportunity to engage in public relations activities (see Chapter 15).

Practical completion (referred to as substantial completion in some contracts) refers to the date the contractor is contractually bound to complete the work. There is some debate as to what constitutes work that is 'practically complete', but it is usually taken as the date the client takes possession of the building (or section of the building). At practical completion the client takes possession and hence responsibility for the building and the defects liability period commences, commonly 6 to 12 months. It is good practice to identify any outstanding work and minor defects prior to practical completion; however, it is common practice to deal with the defects list ('snagging list') at practical completion. The contractor then has 14 days to rectify the work.

At the end of the defects liability period there is a joint inspection of the works to check that everything is in working order. Any defects will need to be dealt with promptly by the contractor. When any necessary defects are rectified, the works is deemed to be complete and the final certificate is issued.

Common problems

The way in which problems are dealt with and their cumulative impact on project success is related to the attitude of those involved. Relational contracting, such as partnering, is founded on shared responsibility and trust, so problems should (theoretically at least) be resolved as a team effort. More adversarial relationships tend to be based on distrust and defensive behaviour. The culture is to blame others for errors and retreat from problems in the hope that someone else will resolve them. Problems during the project tend to be related to physical or managerial factors. Physical problems are related to unexpected ground conditions, difficulties with physical interfaces and problems caused by unexpectedly inclement weather (i.e. too cold, too hot, too windy, too wet). Depending on the project these should have been accommodated in the contingencies; nevertheless they may have implications for the management of the project.

Common management problems are:

- *Programme overruns.* Related to poor estimation of work and poor management of workflow. Design changes also have an influence.
- *Cost escalation.* Related to poor estimation of the cost of the work and poor management of costs during realisation. Design changes also have an influence.

- *Design changes*. Project managers and construction managers taking decisions concerning changes to the design without first asking the design team.
- *Late decisions*. Making a decision to accelerate the work will have a significant impact on the workflow schedule.
- *Failure to ask questions*. The person on site trying to make sense of the information may not have been part of the early team development and may not entirely understand the information. Failure to ask questions (due to insufficient time, attitude, etc) may result in errors, which someone will have to correct and pay for.
- *Failure to request additional information in time*. Late requests for additional and/or missing information can cause conflict between the design and realisation teams and in some cases can lead to incorrect work (and rework if spotted). Usually related to the workers and their manager's inability to think and plan ahead. Location-based planning techniques and the appointment of suitable staff may help.
- *Failure to track design changes*.
- *Changes to key staff*. Changes to key staff during a project can be extremely disruptive to the flow of work, especially for site-based activities. It is not uncommon for prime contractors to move their site managers from one project to another, and although this may make sense to the contractor, it can cause significant disruption on the site (because individuals have different ways of working and communicating). The change of project administrator in the design office can also be disruptive.
- *Communication between the site and the design office*. A great deal of communication on construction sites is channelled via the site manager and his or her ability to understand everything and keep an overview of all changes will be fundamental to a well-functioning construction site.

Post-project problems will also need to be tackled quickly and efficiently and some time will need to be factored into the design office overheads to deal with unexpected problems after the project is signed off. The manner in which the architect and others respond to post-project problems and enquiries will influence the client's perception of the project stakeholders and may influence the likelihood of future work for that client.

Consequences of unresolved problems

Problems can and do sometimes spiral out of control, resulting in time-consuming and expensive action that will usually require some form of independent intervention to resolve the problem. One of the aims of good design management is to avoid, or at least mitigate, serious problems and hence avoid the need for legal proceedings. Few parties benefit from conflict and legal proceedings other than the legal profession, and it is not in the interests of any of the project stakeholders to get dragged into long-running legal wrangles, which will hit profitability and may damage hard-earned reputations.

The project to office interface

The design manager's role during the realisation phase is to manage the interface between the design office and the realisation team. It is inevitable that there will be requests for changes to the design and/or detailing of the building during the construction programme and the design office must have some capacity to respond in a timely manner. It is also probable that there will be problems that cannot be resolved by those working on the project, and intervention by the design manager may be necessary to stop the problem getting out of hand.

In the majority of projects architectural firms have little real control over realisation of the design values, regardless of the contract used. They are, however, frequently judged on the quality of the finished building in addition to the quality of their service provision. From a business perspective architectural firms seem insufficiently attached to the buildings they design; such detachment is unsettling since it emphasises architects' vulnerability in the order of things. The amount of unplanned involvement can also affect the design firm's profitability. The way in which the design office interacts with construction activities will be determined to a large extent by the procurement route chosen. The structure and market orientation of the office will also be a determining factor in how willing, or otherwise, the design organisation is to be involved in the management of construction activities. From a business perspective the amount of interaction needs to be assessed against the business plan, the experience and skills of the office and the firms' exposure to risk. An alternative view is to look at the amount of involvement in production from the perspective of growing the expertise and organisational knowledge of the office. In providing design-only services, it is difficult to benefit from experiential learning. In a conventional model the learning will come from interaction with realisation activities and learning directly from the problems and challenges faced by the various actors charged with doing the physical labour (which can help with constructability and provide valuable experience for project management and construction management activities). At the other end of the scale, by being directly involved in managing construction activities, there is a real opportunity to integrate design and construction knowledge to the benefit of the project and the business.

Chapter Eight
Learning from Projects and Products

There is a natural relationship between the decisions made during the design and construction phases and the functionality and serviceability of the completed building. The manner in which the building performs in use, the options for modification and reuse and the potential for recycling and minimising waste at disposal, are determined to a greater or lesser extent in the conceptual design phases and coloured by decisions made during detailing and realisation. Real estate managers and building maintenance managers will be concerned with durability of the building and frequency of maintenance. Personnel managers will be concerned with the quality of the internal working environment and the adaptability of internal space. It has become common to refer to the building as a facility and its management under the term 'facilities management'. The rapidly evolving field of facilities management has helped to emphasise the link between buildings and organisational effectiveness. Greater attention to the value of buildings in a commercial setting has also helped to re-emphasise the link between the managers of the facility and the designers.

Evaluating the performance of projects and products can reveal a wealth of knowledge for possible inclusion in current and future work. Knowledge transfer between concurrent projects and from completed project to new projects is essential for improving performance of project teams and the organisations contributing to the projects. Feedback and knowledge gleaned from projects should be fed into office procedures to help keep operating procedures current, flexible and above all useful to the design team. To be successful the project and office cultures must be committed to a learning culture in which open communications and the ability to engage in constructive criticism are encouraged. A blame culture at the project and/or organisational level is not conducive to continual learning. Professionals should be engaged in continual learning and updating of skills through regular continual professional development activities, and these should be linked to better performance within the office and project environments. Evaluation and learning form a continual programme with long-term objectives for all stakeholders: looking at how things are, watching how people behave, listening carefully to what people say, asking carefully framed questions and presenting the findings to senior managers and user groups with the intention of effecting positive change.

Feedback must be conducted in a systematic way and form an integral part of project and organisational learning. Time for this important activity should be factored into the office overheads and incorporated into project programmes. The design manager must put into place systems of knowledge capture and implementation so that the design office can collectively learn from individual project and product evaluation. Systematic learning from the process and the product should form part of the office management system. Strategic incorporation of feedback from specific stages in the process is an essential component of a reflective and reflexive approach to management. Similarly, feedback from the building in use will help to identify knowledge for incorporation into current and future design projects. Experience should be incorporated into key project phases, in particular the briefing phase, to help inform new projects, benefiting from good practices and helping to avoid bad practices being repeated from project to project. Appropriate data collection tools need to be used, the data analysed and the knowledge shared within the office, and where appropriate within project teams. Failure to incorporate learning opportunities will usually result in a loss of valuable knowledge, not through any reluctance to analyse performance, but because other tasks become more pressing and the opportunities pass by.

Learning from projects

Learning is taking place throughout the life of a project. The challenge for the design manager is to incorporate specific events into project programmes in which knowledge can be exchanged and captured for use on current and future projects. Project control gateways are designed to discuss progress and hence engage in feedback related to specific activities. Similarly, formally constituted construction progress meetings provide another forum in which progress is discussed. Events at which the project team congregate may help to identify areas for improvement; however, the focus will be on the progress of the project and it is not uncommon for learning from

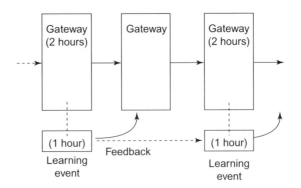

Figure 8.1 Learning events built into the project programme.

the experience to be lost in the noise. For this reason it is recommended that specific learning events are built into project programmes at strategic intervals, where the focus is on reflection and learning, not project progression (Figure 8.1). Learning-feedback loops are crucial to the delivery of effective projects and to organisational learning. Similarly, the use of post-project reviews can help to identify good and bad experiences.

Construction professionals have often been criticised for not engaging in systematic project reviews, the feeling being that valuable knowledge is lost between projects. This appears to be related to the constant pressure on professionals' time rather than any inability to do the review. Some organisations do fail to build systematic project reviews into their working practices and project plans, but this is becoming less common. Failure to review projects may lead to the loss of important knowledge, resulting in the failure to identify and subsequently share good practice. This can lead to the replication of errors and missed opportunities to improve performance.

Reviews need to be facilitated, preferably by someone who has not been involved in the project and therefore lies outside the project culture. This can help actors to be a little more open and candid in their opinions. The facilitator is also more likely to ask some pertinent and perhaps unexpected questions of the project participants. On a practical level, two project architects facilitating each other's projects can achieve this. Similarly, it may be useful for the design manager to facilitate such meetings. The outcome of the project reviews should be recorded in a concise report and sent to all those involved. All review activities need to clearly articulate the aim of the review and state those most likely to benefit from engaging in the event. The key objective may be to focus on team performance, cost control or control of design changes. Some design managers will include reviews at strategic points in projects, to focus on a topical issue. If actors are unwilling to engage in knowledge exchange, or are too candid, then it may be prudent to consider a tactical substitution for future projects.

Through-project reviews

Through-project reviews are normally incorporated into quality management systems and may be linked to routine project evaluation activities at control gateways. The benefit of conducting project reviews at key stages in the project is that there is less reliance on the memory of the actors compared with post-project reviews. Knowledge harvested from such events can also be incorporated into other projects running concurrently, thus making the process more relevant to those involved. Care should be taken to clearly identify learning opportunities and separate this process from routine progress meetings. The advantage of through-project reviews relates to the accessibility of key actors and current knowledge, assuming that the project culture is such that actors feel comfortable discussing areas for improvement. If the project team is different each time it is unlikely that relationships will have developed to such an extent that the actors are willing to discuss issues openly, although this should improve as the project continues. Project team learning is essentially a collection of different learning experiences at group level, and this differs from learning in the more stable office environment. Through-project reviews should:

♦ Involve all key actors involved in the project at the time of the review. There are likely to be changes in some of the actors present between early and later reviews.
♦ Include the client.
♦ Clearly identify the topic that will be discussed.
♦ Disseminate findings to those present.

Post-project reviews

Post-project reviews (sometimes called project post-mortems) are an important component of any good quality-management system. Evaluation at the end of the project aims to measure the success of the project against the goals set out in the brief. This exercise may generate valuable knowledge for inclusion in future projects, which will draw on and adapt the information, knowledge and experiences (both good and bad) generated during previous projects. This helps to keep organisations working efficiently while providing benefits for new projects. The members of the project team mainly hold this knowledge; indeed team assembly is usually based on actors' previous project experience (building type, complexity, cost, performance, etc) rather than professional discipline or educational qualifications. Post-project reviews are usually conducted at the end of a project or after the completion of a major phase of large projects. These meetings are often conducted by the project manager and/or design manager. The review will include input from major contributors to the project and is usually conducted as a meeting or a series of meetings. Participants are encouraged to share their experiences of what went well and what could have been done better, so that future projects can benefit from the learning process. Some organisations may also conduct their own 'internal' post-project reviews to assist with organisational learning.

In situations where post-project reviews are incorporated into the management plan for specific projects, they may be an ineffective means of knowledge capture because:

- Some of the actors may have moved on to other projects and be unavailable for post-project data-gathering. Many actors are only involved for a short period of time, to undertake a specific work package, after which they move to another project. This makes it very difficult to consult them after the event and helps to highlight the need for systematic project reviews during the lifeline of the project.
- Pressures imposed by new projects may override those of completed projects, thus the review may be rather rushed and inconclusive or may not happen, once again highlighting the need for reviews during the process.
- Actors may not remember all relevant facts, and if the review is conducted a long time after the start of a project it is highly likely that the opinions given are not as accurate or as informed as they might otherwise have been.
- Professional rivalry may lead some actors to give a limited account of the project, saving the 'real' knowledge for the benefit of their organisation and their career advancement.
- Professionals are reluctant to admit that they have made mistakes or have not performed as well as intended. Few of us feel comfortable discussing failures and mistakes openly and honestly unless there is an atmosphere of trust and mutual support (which is difficult to achieve within an organisation and even more so in a temporary grouping of project participants).
- Not all clients will be interested in post-project reviews. If the client is not a repeat client, they may have little to gain from taking part in a project post-mortem.

♦ Disagreements, disputes and conflict may make it impossible to conduct a post-project review.

Key performance indicators

Measuring performance is becoming increasingly widespread as organisations contributing to design and construction projects aim to improve their performance through better management practices. A commitment by all members of the organisation to continual improvement is an excellent starting point; however, if performance is to be improved there must be procedures in place to report progress, measure it in a meaningful manner and communicate and incorporate the results. For evaluation to be successful, organisations and projects must have a clearly defined set of objectives, against which performance can be measured. These need to be set out in the strategic and/or project brief, otherwise trying to gauge success becomes a meaningless exercise. It is important to remember that the exercise is not just concerned with metrics; it is also about the right attitude to continual improvement.

To improve performance it is necessary to use some form of measurement. The mantra is 'if you cannot measure it, you cannot improve it'. The Construction Industry Board produced the framework for key performance indicators in 1998. Working with the Construction Best Practice Programme, the Construction Clients Forum and the Movement for Innovation, data is collected, collated and published. The indicators are designed to allow all parties to the construction process to check how they are performing against the industry as a whole. There are ten key performance indicators, seven related to project performance and three to the performance of the organisation.

Project performance:

♦ Client satisfaction with the product (building)
♦ Client satisfaction with the construction process
♦ Defects
♦ Predictability of cost
♦ Predictability of time
♦ Actual cost
♦ Actual time.

Company performance:

♦ Profitability – an important indicator for all organisations
♦ Productivity
♦ Safety.

Learning from the product

Architects and engineers have long been criticised for walking away after the building is complete with scant attention paid to feedback or indeed the use of the building over the years after completion. With increased pressures to reuse existing buildings, through upgrading, extension and repair, architectural firms are starting to reconsider their role and expand their service provision into the facilities management area. The original design team is arguably in the best position to provide advice regarding the maintenance, repair and upgrading of the finished product because of their intimate knowledge of the building design.

From an economic viewpoint buildings represent substantial assets to their owners and users, frequently requiring maintenance, repair and upgrading. Responsible owners have long recognised the long-term financial benefits of regular maintenance of their (often substantial) assets; however, many building owners have no provision for maintenance. More surprising still is that a building owner who has gone to great lengths to employ professionals to design and oversee the construction of their building, taking great care in the selection of the contractor, should then employ a wide assortment of firms (often with no professional input) to carry out alterations and maintenance, often without reference to the original design philosophy. From an asset management viewpoint, such an approach is not particularly sensible. From an environmental viewpoint, the aim of the design team should be to extend the building life for as long as possible, through careful design and material selection, in order to conserve the scarce resources that are locked into the fabric. Once the building is constructed there is a need to consult the original documentation (if not the original team) before alterations or maintenance are carried out.

Facilities management covers a wide range of activities ranging from space management and maintenance management to financial management, operations management and people management. Although definitions vary, the core function of the facilities manager is to support the core business activities of the organisation. The interface between facilities management and design is important if a building's potential is to be realised. The maintenance of a current set of plans and a maintenance database is paramount if a building is to be cared for and utilised effectively during its various lives. The challenge for all parties concerned with building maintenance and asset and facilities management is one of collecting dispersed, often inaccessible, information; this may lead to a loss of design and technical expertise that first created the building.

Of the vast quantity of information generated for individual projects, much is related to the process of building (project-orientated information), with a small amount of information, such as drawings, specifications and maintenance logs being applicable to the actual finished building (product-orientated information). Professionals involved in the building project will retain project information and product information for a set timescale, primarily for legal reasons. But this information is also a source of knowledge for new projects, and data retrieval and data-mining computer software can greatly assist the design organisation's ability to retrieve past project information quickly. Project information may have little or no value to the owners/occupiers of the completed building. Product information such as floor plans, details of construction and legal consents are needed by the building owners and its managers (not necessarily the client or original owners). Such information is easily stored and accessed electronically; however, many designers are reluctant to release this information, fearing loss of future business (e.g. copyright laws and Intellectual Property Rights (IPR)). Increased interest in both building and service maintenance, coincident with the growth of the facilities management discipline, has brought a greater awareness of the value of accurate, accessible information.

Post-occupancy evaluation

There is an obvious link between the way in which we interact with buildings on a daily basis and how well the project team performed. Collection and analysis of data from the building in use is termed post-occupancy evaluation (POE). This may be conducted by members of the original project team and/or by consultants who have had no involvement in the design and realisation phases. Evaluation is usually undertaken at planned intervals after occupation, for example at 12, 24 and 60 months. POE may be used to check that client and user values, as stated in the written briefing documents, were implemented as intended. The problem is that the users may be different from those represented in the early briefing exercises and this needs to be considered when analysing the data. The focus of the data collection may be coloured by the remit of the data collection exercise and the actors' experience of the project. Key areas of concern related to building owner/occupier and building user interests are:

- *Space use.* Is the space functional and being used efficiently and as planned? How has the new facility impacted on working practices and productivity?
- *Time.* Has the new facility helped to improve flow of people within the building?

- *Wellbeing.* Is the perceived comfort and satisfaction of the staff acceptable? Has the internal environment helped with productivity?
- *Esteem.* How does the new facility impact on company image and what do the users feel about the building?
- *Energy use.* Is energy consumption as expected?
- *Maintenance and operating costs.* Replacement of components, cleaning, security, etc.

Collection of reliable data is much easier for some of these factors than others. For example, energy usage will be documented through meter readings, and smart systems can provide a wealth of information for analysis. In contrast, observing how people use space on a daily basis is more challenging. The intention of POE exercises is to report on existing performance and identify changes from the original brief. Recommendations for corrective action and a summary of the lessons learned can be made following analysis and reflection on the data collected. Addressing the issues should justify the expense of the action, leading to improved performance. Concomitant with other data collection exercises the purpose should be clearly defined and necessary approvals sought and granted from appropriate managers before data collection begins. Similarly, methodologies for evaluation should be kept simple, have measurable outcomes, be properly resourced and have a realistic timeframe. Data collection techniques used for POE studies include:

- *Observation.* Participant and non-participant observation can reveal rich data, but it is very time-consuming and building users may resist an outsider's presence. Few of us like to be watched as we work. Remote monitoring and surveillance through closed-circuit cameras raises ethical issues and should only be used with the appropriate consents and safeguards in place.
- *Walk-through surveys.* Observational surveys are used to try and get an impression of how space is being used by looking at, and listening to, users. The term 'walk through' is a little misleading, since data collection usually involves standing or sitting within spaces to observe users going about their daily work, often in conjunction with random informal discussions with users.
- *Questionnaires.* User-satisfaction questionnaires can help to reveal perceptions of building users/owners/managers. Space usage questionnaires are also used, but may not give an accurate picture since they rely on people remembering when (and how) they used specific areas.

- *Interviews.* Interview techniques are useful for gathering user perceptions and opinions.
- *Focus groups.* These can be used to explore specific issues with a variety of stakeholders and user representatives.
- *Measurement.* Hard data collected through measurement is often easier to access and analyse: measuring space usage through electronic sensors, and measuring energy usage, frequency of cleaning, replacement of short-life components, etc.
- *Benchmarking.* This allows comparisons to be made on a number of levels, including other buildings.

Evidence-based learning

It is necessary to balance experiential learning with knowledge gleaned from relevant published literature. More experience does not necessarily lead to learning. For example, repetitive job functions can lead to complacency and lack of interest in learning. Trying to make sense of daily challenges can be enhanced by comparing experience with relevant academic research findings and the views of others. Constant questioning can help to keep knowledge fresh and relevant while stimulating innovative approaches to routine methods and procedures. Many professionals find it difficult to find the time to read research literature, often relying on the professional journals as a source of information and knowledge of the latest trends and innovations. There are many other sources of knowledge that should be explored, some of which may offer more value to practitioners than others. Typical sources include:

- *Textbooks.* Although mainly aimed at students, these represent a useful source of distilled knowledge that is readily accessible.
- *Professional journals.* These deal with topical issues and help to keep practitioners updated with developments in a range of areas, from design through to legal issues.
- *Research journals.* Peer-reviewed articles may offer practitioners some useful information; however, time will be required to search papers that are relevant to the interests of the practice.
- *Conferences.* The conference circuit tends to be occupied mainly by academics, many of whom have never, or seldom, practised. Thus practitioners may find the language used and the applicability of the espoused theory difficult to

relate to daily practice. Conference proceedings may also be difficult to access, although a growing number are now available via the Internet.

♦ *Continuous professional development (CPD) activities.* These are aimed at practitioners and tend to draw on information gleaned from conferences, journals and textbooks, usually enhanced with a fair amount of anecdotal evidence from active practitioners. CPD offers a quick and often effective means of improving and extending knowledge.

The biggest challenge for the practitioner is finding the time to search out and read material relevant to their particular context and needs. For some professionals a good textbook may represent better value compared with attending a conference for a day; it depends on personal interests and level of interaction with the academic environment. Whatever the approach taken, it is necessary to look outside one's immediate field of experience and try and relate it to the experience of others.

Reflection in action

More experience does not guarantee more learning. Learning from experience tends to be most effective when the experiences are painful or novel in some way, but learning from our mistakes is not a good policy if we wish to stay in business (nor is it consistent with the total quality management (TQM) ethos). The opportunity to learn from novel experiences may diminish as time passes. Thus reflective practice after the event is important because the individual will reflect on his or her actions, which may have been rather ordinary and uneventful, rather than waiting to learn from experience. The reflective practitioner has the opportunity to reflect on procedures and habits taken for granted, but which may be open to improvement when analysed. A number of tools to assist with reflective practice range from keeping a reflective journal to organised discussion groups with peers (quality circles). Reflection on practice is an essential component of professional development and the better the management of individuals' direction, the better equipped the firm to respond to change.

The concept of the reflective practitioner is well known to designers and forms an integral part of much architecture and built environment education. The action of designing is itself a reflective activity and design thinking is a fascinating area of research. Reflecting on the progress of projects may be a less attractive proposition than reflecting on our design decisions, but it is here that much can be learned about how design intent is realised. Individual reflection in action is a private activity, largely hidden from colleagues unless we decide to share the experiences. Reflection on daily events combined with evidence from published sources should form a systematic part of a professional's continual learning.

Reflective diary

A reflective diary or reflective log is an established tool for helping individuals to develop their knowledge and ability to respond to situations. The intention is not to record every event in detail, but to record and reflect on events that are significant to an individual, the aim being that reflection puts the individual in a better situation should the same or similar event occur in the future. The reflective diary may be a digital file (kept, for example, on a laptop) or a notebook or sketchbook, which tends to be preferred by designers because it is easier to add small, schematic sketches. Frequency and style of entries is very much a personal choice. Some designers add entries to their diaries following a 'significant' event, for example a project suffering a major problem or conversely a major success. Others add entries on a weekly or even daily basis, recording and reflecting on less significant, but equally important, events associated with their job function. The recommended format is a simple three-stage approach in which individuals:

- *Describe the situation.* A concise outline of the event, problem or success, the actors involved and the issues that are to be reflected on. Keep it factual.
- *Reflect on the event.* What could have been done differently? This tends to be personal.
- *Consider action.* Explore some scenarios. For example, how would you respond if faced with the same event in the future? What would you do differently? Is more knowledge, education or training required to help you be better prepared?

Reflective diaries are personal documents used by individuals to help improve performance. Indeed, many find it useful to reflect in the evening while at home. Diary contents are confidential; however, the process of reflection may result in the realisation that some issues cannot be tackled in isolation. These need to be raised within the organisation and/or within the project team at an appropriate juncture. A reflective diary is also a good tool to identify things that went well and things that need to be improved. These issues can then be taken forward to regular knowledge-exchange meetings and the annual staff review.

Knowledge-exchange meetings

Meetings provide an excellent forum in which to discuss performance. Meetings should be held at regular intervals as well as at the end of the project, thus benefiting as the project proceeds. Each meeting needs to be facilitated (preferably by someone who was not involved directly with the project). The salient information needs to be recorded and clear actions identified. This new knowledge then needs to be disseminated to the appropriate parties and incorporated into practices and procedures at the earliest opportunity. (See also Chapter 12.)

Storytelling

Storytelling is a very useful way of helping to explain situations to others, and its use in architecture is relatively common. Informal dialogues and small-group communication are utilised to tell stories to new members of the office as a means of socialising them into the office norms and to help illustrate good and bad practices. Anecdotal reports sometimes become legends within the office, with the familiar opening line similar to 'did you hear about the time when . . .' opening the way for a tale relating to office and project morals. These stories are highly effective in helping to explain why things are done the way they are, and/or to make a point. Storytelling is an effective vehicle for transferring knowledge within or between small groups of people. Used effectively these conversations can help to expose and develop the knowledge held within offices and project organisations.

Action research and learning

It is through reflection on individual and collective experience, combined with theoretical debates and analysis of research findings, that we are better able to implement improvements to our working practices. This involves planned (considered) change, much of which will be incremental and relatively gradual, but some of which may be more radical and substantial.

Action research is applied research that aims to actively and intentionally effect a change in a system, in this case a social system. This involves the active participation of the researcher(s) in the client system. For action research to have any value it must, like all other research, be conducted in a systematic manner within a defined

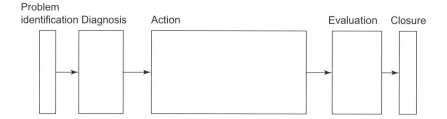

Figure 8.2 Sequence of action research stages.

programme and be adequately resourced. The success of this type of research will depend on the experience and competences of the researcher and the synergy between researcher and client. Success will also depend on the level of commitment shown by those taking part in the research. Ethical issues and the value of the research to both the client organisation and the researcher need to be discussed before entering into an agreement. The ethnographer may be someone with research training already working in the office (e.g. someone with a research degree) or a researcher may be invited into the client's organisation to carry out the research. The main stages in the sequence are illustrated in Figure 8.2 and follow a sequence similar to the following:

- *Start.* The client usually presents the problem, i.e. it is driven by the organisation and discussed with the researcher. Clear goals, resources and timeframe are agreed. The amount of access to often confidential and commercially sensitive organisational settings also needs to be discussed and agreed.
- *Diagnosis.* This stage involves the researcher and client discussing and agreeing to the most appropriate management concepts and research tools to address the problem. An action plan is agreed.
- *Action.* The action stage involves the ethnographer collecting data from the workplace as the client implements the agreed action.
- *Evaluation.* Data is assembled and analysed jointly by the client and the researcher, the outcome of which should be recommendations and advice that can be taken forward and, if appropriate, developed into a new action plan. It is important to recognise that some action research may be inconclusive given the dynamic nature of design and construction projects. However, given the nature of

the research it is unlikely that the effort will have been wasted since it will help to highlight how people act in the workplace.

- ◆ *Closure.* At the end of the programme, generalisations may be made that help to inform business practices and it is likely that new problems and challenges will have emerged to be tackled in related research. Depending on the agreement between client and researcher the results may then be disseminated through publication, or retained for internal use only.

Action learning is a term used to describe an inductive process in which managers seek to solve organisational problems within the workplace. This form of management development involves learning via the process of problem-solving within a group, i.e. learning to learn by doing. As with action research, the problem needs to be clearly defined and the boundaries of the group determined before the process begins. Similarly the results of the study need to be analysed and disseminated within the organisation at the end of the programme. A facilitator is required to facilitate the progress of action learning.

In-company learning can be assisted by consultants and also through interaction with academic institutions. Universities have invested in working closer with industry to share their knowledge through alliances on applied research and work-based educational schemes. The work-based programmes can be student-centred, with the majority of the work being undertaken in the workplace, or teacher-centred, with a structured programme of lectures, seminars and assessment. Many successful programmes combine both approaches and aim to develop the skills of staff around specific projects and/or work tasks. Work-based learning and development programmes seek to:

- ◆ Identify shortfalls in existing knowledge and improve it
- ◆ Identify new areas of knowledge and expertise
- ◆ Encourage staff to share their knowledge (e.g. through internal seminars)
- ◆ Better understand work practices with the aim of reducing waste and improving efficiency.

Learning through looking and listening

An important competence of the design manager is the ability to look at and listen to the activities of the staff in the office and, where possible, the interaction with others involved in projects, which usually takes place in meetings. An enormous amount of knowledge can be gleaned simply by trying to make sense of what is going on in the work environment. For this reason design managers should not occupy an office that is physically separated from the design studio. Detached from the action they will be less knowledgeable about individual projects and will have to rely on what individuals tell them they are doing, which even with the best intentions is likely to differ a little from what was actually done. Being in a position to listen to the hum of the office and see what is being done allows the design manager to spot good and bad practices.

Common problems

The main challenge to learning from both projects and products is related to forward planning and allocating sufficient time to the activity. With constant pressure to deliver creative and high quality services, it is easy to fall into a task-orientated mode with little time to reflect on the things that really matter; and thus fail to profit from the collective experience of the office. Design managers need to encourage and support the design team and ensure that learning events are built into all project programmes. Common problems include:

- *Failure to plan.* This usually equates to a failure to learn.
- *Inappropriate attitude.* Learning is related to attitude and being able to keep an open and questioning mind.
- *Poor estimation* of design effort, programming and monitoring of progress. This usually results in professions having to spend time allocated for other activities, e.g. CPD, on completing project work.
- *Poor communications* within the office. It is surprising how often individuals are unaware of their colleagues' actions, and thus fail to benefit from their experience. Encouraging staff to talk informally about the challenges they face in their daily tasks can help to disseminate knowledge and good practices.

The project to office interface

Following project completion the design manager's role changes to an 'after sales' role. The project will be complete and with the exception of formal visits, for example to sign off any outstanding work and inspect latent defects, there may be no contractual reason to stay in touch with the client. New projects will be exerting demands and pressures on the design office and the design manager will be inter-facing with actors working on new projects. It is, however, extremely important that contact with the client and the building should be maintained. This allows the possibility for the design office to learn from the building in use and also helps to maintain contact with the client and key actors, for example facilities managers, with a view to future work. Although client contact may be dealt with for-mally at partner/director level, the design manager is likely to have developed a rapport with the client or client's representative during the project and this can be an important informal link to new work opportunities.

From a business perspective there is an obvious need to keep in touch with the client and the building manager/owner after the project is finished. Marketing to existing clients will be easier if regular contact is maintained after the closure of the project. Regular contact with facilities managers and maintenance managers is a sensible policy in terms of future work. In addition to any contractual requirements for returning to the building (e.g. at the end of the defects liability period), many offices find it useful to return to the building at regular intervals to see how the building is performing in use. This may be done on an individual and relatively informal level, but it can also be beneficial to arrange formal staff visits.

From a technical perspective the office can benefit from assessing the way in which the building has weathered. This may be assessed from a visual inspection, but it is also necessary to know how much cleaning and maintenance is required, and this can only be gleaned from talking to those responsible for keeping the building service-able. From a usability perspective talking to building users can be an insightful experience, although this is not always possible because of practical difficulties with permissions etc. This type of learning is related to the building product; however, it is also crucial to try and learn from the building process.

The most successful organisations are not just those with strong ideas, desirable products and a commitment to high quality service; they also possess the managerial framework that allows their staff time to think and reflect on their work, while providing the opportunity to discuss topical issues with other members of the organisation, make clear decisions and move forward. If new ideas are to be accom-modated the firm must be so structured as to be flexible enough to allow minor adjustments with minimal disruption. Learning may help to identify business efficiencies and new markets for professional ser-vices. Success of the firm will be influenced by its ability to continually learn from its collective experience of clients and projects. This knowl-edge must be retained by the firm and disseminated to its members, a process much aided by computer-based expert knowledge systems. Acquisition, retention and dissemination of knowledge are a complex process requiring strategic management. In terms of the development of the professional service firm and its ability to respond to external forces quickly and effectively, the knowledge acquired through projects can contribute to competitive advantage.

Part Two
Managing Creative Organisations

Chapter Nine
The Business of Architecture

Design offices are creative, stimulating, exciting places in which to work. The managerial structure of the firm and the organisational culture that develops within the office will have a significant impact on the manner in which individual projects are developed, and hence the profitability of the business. Successful service firms tend to be distinguished by the skills and behaviour of the firm's leader(s), combining design vision, business skills and leadership in a seamless and effective manner. The owners' values will be reflected in the structure and culture of the office. The culture of the office and its market orientation will form part of the organisation's corporate values. These values will influence, and be influenced by, the managerial frameworks used within the organisation, frameworks that should help to encourage and maintain a creative and dynamic atmosphere. The social life of the design office needs careful consideration to create the best possible environment for people to interact, create and share knowledge, and contribute to projects without undue hindrance from onerous management systems, poor working environment or inappropriate treatment. In many respects the issue is about designing and achieving an appropriate fit for the market.

The majority of architectural practices are very small, a characteristic of other professional service firms such as accountants and lawyers. Surveys of architects in the UK and other countries have shown that the make-up of the architectural profession by size has remained relatively consistent over the years. Approximately 70% of offices are in the 'very small' band (1–5 architects), 15% in the 'small' category (6–10) and the remaining 15% in offices with 11 architectural staff or more. Around half of all architectural practices are run by a sole principal. Some of these businesses are one-person enterprises, although many solo practitioners employ a wide range of staff. Alternatively businesses tend to be formed as a legal partnership, comprising two or more partners, or as a limited company with directors. Less common forms of architectural practice are public companies and group partnerships and cooperatives. Given that around 85% of architectural offices employ ten architects or fewer, much of the management literature addressed to large organisations may be inappropriate. Small professional service firms do not have the resources to employ, for example, a personnel manager; it is a job done by one of the senior architects or directors within the office in addition to his or her other duties.

Regardless of office size, design organisations must harness a number of skills in addition to design talent if they are to be successful in business. The office needs clear direction and effective leadership as well as the ability to anticipate future markets and adapt to change. Management systems need to be simple and flexible and also to allow the creative side of the business to flourish. A combination of hard and soft management systems is required. The hard management system is the formal structure and systems employed by the firm, such as quality management, and is task-orientated. The soft management system sits within this and is concerned with the informal, intuitive nature of the firm, concerned with individuals' competences, values and feelings. Ideally soft and hard systems should complement each other and be capable of adjustment and change if the organisation is to become and remain a profitable undertaking. As professionals the architectural business must be true to:

♦ Clients
♦ Oneself and the members of the design office
♦ Society.

The professional service firm

The grouping together of professionals to sell their services to clients more effectively than could be achieved by working alone is known as a professional service firm. These businesses are typically formed as legal partnerships or as limited companies, with partners and directors, respectively, responsible for the management of the business. Their main asset is the people who work within the firm. Other terms such as 'people firms' and 'knowledge-based firms' are also used to reflect the combined skill, knowledge and experience of the firm's members. The professional service firm comprises a number of highly skilled individuals who carry out complex work for clients by means of projects. According to the leading authority in this field, David

Maister (see Appendix 3), there are two special characteristics of the professional service firm: customisation and client contact. Together they demand that an organisation attracts and retains highly skilled individuals. The high degree of customisation causes difficulties in terms of management, especially since situations may be relatively unfamiliar and thus standard management techniques inappropriate. The high degree of client contact, mainly via face-to-face communication, requires very special interpersonal skills for which quality and service have special meanings. This interface deserves as much attention as that given to design activities, because without clients there can be no fee income and hence no business.

Professionals are first and foremost concerned with satisfying their clients' needs and are notorious for regarding the running of their businesses as a secondary part of their work. Architects, for example, are primarily interested in design and the creation of value for their clients. Management of the organisation is too often seen as a secondary activity. Professionals are often charged with ineffective management of their business, squandering profits and missing opportunities to grow the business, leading to lower profits and threatening their organisation's long-term viability. Architectural firms have not escaped from such criticism, seemingly ill at ease with the concept of business management despite the fact that architecture is both a profession and a business. Some authors have claimed that the task of managing a design organisation differs from managing other types of business because it operates under special rules associated with the creative process. In part this is true; however, it should be recognised that design organisations have a number of characteristics that set them apart from other knowledge-based professional service firms such as accountants and project managers. Architectural offices:

♦ Provide a service
♦ Are regulated by professional bodies
♦ Are creative
♦ Are dependent on one market sector: construction.

Figure 9.1 shows the characteristics of an architectural firm.

Service firms

Architectural firms are concerned with providing services to their clients, the extent of which varies depending on the market orientation of the business and the requirements of individual clients. Client orientation and the multiproject environment mean that architectural businesses have to be dynamic and adaptive to changing contexts. The quality of the service provision, as perceived by the client, is

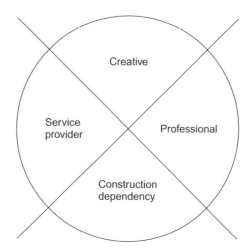

Figure 9.1 Characteristics of the architectural firm.

based on the overall experience of the service provided and, depending on the scope of service, the quality of the finished product. Quality of the service provision is largely in the hands of the design office, although the client's perception will also be influenced by the performance of other design and project team members in realising the building. Service provision must be managed and delivered professionally. To succeed in business requires the same obsession with detail that is needed in the design of buildings: a fastidious approach to every aspect of the business.

Professional firms

Architects and their fellow professionals are regulated by their professional institutions and bounded by their respective codes of conduct. Although the professional institutions were originally set up as a means of protecting their members' interests, some of their professional rules have limited the manner in which their members can trade, for example by restricting the manner in which they may advertise their services. Registered firms must comply with the relevant professional institution's code of conduct; otherwise, the firm is free to act in any legal way it chooses. The professional firm holds integrity and impartiality as fundamental values, aiming to serve the interests of both their clients and society.

Creative firms

Clients commission architectural firms to provide individual design solutions to unique problems, delivering value through architectural design. Architects are primarily concerned with generating and maintaining creativity. Research has found that architects have a strong identification with work that is creative, despite the fact that they often work in highly specialised or very technical areas. The majority of architects also wanted more design work (including greater involvement at the initial design stage) and to be able to work more autonomously. Individual control over design is important to designers. The challenge is to provide a stimulating and creative office environment that allows the space for creativity within a professional management structure.

Construction sector dependency

Architects have a special relationship with one industrial sector, construction. It is the economic climate of the construction sector that influences the economic fortune of architectural practices. Construction sector dependency is further complicated because architectural firms are concerned with issues of design and realisation, themselves culturally different worlds brought together temporarily via a project. Architectural firms cannot isolate themselves from the construction sector because the adoption of new management concepts by other actors will, to varying degrees, impact on their business.

Challenges

Professional service firms face a number of well-documented challenges related to their service provision. The services provided may be seen by clients as intangible, and they are context-specific, have a limited shelf-life and may be difficult to keep consistent.

- *Intangibility.* The product of the design business is often hard to see. Clients may see a set of drawings and a finished building, but the work that goes on to produce these products tends to go unseen and hence is not appreciated. This intangibility of service means that professional service firms must constantly communicate with clients to explain the value of the services they offer. Photographs of current and completed projects, design proposals and design awards are displayed in the office reception and web-based homepage in an attempt to communicate the type and quality of the services provided.
- *Context.* Services are client specific and are usually specific to a geographical location. Many small design offices limit their client base to a defined geographical area around their office(s). While this can help to reinforce a local presence,

it also makes the office vulnerable to fluctuations in local market conditions.

♦ *Consumption.* Services cannot be stockpiled like products. The service is consumed as it is produced; therefore careful workload planning is needed to match the resources of the office to the demands of clients. New projects need to be scheduled to suit the office resources available and hence determine the firm's ability to deliver the work to agreed time and quality parameters. Good client relations are required if the workload is to be planned to suit the office rather than the client. Staff time needs to be utilised effectively to ensure profitability, and this may mean bringing in freelance staff to help with temporary increases in workload.

♦ *Consistency.* Consistency of service is another problem. The solo practitioner may be able to provide a consistent service relatively easily. He or she acts in a similar manner with each project and the consistency of service is relatively easy to control. Put two, three or more professionals together and there needs to be some coordination of activities and values. Establishing and maintaining a good reputation for a high level of service takes a lot of effort, especially if the architects 'together' have different approaches to serving their client base. All staff must have a clear understanding of what is an acceptable and unacceptable standard of work. The use of TQM and regular quality checks can help to maintain a consistent level of service. A stable core of staff can also help.

Clients and the market for services

Architects provide services to a number of clients; they do not manufacture products, and this has implications for the way in which the business is managed. Architectural firms are faced with managing large numbers of small, extremely complex and bespoke projects for a variety of clients. Many of these projects will be running alongside other projects; thus the office comprises a multiproject environment. Clients seek value in their choice of consultants by trying to match quality of service and quality of the finished product with price; design is not the only differentiating factor. Clients also form an important part of the design firm's organisational culture, and affect projects in a positive or negative way. Ideas must be tested against the client's requirements, budget, regulations and programme. Good communication between client and architect is critical, not just to the success of a project but also to long-term client relationships. Satisfied clients are the most important source of new work, either through further commissions or through their recommendations to others.

Client categories

Clients vary in their level of experience of design and construction projects, ranging from expert to inexperienced, and in the way they commission their consultants (see also Chapter 15). From the perspective of the design office, clients tend to fall into one of the following categories:

- ◆ *Cooperative clients* are willing to work with the design office towards a common goal. Emphasis is on sharing values through open communication and maximising value for all stakeholders. Effort will be required from both parties to retain a cooperative relationship through the life of the project.
- ◆ *Challenging clients* constantly demand a high standard of service. Challenging clients are good for the office; they help to maintain focus on standards and a succession of challenging clients will result in an improvement in the level of service provision.
- ◆ *Uncooperative clients* tend to offer constant resistance and criticism and need careful management; otherwise the office is unlikely to make a profit. They will not want to be too involved in the project, and values will not be shared willingly. Uncooperative clients may also present problems when it comes to paying invoices for work carried out on their behalf.

The same client may demonstrate all three characteristics over the lifetime of a project and so the design office needs to remain vigilant and expect some changes in behaviour, especially during challenging periods for the project team.

Managing the client relationship

The architect–client relationship needs to be both nurtured and managed so that both parties benefit from the relationship. Client empathy is crucial to clear understanding and clear communications, which in turn are critical if everyone is to be happy with the finished product. Management of the client–architect interface involves a number of specific and interdependent skills, ranging from the ability to listen to the client (and key project stakeholders) and managing client expectations to developing client trust.

- *Listening to clients*. The most critical skill and an important part of good communication skills is listening to clients; the better the understanding of clients' values and needs, the better the design office is positioned to provide appropriate services. Listening skills are fundamental to effective briefing and to the development and maintenance of a strong client–architect relationship.
- *Managing client expectations*. The key to a good relationship is getting the expectations to match the outcomes. Open communication will help to highlight differences in expectations between client and designer. Clients often need educating about the building process; the more they can be encouraged to become involved in the design process, the easier it is to identify their values and hence meet their expectations. Quality management systems are a useful tool in this regard since they help the firm to keep the client informed of changes and their implications.
- *Building client trust and satisfaction*. The key word here is integrity. Clients place their trust (and their money) in the hands of their consultants and will expect their advisers to be open and honest at all times. Satisfaction with a particular project will be related to the client's perceptions of the services provided. The more involved the client is in his or her individual projects, the easier it is to develop trust and hence satisfy the client.

Service provision

Architectural practices differ in size, the type of services they offer and the type of work they do. Some firms are set up to design one particular type of building only, for example medical facilities. These firms are able to gain work from a specific market niche because of their high degree of specialisation. Equally they are vulnerable to a downturn in activity in that particular sector. Other firms will design any type of building regardless of size or location and tend to be referred to as general practitioners. Research has shown that around 80% of architectural firms specialise in at least one building type, such as housing, industrial or retail. This will affect the type of client that is attracted to the design office. Service provision should match the needs of the clients and the business objectives. In business the key to success is to provide a service of superior quality to a client at a competitive price, and provide it in such a manner that the client will appreciate the value of the service (and the end product). Typical service provision includes:

- *Design only.* Conceptual designers or 'signature architects' are primarily concerned with the creative act of design and the development of highly creative and innovative design proposals, which others then have to detail and make work. These architects become well known for their creative and often daring designs, winning commissions for their design skills. This is a very small market and only a few design offices are able to operate in this way and be financially successful. Most offices have to supplement their highly creative work with more mundane work (which they tend not to publicise), in order to generate enough income to keep the office financially viable.
- *Traditional model.* This covers the familiar services provided by the architect from inception to completion. It is the most common type of service provision for architectural practices. Many practices also provide project management services.
- *The 'one-stop' shop.* Some architectural practices have diversified and offer a one-stop shop to their clients. As a total service provider the services would range from site identification through design to construction, maintenance and facilities management and disposal/recovery management. By their very nature these organisations are also able to offer discrete packages, such as design-only and project management services to suit the needs of a wide client base.

Growing the business

The majority of design organisations will pass through a number of distinct evolutionary phases over time, from inception to survival and then (hopefully) to success. These are relatively predictable stages, often resulting from growth of the design practice in response to client demand, rather than from any specific business strategy. At the inception stage the challenge is to get enough clients and projects into the office to be financially viable; the main concern is staying in business and building a good reputation. This is a very difficult stage and many businesses do not make it. The survival stage describes a period when the office has enough work to stay financially solvent and the business is growing. Staff numbers may have expanded to deal with the increasing workload, and the pressure to be more successful will increase. Some offices will have a deliberate policy of staying small, trying to balance the flow of work with the office resources. Third comes success: the firm has proved itself in the marketplace and has grown in size and complexity. The possibility of failure will exist throughout a firm's life, regardless of its developmental stage. Some firms never make it past the inception stage, while others may get stuck in the survival stage and never reach the third, successful stage.

Some architects are content to operate very small practices and have no intention of growing the physical size of the office. Others may start small with the intention of building a much larger office as the workload increases. Whatever the intentions of the owners and staff, knowing where the business is positioned in the marketplace and where it is heading is crucial to success. Strategies for new service provision range from increasing market penetration, generally regarded as the safest option, through to diversification, which usually carries the highest risk because new skills have to be developed and communicated to potential clients. There are four main strategies:

♦ *Provide existing (familiar) services to existing (familiar) markets.* This strategy involves little in the way of change.
♦ *Extend existing services (familiar) to new (unfamiliar) markets.* This strategy will rely on an effective marketing campaign to raise awareness in a new market niche.
♦ *Introduce new services (unfamiliar) to existing (familiar) markets.* This will rely on interpersonal relations with the existing client base and so less emphasis will be put on marketing.
♦ *Introducing new (unfamiliar) services to new (unfamiliar) markets.* This is the most challenging of the four strategies in terms of establishing a presence, requiring considerable investment in marketing.

Management of the business

The idea that architectural practice requires redefinition and transformation has been voiced on many occasions. To a certain extent change will be forced on architectural practices simply through changes in the environment in which business is conducted. Increased competition combined with the dissemination of professional knowledge through IT will have a major say in shaping the future of many architectural firms. Other drivers, such as government-led reports urging greater efficiency, place additional pressures on professional service firms by making clients more aware of areas for improvement and hence more demanding and critical of the services provided. Technological advances also provide the opportunity for change, with ICTs, integrated design and manufacturing and off-site production helping to revolutionise the way in which the built environment is realised. Advanced technologies have also provided the potential to change the way in which architects manage design and construction projects, for example through new working relationships between manufacturers and architects and a closer connection with clients. Impetus for change will also come from within architectural firms, keen to make a positive contribution to our built environment through the creation of creative designs and the realisation of exciting and stimulating buildings. Sponsors of building projects and building users alike have come to recognise the value that good architecture can bring to their lives. The way in which the project is planned and managed, and the attention to design throughout the life of the project, will have an impact, either negative or positive, on the finished building and hence the building users.

Clients have become more demanding and the pressure to deliver faster and cheaper is increasing. Market forces have forced some design offices to refocus and improve the management of their business in order to survive. Some firms have responded by concentrating on their core competence of design, outsourcing much of the technical work and abrogating responsibility for project management to others. Many other architectural businesses have expanded their core competences and offer a wide range of management-orientated services in direct competition with other providers. Different approaches are reflected in the culture of the office and the types of client and project the office is willing and able to take on. Different approaches are also reflected in office size and ambition. Strategic planning and creative thinking are essential for survival and continued profitability in a highly competitive marketplace. Considerable effort, talent and a certain amount of luck all play their part in the success of the business; so does planning a strategy for the future. Effort is required to distinguish the business as something unique and different to the competition, while balancing the level of risk with the anticipated rewards. This means establishing a strong image supported with a clear statement of values, and communicating a consistent message to clients.

The design organisation's workload and construction output are interdependent with the economic fortune of the country or region in which they operate. The constant challenge for any businesses is that periods of economic growth and recession are not easy to predict, thus some flexibility is required within the organisation. In addition to the global and national economies, there are the local economies related to geographical areas and specific building types. The successful firms are those best able to market their services to the most profitable (or potentially the most profitable) market sector or region. Design practices often have advance warning of swings in the economy (be it on the macro or micro level), reflected in an increase or decrease in enquiries from clients, but there is little they can do other than be prepared to adapt to the changed economic circumstances. The effect of economic fluctuation is reflected in the number of staff a firm employs, with firms increasing their size in a boom and decreasing staffing levels in a slump. These transitions pose challenges for maintaining a quality service and a competent staff.

Developing a portfolio of clients from different sectors gives the design office a better chance of survival in a recession or downturn in one particular sector. As a general rule it is a dangerous strategy to rely solely on commissions from one market niche and/or commissions from a select number of clients. Supply chain management, strategic alliancing, partnering and framework agreements all, to lesser or greater extents, are about working with familiar and trusted partners. The danger lurks in becoming too dependent on too few networks for business. Taking a flexible approach to employing staff and to the amount of space required may help to make the business more responsive to market fluctuations. However, this cannot substitute for clear direction from the owners and the creation of an effective environment in which the project portfolio can be managed. Successful management of the business is based on a thorough understanding of how professional service firms operate and why some firms are more successful than others. This relates to clarification of the business strategy and understanding the challenges facing the business.

Organisational typologies

Organisations tend to be classified as strong delivery firms, strong service firms or strong ideas firms. Organisational typologies are strongly influenced by the values and aspirations of the owners (Figure 9.2).

 ♦ The strong delivery firm is organised for efficiency, relies on standard design solutions and has a formal structure and a relatively stable working environment. This firm tends to specialise in a limited range of building types (for example, speculative office developments or retail), which makes the type of work and the type of client relatively predictable. By reducing client involvement and standardising the production process the firm has little need to change very often.
 ♦ The strong service firm is organised for service and tailors its services to the specific needs of its clients. It has a flexible managerial structure and a highly dynamic internal environment that allows the office to quickly respond to the

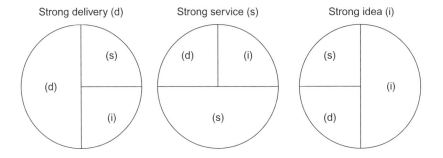

Strong delivery (d)   Strong service (s)   Strong idea (i)

Figure 9.2 Organisational typologies.

differing needs of its clients. Individual and creative solutions are favoured over standard responses, and greater client involvement in the project is encouraged.
♦ The strong idea firm is organised for innovation and seeks to provide innovative solutions to unique problems. It has a flexible, informal structure and a highly changeable environment. Standard design solutions are rarely considered because clients employ the firm for a unique project.

It is easy to find examples of architectural businesses that fit within these categories, although organisations may change their typology over time, or may operate within two or three of these categories simultaneously. For example, many design offices claim they are able to offer strong delivery in addition to strong service and also with strong ideas, thus claiming a foot in all three camps.

Organisational configurations

In addition to the type of firm, the type of organisational control, usually reflective of the principal's personality and leadership style, needs to be considered. Organisational configurations comprise entrepreneurial firms, bureaucratic firms, professional firms and innovative firms.

♦ *The entrepreneurial organisation* is owned and managed by a single partner or director, and with the large number of small firms operating as architectural offices this is a common format. The organisational structure is very simple and the owner makes all major decisions. Because of its size the firm is capable of being very flexible and highly adaptable, but its size also prevents it from dealing with large projects unless some form of strategic alliance is made with other organisations. Quality of the service provision is dictated and dominated by the owner, which makes it predictable if a little idiosyncratic. Employees tend to work *for* the owner rather than *with* them, and are expected to follow their leader's architectural style. Success or failure is mainly dependent on the principal's ability to bring in a steady supply of new projects.

♦ *The bureaucratic organisation* is very organised, highly formalised and described as 'machine-like', and hence is disliked by creative people. This is more suited to medium-sized to large architectural practices, although it can be found in smaller concerns. The standard of service provided is highly professional, sober and predictable. Staff have very clear frameworks in which to work and are not expected to deviate from the *modus operandi* of the office. This type of organisation is regarded as stifling creativity and is more suited to a stable, relatively inflexible environment.

♦ *The professional organisation* comprises a number of professionals, all directors, sharing the same office and staff, but principally working independently of one another. This business is normally constituted as a partnership or a limited company, which is a common arrangement. In this format the directors all work independently, albeit within a common business framework. Care is required if problems of coordination are to be avoided. Clients may be confused by the wide variety of approaches taken by the owners. Similarly, staff may find it difficult to adapt to different directors' working methods and to cope with the overlapping demands placed on them by the different owners. The project portfolio will need sensitive coordination and management to ensure resources are allocated to suit the needs of the business, rather than the individual needs of each owner.

♦ *The innovative organisation* is based on expertise and has the most flexible structure. It is responsive to change and does not use standard solutions. This is regarded as inefficient and demanding on the members of the firm, although some may argue it provides an exciting culture in which to practise architecture. Usually these firms are set up for single projects, perhaps as a result of winning an architectural competition. Because they are innovative and emergent organisations, established and formalised patterns of management are not used and the quality and consistency of service may be difficult to predict.

Design firms are not stable entities; they change over time in response to external pressures (e.g. clients and projects) and internal pressures (e.g. changes in staff). It is not uncommon for the office to change as it matures and responds to its business environment. An innovative firm may eventually morph into a bureaucratic organisation. Many design firms are quite adaptive and can adjust their culture to suit a particular client's needs. It is not unusual for architectural firms to have their culture changed by their interaction with, for example, repeat clients.

Control and leadership

The management of staff and the running of the business are very closely linked in professional service firms. An essential requirement is that the management intentions of the directors or partners should be clear and effectively communicated to all staff. Effective management of the firm should be concerned with both the organisational structure of the firm and the motivation of its members. The organisational structure of the firm is concerned with the 'control' of its members' activities, through job descriptions and bureaucratic rules. However, individuals will exercise free will and may choose not to comply with the constraints placed on them if the controls do not fit their work ethic. This trait is strong in creative individuals, such as designers and architects, who appear to take pleasure in 'bending the rules' and/or ignoring managerial controls. Design offices should be stimulating environments that encourage people to work creatively and communicate easily with one another within a managerial frame. This demands consistent and unambiguous leadership. The objectives of the firm, the range of services it offers and the purposes of its managerial controls need to be clearly defined and adhered to by all members of the organisation. Mission statements and the statement of goals will form the basis for management decisions and will also help with day-to-day management decisions.

Regardless of size or orientation, every design office needs to have someone in control. This person is usually the senior partner or managing director of the office. It is not uncommon for individual members of the office to have only a partial understanding of, and interest in, what the firm is doing. Designers will be primarily concerned with their individual workload and their projects, but many will also be interested in helping to keep the business profitable. Communications within the office should facilitate interaction between the owners and the staff so that all members of the office can share the same values and goals, perhaps reinforced by reward systems based on both individual and organisational performance. Managers will influence the behaviour of individual designers through general policy decisions, individual project management and the day-to day design-office management. Managers will also influence the process through their managerial style, be it autocratic or democratic. Control can be divided into three levels, ranging from policy decisions to individual project control and day-to-day managerial control.

- *Policy decisions.* Policy determines how the office is managed and how design activities are coordinated and quality levels controlled. This is facilitated by the use of quality management systems and ITs.
- *Individual project control.* This will be tailored to suit individual clients and the specific characteristics of the design task. Quality parameters will be set out in the project quality plan.
- *Day-to-day managerial control.* Management of individuals within a design office varies widely, from leaving staff to make their own decisions with minimal input from their managers, to very tight control where decisions are closely monitored and approval is required from the design (or technical) manager for the slightest variation in office procedure.

The business plan

The business plan is an important element in establishment and maintenance of a strong image. The business plan should contain a clear mission statement and the main objectives and strategy for the firm. This plan is sometimes referred to as a statement of values. The business plan will result from a strategic evaluation of external and internal factors. The external factors are:

- Clients and the market for services
- Competition for clients and services.

The internal factor is:

- Office structure and ambition.

From this, decisions can be made on the target clients/market segments, the type of services that can be offered (specialisation) and the price to be charged for the services.

Architects must learn to separate the design side of the firm from the business side. A good business plan should allow the freedom for a firm to respond to a situation spontaneously and creatively. A poorly considered plan is likely to inhibit, rather than assist, the creative potential of the firm. The design of the core business and the planning of the firm to achieve its aims and objectives should not be carried out until the directors have carefully investigated and evaluated the market for the firm's professional services, considered the balance between risk and reward, and investigated issues concerned with specialisation and diversity. The firm will then be in a position to plan its priorities and goals, instigate strategies for achieving them and write a mission statement. Priorities should be established and considered against known resources and then committed to paper as part of the business plan. The strategic plan and the mission statement must be regularly evaluated and revised to reflect changing market conditions. It is only when the strategic plan and the mission statement have been committed to paper that the marketing strategy can be considered.

- *Strategic plans*. The strategic plan is a tool to guide the business on a day-to-day basis; it should be concise and accessible. An overlong document that employees ignore is of little use. The strategic plan should form an essential part of the office manual or quality plan. It should clearly show the aim of the business in the next twelve months and over the longer term, say the next three years. It is only by agreeing and committing these plans to paper that the necessary resources can be put in place, training programmes identified and marketing strategies established. Once agreed, strategic plans provide a useful framework on which human resources can be allocated and assessed against cash flow projections (Figure 9.3). The managerial style of the firm's owners will influence the development of the strategic plan. In a top-down approach the owners will determine the plan and impose it on the employees. A bottom-up style of management involves all employees in the decision-making process. Although there are advantages and disadvantages to both approaches, it is important that all members of the firm are consulted so that they can develop a sense of ownership. This will help the firm move forward as a cohesive unit with well-defined and well-understood aims and objectives.
- *Mission statements*. The purpose of a mission statement is to put down in writing, clearly and concisely, the firm's direction – its aims and objectives. Some mission statements are designed for use only by the firm's employees, while others are designed to be read by clients as well as the staff, i.e. they are designed to be part of a firm's marketing strategy. A statement of values would be a good example. The mission of the firm can only be committed to paper once the directors and staff have a clear understanding of

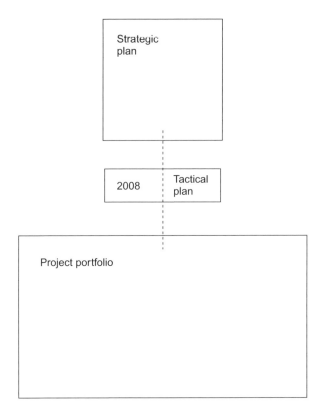

Strategic
plan

2008 | Tactical
plan

Project portfolio

Figure 9.3 The strategic plan and the project portfolio.

where the firm has come from and where it is heading, have analysed the market for their particular services and have discussed and agreed the strategy for the firm – the strategic plan. Mission statements must be realistic, representing the values of the owners and the resources available to achieve the mission.

Strategic alliances and joint ventures

One way of growing the business is to enter into a strategic alliance or joint venture with firms that offer complementary services. Collaboration as part of a virtual team is becoming common, as different professional service firms group together to offer a more comprehensive service than they could if working independently. This means that solo practitioners and small architectural offices are able to operate as much larger concerns for some projects, without physical office location or office size being a barrier.

Outsourcing

Outsourcing specific work packages offshore to benefit from cheaper labour has become common practice in many business sectors, especially the service sector. Professional firms have been quick to realise cost savings and increased organisational flexibility afforded by outsourcing their non-core services. This started with some administration work, but has grown to cover a great deal of technical work, for example the production of working drawings. Some design offices have outsourced aspects of their work for a long time, for example specific detailing requirements outsourced to consultants with whom they have developed informal working relationships. Outsourcing packages of work to others can form an effective way of managing the design organisation. Some design practices are starting to specialise in design and information management, i.e. they do the conceptual design work but outsource the task of producing the project documentation to a variety of specialists ranging from technically orientated professional design organisations to specialist subcontractors and suppliers. While this may be a cheaper option than producing the work in the office, care must be taken with the quality of the work provided. This means investing time in developing relations with the service providers, checking out their systems and meeting the people. This upfront cost is usually recouped quickly. Advantages of digital outsourcing include the ability to respond quickly and efficiently to client demands. Disadvantages tend to relate less to technical challenges and more to the cultural issues and the sharing of design values.

Risk and reward

A balance must be maintained between the firm's level of exposure to risk and the level of the reward (fee income). Generally, the success of a business venture is proportionate to the risk that the owners of the business are willing to take. As such it is essential to recognise the anticipated level of risk and set the goals of the firm within these parameters. New service provision and new market niches represent a real enhancement in risk, but they may promise high rewards. The challenge is to try and forecast the degree of return against the amount of risk, usually with incomplete information. A number of tried and tested techniques are available for forecasting, from probability to sensitivity analysis and scenario-planning. Scenario-planning is a useful way of considering likely outcomes of different variables, from the optimistic to the pessimistic. Risk management techniques can help to minimise the risk of a claim against the business. Assessing the risk associated with each client and each project is another useful approach to identifying potential hazards and mitigating them. In extreme cases this may mean pulling out of a project before entering into a contract with the client. Questions about the firm's ability to respond to change, the applicability of the firm's skills and the client's reaction to any planned changes can be explored through such methods. Unfortunately, the further ahead one tries to forecast the less accurate the prediction is likely to be.

Market analysis

New opportunities and threats to the business should be assessed at regular intervals. New opportunities may arise quite quickly and the business must be in a position to respond. Other consultants pose a constant threat to an organisation's market share and consequently to its survival and profitability. When sufficient information has been collected the firm can carry out an analysis of its strengths (S), weaknesses (W), opportunities (O) and threats (T), known by the acronym SWOT. Many people, including the owners of the firm, find evaluation to be a stressful experience but if the firm is to develop, all of its members must be prepared to learn from their collective experience and then act. Evaluation can be carried out on a number of different levels:

- ♦ Evaluation of the entire firm, the complete system
- ♦ Evaluation of particular business strategies
- ♦ Evaluation of projects (and clients)
- ♦ Evaluation of staff performance.

Evaluation should be appropriate to both the size and development stage of the firm. Timing of the evaluation needs careful consideration; some firms may feel it should be carried out monthly, some quarterly and others annually. Again, it will depend on the size and age of the practice.

- ♦ Evaluation is expensive because of the time it takes to carry out the evaluation effectively. The process should be kept as simple as possible; the production of a series of lengthy documents which few people have the time or inclination to read may well have a negative effect on staff morale.
- ♦ Data is historical and should be used in a positive manner to shape the future direction of the firm.
- ♦ There must be an effective and meaningful feedback system to all staff.
- ♦ Take action. Do not put off difficult decisions until the next evaluation; intervention may be the only solution.

Market analysis will involve an examination of the markets in which the firm currently operates (and which it would like to enter in the future), known as an external analysis. An examination of the firm's own strengths and weaknesses constitutes an internal analysis. This information can be used to inform benchmarking activities.

External analysis

Market analysis should be carried out regularly, for example every four to six months. The market will be changing and competitors will also be attempting to gain an edge and increase their market share. Competitors open and close offices, reinvent themselves and offer new services every day of the year; if the situation is not monitored the firm could very easily miss an opportunity or, worse, find itself in trouble because of new (and unexpected) competition. Anticipation is an important business skill. An external analysis of the market needs to consider the following:

- *Economic and political climate*. Government policy, government spending and changes in legislation will affect building activity, as will economic growth and interest rates.
- *Social and technological climate*. Social changes may lead to a demand for certain building types, while changes in technology may lead to new building products.
- *Market for services*. The market for services is related to building types and service provision. Growing and shrinking markets need to be monitored carefully with regard to client behaviour and client characteristics, referred to as market segmentation. A large proportion of the information is available in the national press, specialist journals and from professional bodies such as the RIBA and the Royal Institution of Chartered Surveyors (RICS). However, information relating to client wants and needs is difficult to appraise without talking to them directly.
- *Competition*. Competition will come from within the architectural profession and from other trades and professions. Their strengths and weaknesses must be considered.

Internal analysis

Coinciding with an assessment of the market should be a careful audit of the firm's skills, client contacts and opportunities. A regular analysis of employees' strengths and weaknesses will identify areas to be strengthened through further training and education. Analysis of marketing activities and client satisfaction will help to identify areas to be consolidated. The firm will build on its collective experience, and a frequent evaluation of its successes and failures – its strengths and weaknesses – is just as important as an evaluation of the market for the firm's services. Clients will also be looking at the firm in a similar manner; therefore it is important to recognise and manage the image that the firm is giving out to people outside the firm.

Performance criteria and benchmarking

Whatever strategies are adopted to meet and anticipate market forces, the firm's success will depend on the consistency of the service provided to its clients. Clients will expect their consultants to deliver what they promised. The professional service firm must perform well across a number of key areas. There will be a number of 'essential deliverables' related to each client. Failure to live up to the client's expectations may cause problems and could result in the loss of future business. The essential deliverables will include:

- Responsiveness and quality of the service provided
- Quality of the design
- Quality of the completed building
- Cost certainty
- Time certainty.

Benchmarking is a comparison-based management tool that can be used to help an organisation gain competitive advantage. There has been a lot of emphasis on the value to be derived from benchmarking activities, less on the amount of time and resources required to undertake benchmarking in a meaningful way. Advocates of benchmarking claim that the true measure of a firm's performance can only be gauged by using all three of the following:

- *Internal benchmarking.* The firm needs to examine its working methods and make any necessary improvements. For the architectural firm, internal benchmarking may be interpreted as a comparison between different projects where a quantitative comparison is possible based on an analysis of staff hours against profitability. This is the easiest to carry out since the information is readily accessible within the office systems. It is, however, often the most difficult area to come to terms with for directors and staff alike.
- *Competitive benchmarking.* The firm needs to look at the industry in which it operates to learn from examples of best practice demonstrated by others. This area of benchmarking involves comparison between the architectural firm and other consulting firms operating in the building sector.

Assuming that accurate information can be obtained, the firm is able to compare its performance with other service providers. Care should be taken to compare the firm with one of a similar size and market orientation.

♦ *Generic benchmarking.* The firm must look outside its market niche to learn best practices from other sectors/industries. Although the benchmarking literature refers to generic benchmarking as a comparison between business processes regardless of the industry they come from, the architectural firm needs to exercise a certain amount of caution when borrowing ideas from manufacturing processes based on mass production and repetition. Architects should consider other consultants, such as accountancy and advertising, to see if lessons can be learned from them. For example, the manner in which advertising agencies compartmentalise jobs to maximise individual talent may be suitable to some architectural businesses. By carrying out the benchmarking exercise on a regular basis a firm may well broaden its knowledge base and pick up different ways of doing things.

The office to project interface

Architectural firms depend on a steady flow of projects in order to survive and prosper. Each project is an income-generating activity when well managed, but a loss-making venture when poorly planned. In this multiproject environment each project will exert particular demands on the office resources. Similarly, each project will influence the culture of the office through interaction with the client and other project participants. It is important for the success of the project and the profitability of the office that the client and the project fit the office culture. Failure to achieve a suitable fit will usually result in unprofitable projects, and difficulties for the office in terms of unnecessary rework. Management concepts such as TQM and lean thinking must be applied to the office and all projects to be successful.

The business strategy will influence the type of clients that the office engages with and the type of buildings that it specialises in. This will colour the profitability of the business and to a certain extent will influence how individual projects are comprised and delivered. Offices that constantly complain that their clients are too difficult and unprofitable and that their projects are fraught with difficulties need first to re-examine their business strategy. It is about the fit between client and project values and the values of the design office; the better the fit, the better the satisfaction of all parties. When problems with compatibility of values occur and subsequently reoccur between the projects and the office, then it is time to reassess the business strategy. The project portfolio must fit the collective values of the office and the business plan, otherwise it is unlikely that the firm will be profitable. Over a period of time the interaction between the office and a variety of projects will influence the culture of the office and help to colour the business strategy. Some offices will change little; others will morph into quite different organisations as they seize opportunities for new business.

Chapter Ten
Managing Creative People

Good people are the design organisation's principal asset and also the most expensive resource. Depending on size and structure, staff may account for between 50 and 80% of the total running costs of the business. Somewhere around 65% is a useful guide figure when calculating costs. Putting together a collection of individuals with complementary skills and competences and keeping them together is a fundamental concern for the professional service firm. Once assembled, all members of the office must be deployed effectively to ensure profitability and be motivated to continually search for improvements in working methods. The collective knowledge and combined skill-base must be managed sensitively, to maximise the potential of the office while respecting the wellbeing of its staff. Individual knowledge, skill and experiences of the staff combine to give the firm its unique culture, and the manner in which they interact will directly affect the quality of service provided.

A professional service firm's most distinctive characteristic is that it only has the assets of its staff with which to trade, which makes the business very difficult to value financially. The assembly and maintenance of a dedicated staff are crucial to a firm's success in the marketplace, and to stay competitive requires frequent evaluation and adjustment of staff skills and competences. This is particularly true of the knowledge-based firm where the proper selection, training and development of staff are essential if a high-quality service is to be delivered. Design managers must be involved in staff selection and staff development programmes since these determine the firm's culture and hence its effectiveness and profitability. A well-managed, professional service firm will draw on various interdependent, and complementary, types of intellectual capital. This is primarily human capital and system capital, although for project-orientated businesses

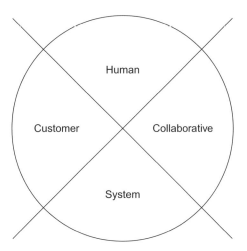

Figure 10.1 Intellectual capital of the architectural firm.

the client capital is a crucial component, as is the capital resulting from collaborative and integrated team-working (Figure 10.1).

- *Human capital* comprises the knowledge and talents that reside in the human brain. Architectural practices are heavily reliant on their human capital. This type of capital walks into the office in the morning and out again in the evening, or logs on and off the ICT system. The firm does not own human capital; it is rented via the payment of salaries for an agreed number of hours per week. Human capital is fickle and at times unreliable. Human capital must be managed with respect for the individual, otherwise it is highly likely that this valuable resource will move to another employer, taking vital knowledge and contacts with it.
- *System capital* is know-how contained in a firm's processes and documented in past projects held on databases. System capital changes as working methods and procedures are adjusted to reflect the experiences of the firm. The more a firm can incorporate knowledge into their systems, theoretically at least, the less their reliance on human capital. Quality management systems are a good example of system capital and ICTs provide a vehicle to build system capital through intraweb technologies and data-mining techniques. Knowledge capital is encoded in standard details and the master specification.
- *Customer (client) capital* describes the value of a firm's relationship with its clients. This is shared knowledge and not

owned by either party. The type of client and the frequency of interaction with the design office are unpredictable.

♦ *Collaborative capital* is shared knowledge between collaborating organisations. It is generated through interactions between individuals working towards project goals. This knowledge is mainly project specific, unless firms are working within strategic partnerships and alliances. This is shared knowledge, much of which is embedded in project processes and the heads of the actors participating in the project.

Getting the balance correct

Design organisations are constantly adjusting their size and focus to meet external pressures, often reinventing themselves through adversity, growing and shrinking to suit fluctuations in demand for their services. Because of the need for flexibility it would be misleading to write about design organisations as if they were stable organisations. Architectural firms are collections of individuals working with one another to achieve their goals and, more importantly, to survive and prosper. These social systems are seldom stable, but are usually quite hectic, dynamic and highly adaptive to suit differing client needs. To be competitive a balance has to be achieved between stability and adaptability. Within any design office there is constant tension between the needs of the office and the needs of particular projects. There is also a fair amount of friction between the needs of designers and managers, and a balance has to be found between creative and destructive forces. Design management could be viewed as a means of helping to keep things together, something that allows for a gentle shaking and trembling and allows space for individuals to realise their creative potential.

A well-balanced team would comprise a number of individuals with different education and a wide variety of skills, drawing on the combined knowledge of the organisation. As a general guide the office should comprise individuals with different competences, often referred to as the finders, minders and grinders (Figure 10.2).

♦ *Finders* are individuals who go out and get work from clients. These are usually the partners and directors of a firm, supported by other senior members of the office.
♦ *Minders* are the individuals who nurse the project through its development to successful completion. The design manager would be a minder, as would those responsible for administering individual projects.

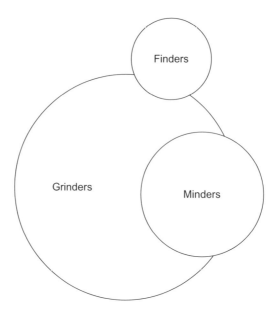

Figure 10.2 Office roles.

- ◆ *Grinders* are those who do the work, e.g. the architects, technologists and technicians charged with designing and detailing the project, along with supporting administrative and secretarial staff.

Staff competences

Architectural practices tend to comprise different mixes of professionals to suit their market orientation and the needs of their client portfolio. Some firms will employ only architects, some of which will be design-orientated, some technology-orientated and some with a flair for management. Others may comprise a mix of architects, architectural technologists and computer-aided design (CAD) technicians, sometimes supported with project managers and cost consultants. Solo practitioners tend to have rounded skills in design, technology and management, employing additional labour to suit the demands of individual projects.

Competitive design organisations need professionals with different skills, all working towards a common goal within a professionally managed office. The correct balance is linked to good recruitment decisions and the ability to retain talented and motivated staff at all positions and levels. The balance of staff in terms of staff profitability is also important from a financial perspective (see Chapter 14). Secretaries, administrators and personal assistants to senior managers also

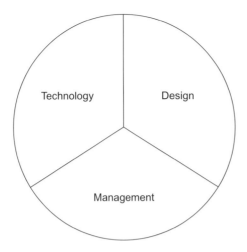

Figure 10.3 The balanced professional.

play a vital role in helping to keep the business functioning smoothly. The ability of support staff and designers to work seamlessly will make a considerable difference to the effectiveness of staff.

The balanced professional (Figure 10.3) is a rather elusive individual, since most of us have strengths in one or two areas and weaknesses in others. Thus balancing design, technical and managerial skills in the office requires a collection of individuals with different competences that balance and complement one another. Putting these individuals together in different combinations will result in firms with a bias towards a particular area, for example design or management. This bias should reflect the firm's market orientation.

Office culture

Every firm is unique; its character is drawn from the unique individuals that make up its workforce and the organisational structures that exist to control and manage their collective talents. Culture is manifest in the interaction of its members (the collective values of the directors, professionals and support staff) and those positioned outside the firm (the values of multiple clients, a wide range of consultants and suppliers of equipment and support services), as represented in Figure 10.4. The culture of the firm will colour how its members communicate and how they make decisions. Perceptions of the firm's past, present and future will influence the development of the firm's cultural climate. Excellent organisations have a bias towards action and are close

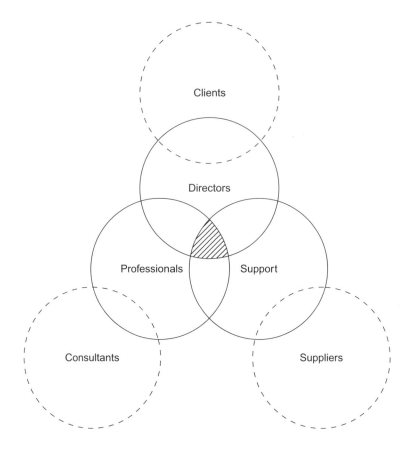

Figure 10.4 The design firm's culture.

to their clients; they emphasise entrepreneurship and productivity through people and have a hands-on approach to management. Successful organisations also tend to stick to what they are good at (their core business); have simple and lean staffing levels based on small work groups to improve communication; and demonstrate 'loose and tight properties' simultaneously, i.e. liberal enough to encourage creativity while tight enough to ensure a consistent service level.

A firm's culture is developed through interaction and communication. The firm's culture is expressed in Figure 10.5, where the three main contributing factors – clients', firm's and individuals' values (and needs) – are illustrated. The manner in which all three factors interact will influence the firm's culture and effectiveness. Positive cultures can help to promote the firm's growth and create exciting places to work. Conversely the development of a negative culture can be detrimental to the business. The way in which people are treated in an architec-

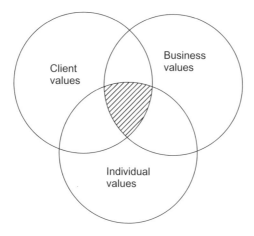

Figure 10.5 The design firm's values.

tural practice is related to its structure and personality and the inter-personal skills of the managers. There is plenty of anecdotal evidence claiming that people are treated badly in some architectural offices, with stories of excessively long hours for little reward. Such offices usually have a problem with turnover of staff and recruitment.

Those able to motivate and reward staff fairly are well on the way to establishing a healthy and competitive business. Productivity and quality are related to the degree to which the professional is 'engaged' and committed, and to delegation and individual control over design quality. Two important factors central to motivation are known as intrinsic rewards and extrinsic rewards. Intrinsic rewards are based on the fulfilment of individual beliefs and values and are rather illusory. Intrinsic rewards include personal career advancement, recognition, achievement and enjoyment. Extrinsic rewards are more obvious since they are based on economic rewards. These include salary, pension, paid holiday entitlement, job security, working conditions and status. A good salary, benefits, bonuses and profit-sharing are important, but so is status within the firm, recognition of a job well done and recognition by fellow professionals. Financial rewards are most effective when related to performance that is better than expected; thus a bonus paid based on project profitability can be particularly effective in reinforcing teamwork and efficiency. Rewards may also be given as social events and or days out paid for by the architectural practice.

Senior managers' expectations of their staff must be realistic and set at a level that respects staff psychological and physical wellbeing. Expectations must be communicated to employees through regular feedback, formal staff reviews and associated support activities. In a similar vein the staff's expectations of their design managers and the firm's senior managers are equally important. Staff expect strong leadership and clear lines of communication and delegation, i.e. they require commitment from their managers. In many professional offices with problems of staff morale and motivation there is a clear mismatch between the directors' expectations and those of its staff, usually a direct result of the two groups failing to communicate and in many cases failing to develop trust.

Psychological wellbeing

There is growing awareness about, and concern for, the psychological wellbeing of employees. This trend can be seen in all areas of commerce, from manufacturing through to service industries, with reports of stress and burnout featuring highly in research studies. Rapidly changing conditions, the demand for more work in less time and increasing job insecurity are contributing factors. So too is poor management. A growing number of studies from construction sites, engineers and architects' practices are helping to highlight a growing concern about the level of stress that employees are subjected to, and the growing incidences of burnout. A similar observation can be made of many support staff, partners and directors of professional service firms.

- ◆ *Burnout.* Working too hard over too long a period will result in individuals becoming tired and less able to function effectively. Mental exhaustion resulting from too much work is known as burnout. Burnout can have a negative effect on performance and can affect stress levels, since tasks become increasingly difficult to achieve within the timescale (hence creating stress). Sensitive work programming that allows some space for quieter, less demanding, more reflective activities can help to balance the high-pressure times (which are inevitable) and allow individuals to recover. Allowing time for CPD between the end of one project and the start of another can also be an effective way of mitigating burnout and reducing stress.
- ◆ *Stress.* When individuals are given tasks to do that lie outside their area of expertise, are not given appropriate authority over decision-making and are expected to deliver too much within the time available, it is highly likely that they will experience some stress. Uncertainty over what

is expected by their line managers can also create stress. Although a certain amount of stress in daily work is to be expected, high levels of stress can lead to problems. Stress can be readily mitigated through open and clear communications within the office and good managerial practices.

Psychological wellbeing is related to an individual's perception of job satisfaction, the psychological and physical demands of their job and the work/life balance afforded by their employment and personal circumstances. Employees are likely to seek alternative employment if they are dissatisfied with their salary, have to work very long hours without any flexibility, suffer from burnout, are subject to stressful working conditions and feel undervalued by their employers. Some of these factors may be influenced by an individual's relationship with work colleagues and compatibility with the prevailing office culture. Other factors are directly and indirectly influenced by the way in which the business is managed and the allocation of individual workloads.

Architecture is a high-pressure environment, but this does not mean that work has to be stressful. Nor does it follow that staff should constantly be subjected to unrealistic deadlines and unreasonable work demands that leave them mentally and physically exhausted. All businesses must take measures to provide a supportive and healthy working environment; this includes both the physical and psychological wellbeing of all employees, regardless of their position and job function. Realistic allocation of individual work programmes is the responsibility of the design manager. It is good practice to discuss workload with individuals before confirming programmes since not all individuals are the same and some may take more or less time to achieve certain tasks than their co-workers. Discussion of work programmes with staff can also help to provide individuals with a sense of ownership for the work and help to reduce uncertainty and unnecessary stress.

When things do go wrong, the tendency of senior managers is to blame the staff. This is a little unfair for a number of reasons, not least because of the complexity of the designer's task. First, the organisation should have employed staff that are competent and then allocated them to tasks appropriate to their levels of experience and knowledge. If inexperienced, then they should be adequately supervised. Second, the managerial systems should be designed and put in place to prevent errors. Quality management systems and office quality-control checking procedures are essential tools, as are regularly maintained and updated office standards. When mistakes are found, it is essential that the office procedures are checked and actions checked for conformity with procedures. Once analysis of the process is complete, the system(s) can be revised to prevent similar mistakes happening again. The better-managed architectural practices operate as a team with shared responsibility and a high level of trust, sharing responsibility for the quality of the work and overall health of the business.

For many professionals the boundaries between work and life are blurred; it is one of the characteristics of being a professional. Few professionals work standard office hours, and they continue to think about projects and design solutions in the evenings and at weekends. The balance between family and work, the work/life balance, must be considered in the overall planning and resourcing of the office workload. Even in the best resourced and managed offices there will be occasions when staff are expected to work extra hours to complete work to a project milestone. This is a characteristic of professional work and the majority of professionals are happy to do this provided that it is not a regular occurrence and there is some trade-off (in the form of time off in lieu or additional payment for their time). Usually programmes allow for some flexibility in working hours to cover temporary and unexpected fluctuations in workflow. When staff are expected to work long hours on a regular basis, or feel under a tacit obligation to work for longer than stated in their contract of employment, this is a sign of a badly managed office, and high turnover of staff is to be expected. Given the nature of professional work, many professionals find it difficult to 'switch off' after work. Normally this is not a problem, but in some cases this can affect an individual's family life, which in turn may have a detrimental effect on performance.

Burnout and stress are not necessarily related, although both are signs that there is a management problem and the senior managers must take action to mitigate both. There is a correlation between physical fitness and cognitive behaviour; a characteristic often overlooked is that the sedentary lifestyle resulting from sitting in front of a computer, at a desk or in meetings, is bad for our health. It is important that staff take regular breaks and regular physical exercise.

Recruitment and retention

Over their lifetime all organisations experience fluctuations in size, changes in direction and changes in personnel. Some of these changes may reflect planned incremental change as set out in the organisation's strategic plan, for example expanding into a new market niche.

Other changes may not have been anticipated, for example losing a key client or a key member of staff. Fluctuations in the client portfolio will be reflected in changes to the competences of the staff. Staff may join and leave the office for a variety of reasons. The most usual reasons for moving to another office are usually to improve their salaries and/or to progress up the career ladder. Other reasons may be associated with poor job satisfaction or personal reasons that have little or nothing to do with the job. Some attempt must be made to manage the comings and goings, both in the short term and strategically over the longer period. The workforce is more mobile than it has ever been. Loyalty to employers is less than it used to be and employers are less prepared (or less able) to be loyal to their employees in an economic downturn. With every departing member of staff a vital source of personal knowledge leaves and new, different knowledge enters with new appointments, thus changing the organisation's collective skills and knowledge base.

Staff turnover

Staff turnover is usually viewed as a problem rather than an opportunity for change. It is easy to see why. Apart from the loss of a valued employee, taking hard-earned knowledge with them (usually to a competitor), suitable replacements need to be found as quickly as possible, thus minimising any disruption to programmed work. The vacancy may need to be advertised and time invested by the senior members of the design office to filter the applications, interview those short-listed, select someone appropriate, agree the contract, agree the starting salary and confirm an appropriate starting date. Once appointed, the new member of the office must then be quickly integrated into the firm's organisational culture via an induction programme and informal supervision from a colleague and/or the design manager. This is a costly, lengthy and often stressful process for all concerned because there can be no guarantees that the newcomer will 'fit' the office culture. References from previous employers and performances in job interviews can, as many of us have found to our cost, be misleading, hence a probationary period for new staff (usually three months, or longer for more senior appointments) is necessary. If the new staff member is unable to work effectively with existing procedures and colleagues during the probationary period, it is important that the problem is tackled quickly. If the appointment is not working out, this is the time to part company and start again.

The competitiveness of the organisation will be affected by short-term and permanent staff changes. In a boom period staff may move to increase their salary and their promotion prospects, with good staff being poached by competitors. In an economic recession staff are more likely to stay (unless made redundant), partly because there are fewer opportunities to move and partly because of fears over job security. Staff turnover can be controlled through good management, motivation, and reward, training and effective interpersonal communication between the firm's members. Keeping everyone informed of both threats and opportunities is one way of reducing uncertainty for all employees. High staff turnover is usually a pretty good indicator of a poorly managed firm.

Although individuals initiate the majority of staff changes (often to the surprise of their managers), there are occasions when managers need to make changes for the good of the business, i.e. to make people redundant or to dismiss them. All members of the design office, whatever their responsibilities or position, must accept that organisations change over time. Some staff may find that, for a variety of reasons, they no longer fit within the team; some may leave of their own accord and find more suitable employment, while others may have to be dismissed. Management's only real social responsibility is to pursue their and their firm's economic self-interest. While this may be true of some design organisations, others are often driven by a larger responsibility for their staff, tending to put off difficult decisions because of their concern for the wellbeing of their employees. This is an admirable policy but it is sometimes done at the organisation's expense, and care has to be taken not to damage the business. A professional service firm, especially the small to medium-sized business, is only as strong as its weakest member. It is unfair to others in the office to carry ineffective staff, often leading to problems of motivation and always leading to a reduction in the firm's overall productivity. Identification and recognition of the problem is the first step, followed by consultation with the employee to find a solution. Efforts must be taken to realign duties, reinforce organisational values and refocus ineffective members of staff. If this fails to get results then they must be dismissed. A tough but fair and open policy is required within the spirit of prevailing employment legislation.

The flow of staff from one business to another should be seen in a positive light. Movement provides the opportunity for individuals to gain new experiences and develop their careers, while bringing new knowledge to their new environment. Changes in staff also provide an opportunity to redefine roles and adjust the skills and knowledge to better suit the strategic development of the business. Modest staff turnover can help to prevent firms from becoming stale and can assist with the retention of a competitive edge.

Recruitment

Recruitment policy relates to the development and growth of the firm, whether it is the appointment of new staff because of business expansion or the replacement of staff that have decided to move on. Design firms compete for staff in the same way as they compete for clients, and the firm's reputation as a place to work and for the quality of the service provided will affect the type of employee it attracts.

Staff should be hired with a view to the future growth of the business as set out in the strategic plan. Staff should not be hired as a knee-jerk reaction to the loss of a valued employee. The job function of the incoming member of staff needs to be carefully considered against the firm's strategic plan before the job is advertised. Temporary staff can be brought into the office while the longer-term aspirations of the business are addressed. New staff with new skills and different approaches can help the firm to develop in a positive manner. Before recruitment starts, the firm's directors must agree on the qualities they are looking for and, just as importantly, discuss the issue with those who are going to interact with the new staff on a daily basis. New staff may be viewed as a threat by established employees, and therefore it is essential to keep everyone informed to limit any negative feelings; a good manager will discuss the issue with existing staff before the vacancy is advertised.

A flexible workforce

Temporary workers are an important part of many business plans since they give a considerable degree of flexibility, allowing the firm to respond more effectively and quickly to changing demands. Temporary staff may be contracted in when (and only when) required to cope. This is a valuable yet disposable resource, used to cope with short-term increases in workload and/or to provide specialist skills and knowledge otherwise unavailable in the office. Specialist employment agencies may be used, although many small offices may rely on help from other small businesses that may be less busy. Offsetting the advantage of flexibility is the lack of consistency, which can lead to ineffective communication and unbalanced groups and teams, even when an effective management system is in place. Temporary workers will often lack firm-specific knowledge, i.e. they will not know the firm's operating practices and may require a greater degree of managerial support than the permanent employees.

Integration of new staff

The smooth integration of newcomers into the design office is essential if the firm is to function effectively. Induction into office practices and procedures, a process described as cultural socialisation, needs to be managed by the design manager. New employees will bring expectations and experiences to the firm that will be evaluated against their actual experience, which should, in turn, lead to adaptation to (not adoption of) the firm's cultural norms. The ability of the newcomer to adapt quickly to the office culture is important for the continuity of the cohesive firm and is vital to continued success in the market. The new staff member will expend a lot of energy getting used to how things are done in this unfamiliar culture, how jobs are administered and how he or she fits into the existing social structure within the office, a challenging and stressful time for the newcomer and also for the existing members of the firm. In the early days the design manager must provide support for the newcomer and allocate work to allow for socialisation activities.

The faster a new member of the office becomes familiar with their new colleagues and with office procedures, the better for the entire organisation. Failure to provide relevant information and guidance quickly can result in the newcomer struggling to identify with the office culture. If this is allowed to happen the individual will take more time to socialise and identify with the organisational culture, with a resultant negative effect on the performance of the unit as a whole. In some circumstances this can lead to alienation of the newcomer and resentment among the existing members. There are a number of simple, yet effective, ways of encouraging socialisation. They should be set out clearly in the quality manual and discussed with the organisation's new member. They are:

- *Inform existing staff* via formal weekly review meetings and discuss job roles and workloads before new members join the firm. This helps stop existing staff feeling threatened by the arrival of a new and unfamiliar person.
- *Assign an experienced member of staff* to oversee the new member of staff for the first three months, to offer informal advice. This is sometimes referred to as the buddy system.
- *Provide training* in the office management procedures, quality assessment (QA) systems and health and safety procedures through a formal induction programme.
- *Keep a record* of the induction training.
- *Review performance* after the end of the probationary period. Set a date and stick to it so as to avoid uncertainty. At the end of the review one of three decisions has to be

made: either (1) confirm the individual's employment via a permanent contract, (2) continue with a further probationary period (only if there is good reason to do so), or (3) terminate the contract.

Interpersonal communication between new and existing staff is an important tool for introducing new members into the cultural norms of the office. This is done formally through job instruction and informally through the telling of stories and legends.

The effectiveness of the new member of staff can be improved by dedicating time to the integration process from day one of their employment, which is the familiarisation of both formal and social controls. It is no use sitting them at a desk with a copy of the office manual to read, or just as bad, giving them a lot of urgent work to be completed by the end of the week. The first few weeks should be seen as an essential training period, not just for the new employee but also for the existing staff. Time must be allocated so that all of the firm can be involved in this integration process because it is just as important not to alienate the existing staff as it is the newcomer; be open and clear about responsibilities and the role of team members. New members of the firm should be helped to grow into their new role. One technique, which transfers well to smaller firms, is to use the staff review system from the first week. The new staff member is asked to assess their own skills against the skills needed and to agree three objectives they hope to achieve in their first three months (usually the probationary period). At the end of the three-month period a staff evaluation is conducted.

Few architectural firms are large enough to justify the employment of personnel managers, so this job is carried out by the design manager or one of the firm's more experienced staff members. This role is additional to an individual's existing commitments and time must be made available for it – an investment that will quickly be repaid. If new members of staff are integrated quickly and smoothly they perform better sooner, a benefit to both the firm and the employee in terms of job satisfaction. Even if they decide to move to another firm after two years, they have been an integral productive part of the team during that time.

The office environment

Although it is common for architects to work as solo practitioners, the majority of designers work with others in shared physical office space, and/or with others in cyberspace. Not so long ago, setting up and running an architectural business was relatively straightforward. Suitable accommodation was found and a brass plate put up on the door to announce one's presence. Now ICTs provide the opportunity to work effectively and flexibly from remote sites. Many offices have taken advantage of the technology, allowing staff to work from home or the building site, providing employees with greater flexibility while at the same time reducing the amount of physical space required and hence reducing overheads. This tends to raise questions about the amount, function and location of physical office space. ICTs also allow individuals to work as part of a networked team from remote sites, in the 'virtual office', perhaps only coming together for design reviews and other meetings. There is, however, the need for face-to-face communication when developing designs, and this can be achieved by renting office space as and when required and/or by maintaining a small amount of architectural studio space. The main concern is that of clients. Many clients still like to visit the design office in person and meet some of the people who work on their projects. Thus some form of office presence is required. A well-positioned office that is accessible by clients and which acts as a 'showroom' for the work of the office may be sufficient for some organisations, with the majority of staff working remotely.

Remote working has a number of advantages and disadvantages. The principle of remote working should be familiar to the majority of professional design offices who use external consultants to help in busy times and/or to add specific talents for certain jobs. These flexible workers often carry out work outside the firm's office, either from their own offices or from home. There are, however, a large number of people who enjoy the social interaction afforded by working together in an office; somehow communicating by telephone or by email fails to satisfy their desire to be with other human beings. There is growing evidence to suggest that people who work from home are prone to feeling isolated and are more likely to be overlooked when it comes to promotion – the out of sight, out of mind syndrome. Working from home does not suit all staff and it is easy to become distracted by, for example, pets and children. Another problem is that of doing too much work, leading to burnout and thinking that they should be doing more (resulting in stress).

Working from home can be liberating and rewarding. In reality the majority of people who work from home tend to overwork and may feel isolated since they are not visible in the office and may suffer from social exclusion. Design managers must be aware of the advantages and disadvantages, discuss working preferences with each staff member, continue to monitor and evaluate performance, and adjust working practices accordingly. Quality of work must be monitored for consistency with the office standards. Current opinion is that a mixture of office interaction (interpersonal communication) and remote working is the most appropriate option for all concerned, the balance being a personal matter. For the owners of a firm the main issues centre on trust (to put in the work), quality of the work (more difficult to supervise at a distance) and delivery (on time). Tele-commuting can be employed effectively. If appropriate management systems are in place and the available technology is utilised, there is opportunity to reduce the amount of floor space rented or purchased, with reduced overheads. So there may be significant savings in the cost of space needed to accommodate employees. Another bonus is the flexibility afforded to the firm's members; happier employees equate to better quality of work and greater commitment to the firm.

Skills development

Professionals have a duty to keep up to date with the rapidly increas-ing and changing body of knowledge; expertise based solely on expe-rience is not sufficient. Practitioners must continue to validate their knowledge against current information, i.e. they must be committed to lifelong learning. Knowledge and practice become obsolete, often faster than we would like to acknowledge, and to stay in business it is inevitable that some form of planned professional development must form an essential part of our daily activities. The use of the words 'planned professional development' is deliberate since the needs of the individual and those of the organisation must clearly be identified before continual professional development programmes are instigated. Areas for enhancement and improvement may be identified by the firm's management through an annual staff appraisal, or identified by individuals through reflection on their daily prac-tice. Professional development of staff during their working career is important because:

♦ It helps to ensure staff are knowledgeable about recent developments and helps them to stay abreast of current information and practices with regard to their own area of specialism.
♦ It is essential in helping staff to develop new areas of spe-cialism (thus going some way to keeping staff happy and motivated).
♦ It helps to keep the office knowledge fresh and the business more competitive. Mistakes (through ignorance) are less likely.
♦ It is required by clients (seeking reassurance that the professionals they commission are competent).

◆ It is demanded by professional bodies for continued membership.

Knowledge acquisition and the development of new skills may go some way to keeping individuals happy, while at the same time helping the design office to maintain a competitive edge through its collective development.

Career development

Society has become more mobile and few people expect to stay in the same job or same firm for their whole working life. Some people may be happy to take a relatively relaxed view of their career, responding to challenges as they arise, but the majority will attempt to manage their career. This means setting targets for career development and balancing them with family life. A personal profile can help to identify skills and experiences, strengths and weaknesses. This can then be matched to the marketplace to identify opportunities that are most likely to bring the greatest satisfaction.

◆ *Priorities*. The most important aspects need to be listed, for example salary and perks, job flexibility, balance with home life, professional standing, type of projects, location of office in relation to home, etc.
◆ *Formal qualifications*. Academic qualifications and professional standing provide a solid foundation from which to build a career. These generic academic skills will be adapted to suit the job when starting work and developed through additional training and education while in work.
◆ *Transferable skills*. In addition to vocational skills there are a number of key transferable skills that need to be developed. Those key to managers are described below.
◆ *Work experience*. List the type of businesses worked in, and achievements (which can help to identify strengths and weaknesses).
◆ *Work satisfaction*. Identify the greatest sources of personal satisfaction.
◆ *Personal attitude*. Personal characteristics and values are important. Personality traits, such as whether an individual is an introvert or extrovert, organised or chaotic, spontaneous or considered, will influence how well they fit a particular office culture. Personal values should also fit the office values.

Transferable skills

In addition to experience of, and sensitivity to, architectural design, all design managers should be skilled in the following areas. This will help individuals in their current job and will play a significant part in allowing them to adapt to new jobs:

- Communication
- Information management
- Organisation
- Self-management
- Team working
- Technology.

Continual professional development (CPD)

Most design offices will recognise the benefits to their business that dedicated, motivated and ambitious individuals contribute. However, in the background is the concern that valued employees may leave and take their knowledge and skills to a competitor. The true professional recognises that professional development is never complete; there is always something new to learn and a new situation to experience and respond to. The RIBA's interest in CPD started in 1962, although it was not until January 1993 that the institution made participation in CPD a duty of membership, helping to maintain the value and integrity of the professional qualification. Chartered architects are obliged to undertake a minimum of 35 hours' CPD activity a year, to draw up a personal development plan and to keep a record of the activities undertaken. Members of other professions, such as the Chartered Institute of Architectural Technologists (CIAT), Institution of Structural Engineers (IStructE) and RICS are also required to pursue CPD and keep appropriate records of achievement as set out by their respective institutions.

CPD helps all staff to stay knowledgeable and provides a vehicle to strengthen the business acumen of the firm. CPD can also act as an agent of change by introducing new managerial techniques to practitioners. Organisations must establish a policy to maintain a fair system for all employees, regardless of position. A carefully designed and adequately resourced staff development programme will not only help to keep existing employees motivated, but will also help to attract new staff. The better the knowledge of the individual members of the office, the better the collective knowledge of the organisation and the better it is able to compete. There are four main steps in managing CPD activities.

♦ Identify areas and prioritise CPD activities to suit both individuals and the business.
♦ Coordinate individual CPD activities to suit individual work programmes.
♦ Evaluate individual CPD activities and discuss within the office to help share knowledge.
♦ Evaluate CPD and discuss future plans during the annual appraisal.

CPD is one of the keys to gaining and retaining competitive advantage through the constant updating of the design organisation's collective competencies. But there is a catch. Both time and money must be allocated (and fairly distributed) for education, training and staff development. The boom or bust nature of the building industry can make it difficult to adhere to previously agreed and planned time and financial budgets for CPD. In a boom the money may be available but time may be in short supply as the firm struggles to meet the growing workload, while in a downturn the time may be available but the finances to cover the fees associated with formal CPD activities may be limited. For many small design firms operating in a climate where fee levels and profit margins are low, the allocation of valuable resources to CPD may be very limited, and some firms look to their employees to assist with the cost of some educational and training programmes. Costs must be factored into office overheads and time must be factored into individual work programmes. The office will need to:

♦ Provide an annual budget to cover the cost of staff education and training programmes
♦ Allocate someone in the office to monitor CPD activities, i.e. keep records and motivate individuals to continue during difficult times.

The aim is to ensure that:

♦ CPD activities are beneficial to both individual and organisation
♦ Individual and organisational needs are discussed at the annual staff review
♦ Individuals share their new knowledge and skills with their colleagues.

Motivation to learn should be part of the psyche of professionals. Pressure to perform one's role more effectively, pressure to get promoted to more responsible positions, the fear of losing one's job, and professional body requirements for CPD, all form part of the motivation to learn. For motivated professionals the design manager will need to do very little other than provide some informal support when needed. However, there are periods when even the most dedicated of professionals goes through some difficult times. This may be related to their work, the office culture or personal circumstances outside the remit of the office, and learning may not be the most important criterion. The design manager needs to be able to identify when individuals are not performing efficiently and try and help.

Performance review

Linked to the issue of motivation and reward is the staff performance review (staff appraisal). The performance review should be conducted as a formal interview between the employee and his or her manager. In the majority of offices the senior partner will conduct the review, preferably in conjunction with the design manager. In large offices the task may have been assigned to a partner or senior manager responsible for staffing matters. The interview is usually carried out with employees once a year and prior to the annual review of salaries (which should be a separate event). Points to address from both the employee's and the manager's perspective are:

♦ *Quality of work.* Has the work met the expectations of the office and clients? What are the individual's strengths and weaknesses? Could the strengths be utilised and supported more effectively? Do the weaknesses need to be tackled through education and training and/or more sensitive delegation of duties?

♦ *Contribution to teamwork and office morale.* How has the individual influenced the culture of the office? Have they demonstrated leadership abilities? Do they have a positive, neutral or negative influence on other staff members? How do people outside the office, i.e. clients and key project team members, perceive them?

♦ *Contribution to the profitability of the firm.* Has the individual brought new business to the firm or suggested cost-saving ideas (and if so, how is this to be rewarded)?

♦ *Staff development.* What new skills has the individual acquired since the previous review? Have CPD activities been met?

♦ *Staff grievances.* Are there any areas of concern or problems? Can they be resolved to both parties' satisfaction?

◆ *Personal factors*. Are there any personal/family issues that have affected, or are likely to affect, performance? How can they best be accommodated to suit the individual and the office?

Adequate time should be set aside for the discussion (minimum one hour, maximum two hours) and to make a record of what was agreed. Managers and staff must make a commitment to try and meet their obligations over the next twelve months. The meeting needs to be conducted in an open and supportive environment that allows an honest exchange of views on a one-to-one basis. Carried out properly, it will benefit both the firm and the individual. Staff reviews may be perceived (and sometimes used) as a tool to reinforce hierarchical systems; they can be self-defeating if not handled with a degree of sensitivity and common sense. The staff performance interview provides an excellent opportunity for vertical communication and should be carried out prior to an evaluation of the organisation's health. Feedback through regular knowledge-sharing activities and project reviews is also important but should be kept separate from the individual staff review. It may be appropriate to undertake a project-specific performance review either at the completion of a job or at a stage during its life cycle. This is in addition to individual staff reviews and is a natural development/extension of the design review.

The office to project interface

It is the interaction of individuals from different organisations that makes up the social network of the temporary project team. Healthy projects need dedicated, enthusiastic and happy participants who have complementary skills and experience. Getting the right mix of people and organisations is a concern for the project manager. The design manager will also be concerned with the smart resourcing of the project portfolio and delegation of tasks to those most competent. This will help to keep a healthy balance between the demands of multiple projects and the office resources. Managers must recognise that the interaction of staff with project members located in other offices and locations may affect individual performance, both negatively and positively. The ability of staff to communicate clearly and effectively across different levels and with various types of organisations and individuals is an important competence.

Chapter Eleven
Managing the Design Studio

Successful design organisations instinctively know that complex management systems with mountains of paperwork and numerous form-filling exercises can detract from the firm's core business, alienate employees and lead to a downturn in productivity. Good design managers also realise the value of their staff in achieving strategic goals. An empowered, knowledgeable, proactive and well-resourced staff working with simple managerial frameworks and systems is fundamental to the development of creative architectural design and delivery of a high quality service. Design must be managed to ensure successful outcomes. Successful architectural practices employ managerial frameworks that put individuals in control, yet provide the necessary supporting framework to help staff achieve a high and consistent standard of work and encourage creative thinking, i.e. they employ creative management, which allows for a certain degree of 'roughness' in the system. Individuals working in design offices tend to be extremely committed professionals, constantly striving for perfection. Ensuring a good fit between individual needs and organisational support will help individuals to be self-managing, making the job of the design manager considerably easier. Apart from recognising human needs in the workplace, the three criteria for stimulating effective design work are:

♦ *Control over design.* The amount of control an individual has over 'their' design project can be an emotive issue. A high degree of autonomy relates to a sense of ownership and pride in the job, and a low degree of control relates to individuals feeling helpless and undervalued. It is not uncommon for conflict to occur between the amount of individual control required by designers and the level of control that is exerted by managers. The vast majority of architects are highly motivated, like doing things their own way and are particularly resistant to overzealous management. Other professionals that share the creative design office, such as architectural technologists and technicians, may be a little more pragmatic in their approach, yet they too dislike restrictive controls. Lack of control, either perceived or real, caused by too much managerial interference may result in staff becoming less proactive.

♦ *Organisational support.* This relates to clear leadership from managers and appropriate frameworks for undertaking the job. Related issues are the availability of design information to avoid guesswork and allow informed decisions to be made, and the ability of the design office to learn from its collective experience. This involves the use of feedback opportunities to ensure continued learning and ensures all individuals are included and do not feel ignored.

♦ *Design of the architectural studio.* This has a role to play in the effective production of work. The layout of workstations and associated space may depend on the physical architecture of the office, and may not always be ideal. However, recognising the need for designers to interact while working can help with the layout of the studio space. Space will be required for computer workstations, displaying and discussing designs, quiet study, meetings, making and storing physical models, and storage of paper files and drawings, etc. The way in which projects are organised also has a role to play and some flexibility is required to allow small design teams to work in close proximity on specific projects. Designers need to be able to work together on and across projects, and the ability to communicate and share knowledge informally is necessary to avoid design errors and wasted time searching for information.

Understanding how designers interact within the design office is paramount in the creation of excellent architecture and the profitability of the architectural business. By observing designers undertaking their daily work and encouraging feedback, it is possible to implement and/or adjust managerial frameworks to better assist the designer in his or her task. Failure to understand the needs of the professionals working within the office may have an adverse effect on the ability of the office as a whole to perform. Similarly, understanding the relationship between independent projects as they pass through the office can greatly assist with the resourcing and coordination of design work.

The project portfolio

Appreciating the value of and risks associated with each project is fundamental to effective portfolio management, and hence the profitability of the business. Despite employing competent professionals it is not uncommon for design projects to exceed the allocated time, run over budget and/or fail to deliver the expected results. Although the causes can be complex, it is not uncommon for the problem to be related to the inability of the design office to prioritise projects and manage resources to fit the projects within the project portfolio. This requires an understanding of each project to assess its value to the office and the level of risk associated with that project. It also requires some effort to position new projects within the project portfolio. Project portfolio management requires some hard decisions to be made based on the perceived value of each project to the design office. This sometimes means saying no to a client because the project cannot be accomplished with the available capacity of the office. It also means that projects may need to be reprioritised to accommodate a high value project. Portfolio management requires all projects to be prioritised in terms of the value they deliver to the office (financial value, esteem, etc.) and the risk they represent. This is partly related to the characteristics of the client and also the characteristics of the project. A database of all projects will greatly assist the design manager in allocating resources to individual projects, but this must be related to the strategic plan of the business and hence the attitude to various types of project.

Managing multiple projects

Understanding the relationship between independent projects as they pass through the office can help with efficient resourcing. Projects can be managed more effectively if their characteristics are understood. Two characteristics can help with managing resources within the office: the urgency of need or the priority, and the value that the project provides to the design business.

♦ *Priority*. The priority of each project is the client's urgency of need. Tension is created within the office by projects having different levels of priority, which creates internal competition for resources. Mapping all projects against a master schedule (Figure 11.1) will provide an overview of project deliverables (project closure). The mapping can be carried out on different levels, for example splitting the projects down to key milestones, e.g. the completion of the concept design work.

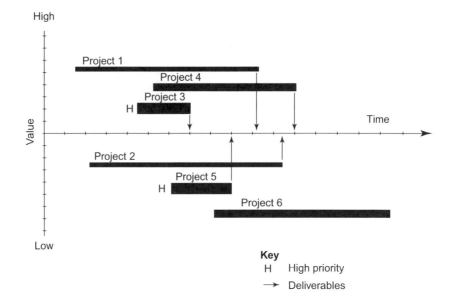

Figure 11.1 Mapping the multiproject portfolio.

♦ *Value*. The value of each project relates to its size, esteem, fee income and overall contribution to the smooth running of the office. By ranking projects according to size, esteem, fee income and contribution it is possible to make an objective assessment of the importance of the project. This is usually undertaken using a simple scale from high to medium and low value.

The characteristics and number of projects can have a significant effect on the ability of the office to make a profit.

♦ Small, high priority, low value projects may help to fill a gap in capacity, but too many will place an unnecessary burden on the office. The same activities need to be followed in the majority of projects and a large number of small projects can make it difficult to return a profit. The large number of clients also places considerable demand on interpersonal communication and hence time.

♦ Large, longer term, high value projects are the target of most offices, although given the amount of competition these are harder to acquire compared with the smaller projects. Large projects provide stability to the office since they are easier to resource and they provide a relatively continuous flow of money into the business and work for the staff. A portfolio of large projects also means fewer projects and hence fewer clients compared with a portfolio of small projects.

Responsibilities and reporting

The project portfolio should be managed by one person in the office, and this job is usually undertaken by the design manager. The design manager will be responsible for assessing the value and priority of the project and for keeping the master schedule updated. The design manager will also be responsible for allocating resources and for balancing competing projects to avoid conflict. Individual projects will be managed by a project administrator, usually an architect or architectural technologist. The project administrator will be responsible for the project and will report to the design manager on a regular basis about individual project progress. Reporting should include any problems (known and anticipated) that may affect the completion of the work and the anticipated impact on the completion date of the project.

The design manager's role

The design manager's challenge is to stimulate, facilitate, motivate and enable creative activity to flourish through effective programming, clear communications and mutual trust (see also Appendix 2). The design manager's role is not to micro-manage project work; the staff are hired to do that. Design managers need to maintain a distance from individual projects in order to retain an overview of the entire project portfolio. High quality work will be helped and assisted by smart staff recruitment and retention strategies. One individual in each organisation must take overall responsibility for the quality and timely provision of design information for the entire project portfolio. In small offices this role is often undertaken by the senior partner, in medium-sized offices by a partner or associate and in large offices by someone who carries the title design manager. Whatever the job title, the design manager should have the following competences:

- *Motivation and leadership*. Ability to stimulate and motivate team members through commitment and personal enthusiasm. Ability to establish and build effective working teams and clearly define responsibilities within the overall project framework. Ability to build trusting relationships and develop mutual respect.
- *Planning and delegation of work*. Assessing and managing individual workloads with due concern for other team

members. 'Helicopter perspective' – to stand back from the immediate concerns and take an overview of priorities. Organising and chairing meetings. Realistic delegation of work packages to others.

♦ *Communication.* Communication skills to explain concepts and ideas as well as to transmit changes in individual tasks, responsibilities and project goals often through drawing and sketching. Interpersonal skills include the ability to listen to the team members, give and receive constructive criticism and include feedback to individuals and the office in general through knowledge-sharing activities. Communication skills are essential, especially where design activities are separated from the production team; also crucial are integration, teamwork and effective communication.

♦ *Flexibility.* Flexibility in responding to changes, both from external and internal sources within the framework of a quality management system. Tolerance and ability to work in uncertain areas.

♦ *Problem-solving.* This is where an individual with design training has the advantage over one with managerial training. Design managers must be able to advise staff on design, technical and managerial issues. This means being able to answer questions that relate directly to projects and (indirectly) to office standards and procedures.

♦ *Ability to deal with stress.* The amount of time to produce work is under constant pressure, and coupled with increased complexity of buildings it is probable that some staff will, at various times, experience a degree of stress. The sequential model does offer one substantial benefit here since each individual within the team has assigned boundaries, controlled by the preprogrammed design reviews; there is more stability in the system and therefore less uncertainty. The stress must, however, be 'absorbed' by the design manager and supporting management systems. It is important to manage stress through effective and considerate delegation to avoid a negative stress situation.

The actual role will vary between different organisations; however, a design manager would be expected to lead and coordinate the design and project teams and report directly to senior management. In all but the smallest of offices the design manager will form a link between the designers and the senior management team and in some cases will be the link to clients. Thus design managers occupy a boundary role, essentially providing a buffer between the staff and the managers. In addition to demonstrating leadership, typical responsibilities of the design manager include:

- ♦ Allocating and coordinating work and team resources
- ♦ Maintaining and monitoring progress and work programmes
- ♦ Maintaining and developing standards and systems to achieve all key targets and promote continual improvement
- ♦ Liaising with clients, interpreting briefs and design requirements, assessing feasibilities, preparing working drawings and supervising works on site
- ♦ Assessing and analysing tender submissions and draft reports for approval.

Enabling and encouraging

Individual members of the organisation will each have a number of strengths and weaknesses. The challenge for the design manager is to tease out and enhance individual strengths and identify and mitigate the weaknesses. Individuals usually have pretty strong views about what they want to do and not do as part of their job function, but such desires may not always equate to their strengths and weaknesses. Good design managers are sensitive to individual skills and needs and will try and balance these against the overall demands of the design office. It is good practice to talk about this with individual designers and share observations. It is through open, trusting and honest relationships that the office can maximise its potential, to the benefit of all concerned.

Some staff will be more motivated, more talented and better at delivering their particular package of work than others. Design managers must understand this and allocate duties accordingly. Good staff should be rewarded and their good habits shared with others. Individuals that are underperforming need to be identified quickly and appropriate action taken to help rectify the problem. The problem may be relatively simple and easily rectified through advice and discussion with colleagues. In more serious cases it may relate to updating of skills through training and education programmes and/or the reallocation of duties.

Models of design management

The task of designing and producing contract documentation is difficult to define since it continues, with varying degrees of frequency, throughout the design and construction phases. Many of the actions that the designer goes through are, in the main, subtle and difficult to observe. As a result, the process may be difficult to manage unless it is fully understood and the implications of decisions taken recognised by designers and managers alike. Getting it wrong can be expensive (the cost of correcting the mistake and damage to the reputation of the office), and therefore adequate systems need to be in place to prevent mistakes extending beyond the office boundary.

The point was made earlier in this book that management is about action. It is, however, necessary to have some form of framework in which to work. Frameworks will vary between different design offices, ranging from very loose to very rigid procedures and associated controls. For example, quality management systems can be, contrary to many people's belief, designed to allow a great degree of creative freedom. Unfortunately, many systems have not been given adequate attention and end up as a poor fit to the *modus operandi* of the design office. This is usually a result of a top-down approach with little regard for those actually doing the work. Working from the bottom up tends to result in a better frame that fits the working habits of the office and encourages work of a consistent quality. Design management is inextricably linked to, but often independent of, the management of the organisation and its profitability. It is an area in which the conflict between designers and managers is potentially greatest. Good design management is concerned with finding a balance between creative freedom and managerial controls, and this can only be done in relation to the specific context of an individual design office and the type of clients it works with. One of the design manager's key functions is to use a design model that the members of the office are comfortable with, which helps to maximise resources and promote creativity. Process models should provide a clear framework and thus a supportive environment in which design and designers can flourish. Consideration must also be given to the model used for specific projects, so that coordination problems are avoided. In architect-led projects this should not be a problem, but for projects managed by others it may necessitate some project-specific amendments to the design management model.

A quality framework

Consistency and quality of the service provided will be influenced by the effectiveness of the design management model. A quality management framework can provide appropriate controls in which to manage design activities in a consistent manner. It provides the backbone of a well-managed practice and may allow a firm to adopt other management innovations. Quality of service provision will depend, primarily, on:

- ♦ Management structure of the office
- ♦ Skills and dedication of the staff
- ♦ Interaction with clients
- ♦ Interaction with other project participants.

Quality control aims to ensure work conforms to predetermined performance specifications. Quality control procedures work well in manufacturing because it is easy to check products against predetermined standards during the production process and also at the end of the process when the product is finished. The intangible nature of a professional design firm's output makes quality control more problematic, but this cannot be used as an excuse for not implementing checking procedures, for example before the issue of a set of drawings from the office.

Quality assurance is a formally implemented management system that is monitored by external certification bodies to check that the firm is complying with the ISO 9000 series of standards. Quality assurance means assurance that the process is managed. It is a hard management tool that can offer a reliable and consistent quality of service to the client while helping to minimise the firm's exposure to risk. Quality assurance comprises a series of procedures, a uniform system of working that is reviewed on a regular basis, has senior management support and is utilised on every project. To become certified, the firm must set up and maintain a formal quality assurance system that comprises a series of controls designed to ensure the delivery of a quality service to the client. These controls include the appointment of a senior member of the firm as a quality manager and the writing of a quality manual. Each project will have a quality plan.

TQM encompasses everything the design firm does. The quality of the working environment is seen to be an important influence on the quality of what is produced. It is a people-focused management concept that aims at continual improvement and greater integration, with a focus on increased client satisfaction. It is a very simple, holistic approach to quality that transfers well to professional service firms because it is a philosophy rather than a technique – essentially a soft management system. However, the philosophy of TQM needs to be introduced to everyone in the firm and extend to include suppliers, contractors and even the client, which in many cases may require a cultural change. Within the architectural firm a change to TQM can be achieved through a combination of leadership by management, the implementation of systems (QA), CPD and, most importantly of all, employee involvement through teamwork. The Japanese refer to this as *Kaizen*, a step-by-step approach to continuous improvement, and it has similarities to the concept of having pride in one's work.

If a firm is to achieve competitive advantage through TQM, both its customers (clients) and its suppliers (consultants) must be involved in the process.

Adoption of TQM is important from a business viewpoint, but it is also important to look at it in terms of the quality of life for those involved. A well-designed quality management system has the potential to make life at work easier and more enjoyable and allow more time to be spent on delivering exciting buildings. Good QA systems can also help to manage stress (more certainty) and burnout (tasks are clearly defined and managed). Quality service can be achieved by giving attention to the following:

♦ Consistent standards for individual projects
♦ Consistent approach to client relations
♦ Consistent quality review processes
♦ Clear responsibility.

One of the most important attributes of a simple, well-designed and easy-to-use quality assurance system is that it can be used as an underlying framework for all of the firm's activities. Such a system provides the firm with:

♦ A clear management structure that is understood by all of the firm's members
♦ Policy and procedures to enable the delivery of the service promised to the client
♦ Control and review of the design process and production information
♦ Control of job documentation via the 'job quality plan'
♦ A training policy for all staff and directors
♦ A comprehensive risk management system.

Implementation and development costs relate to the appointment of an external consultant, purchase of reference documents, production of the quality manual, training, formal certification, auditing and maintenance costs. Quality management should be introduced gradually so that staff, external consultants and clients are comfortable with resulting changes and improvements in service delivery. Once it has been adopted, it is important to maintain the momentum through review of the quality business plan and the commitment of all staff to continuous improvement. Commitment comes from initially raising staff awareness about quality management, through specialist training for both the quality manager and the auditors, to general training and updating as jobs progress through the office. All members need to appreciate that this is a collective effort and they must understand, agree and commit to a constant drive for improvement. TQM cannot be enforced through management checks and instructions; it has to be desired and worked for with examples set by senior management. The firm must invest in adequate education and training if this is to be achieved. The use of in-house training sessions and CPD is an essential factor in the education and motivation of all the firm's members. The quality manager and the directors of the firm must be able to set examples and motivate all of the firm's staff because TQM is a team effort.

A question of fit

The manner in which individual design projects are managed in the office is very much a matter for the office management team. Some models may be more productive and profitable than others. Essentially there are two main design management models: the traditional model and the sequential model (Figure 11.2). The traditional model is based almost exclusively on the RIBA Plan of Work. This is also called the 'job running' model, the 'whole architect' model and the 'generalist' model. It relies on the skills of one individual to do the work and administer the project from inception to completion. This model can be found in the majority of literature on job running and underlies the manner in which architects are taught to design in architectural education. The sequential model (or process model) relies on the

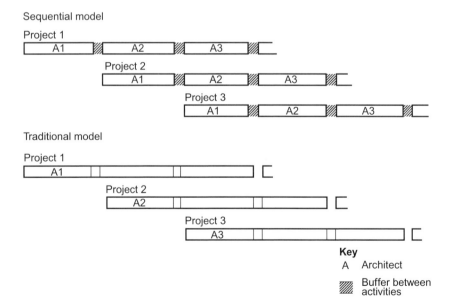

Figure 11.2 Comparison of traditional and sequential models.

complementary skills of individuals working on specific areas of projects. Individuals work within their area of specialisation, for example
architectural detailing or contract administration. This team of specialists may be self-managing, but it is more common for a design
manager to oversee the coordination of the work packages. Design
offices may use one approach exclusively or different approaches to
suit the project context. For example, the traditional model may be
used for refurbishment and small, new-build projects, with the sequential model used for repeat clients and commercial new-build projects.
Subtle differences may be found between comparable design offices
using the 'same' model depending on how the office is managed and
the degree of flexibility afforded by the systems in place.

   A demand of both models is that the strengths and weaknesses of
each individual working in the office are identified. This is perhaps a
little more important for the sequential model, but regardless of the
approach used, the design manager needs to know who is working
on what and how it fits with their individual skills. Mapping the ability
of staff against their experience (Figure 11.3) may help to provide a
relatively crude but effective visual guide for the design manager.
When mapping staff competences it is necessary to update the matrix
at regular, say six-monthly, intervals to reflect the development of
individuals as they mature through project experience and CPD
activities.

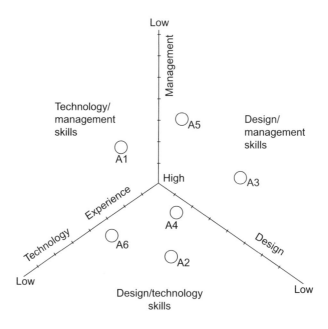

Figure 11.3 Mapping staff skills and experience.

The traditional model

The traditional model is relatively simple, familiar and convenient to use for a wide variety of project types. It tends to be used extensively within the architectural profession in the UK, from solo practitioners through to the majority of medium-sized offices. When a commission is received, a project administrator (also referred to as a 'job archi-tect' and a 'project architect') is appointed to take the project from inception through all of its different stages to practical completion. In this model the project administrator often acts as a project manager by default. The project administrator is relatively autonomous in the administration of the project, with the design manager overseeing the progress and coordination of all projects. Depending on the size of the project and the size of the office, the project administrator may have assistance from other members of the office. In this model the individual is required to exercise skill throughout all stages of the project, thus acting as a generalist rather than a specialist.

Advantages

The benefit of this system is that it is familiar to designers and others contributing to the project. It is consistent with the manner in which architects, technologists and surveyors are taught, with little interaction with other disciplines through their training. An architect, sometimes with support from technologists and technicians within the office, is responsible for administering the project from inception to practical completion and final certification. The design manager oversees prog-ress of all projects within the office. Thus the design manager tends to be concerned mainly with delegation of work, problem-solving and reporting progress to the firm's directors.

Disadvantages

While this is usually the only option for solo practitioners and very small architectural firms, it could be viewed as wasteful of skills and time in a larger office because it is rare for an excellent designer to excel also at other quite different functions, such as detailing, contract document preparation or project administration – tasks that could be carried out by someone who has better skills in this area. Thus there may well be a weakness in the service reflected through an inappropri-ate use of resources; it is certainly not cost-effective and not a strategy to employ if competitive advantage is required. Another problem arises if a member of staff leaves the firm (taking knowledge of the job with them that may not necessarily be recorded) or for some reason has to be replaced with another job architect; continuity is lost and time is required for another architect to 'pick up' the project.

Suitability

The traditional model is most suitable for small projects, especially work to existing buildings such as extensions and improvement work and repair and conservation projects, where continuity of thought is particularly important. Small-scale new-build projects also suit the traditional model. This model tends to be used by solo practitioners and small to medium-sized offices.

The sequential model

The alternative approach is to assemble a group of individuals with a variety of specialised skills, who are capable of working as a team under the control of a design manager. With this system each individual is responsible for clearly defined segments of the project, and since his or her administration duties are reduced there is more time to specialise in their chosen area. The sequential model is based on the earlier observation that every project has four distinct phases – briefing, design, production information and construction – and each phase requires individuals with specialised skills. Such a system demands individuals not just with different abilities and interests but also with different training; it is unrealistic to expect qualified architects to be the best people for all of the jobs. For example, a simple sequential model would require individuals with specialisation in the following phases:

- ◆ *Briefing phase*. Requires project management and design skills – architects with additional project management experience, or project managers/construction managers with design experience.
- ◆ *Design phase*. Requires design skills – architects.
- ◆ *Detailing and production information phase (detail design)*. Requires detailed knowledge of construction, materials and building methods – architects and architectural technologists.
- ◆ *Construction phase*. Requires contractual, legal and time management skills – construction managers and project managers.

Although it may be argued that such an approach is only applicable to medium-sized to large offices, from the breakdown above it is clear that four individuals could operate as a very effective firm. Add an additional member to deal with the financial/administration side of the business and the total is five – a small practice. In larger offices it is possible to delegate specific tasks within a certain phase; for example, large design departments have specialists in areas such as feasibility studies, client briefing and specification writing, which is usually termed 'functional specialisation'. This model has parallels with the building sector, where specialist sub-contractors are employed to supply specific items, for example cladding or brickwork.

Good managerial skills are required to ensure such a system operates smoothly and the links between the specialist disciplines are as seamless as possible. This requires a dedicated design manager capable of getting the best out of the team, which itself must be fully integrated. Clear communication is essential, as is the ability to keep everyone informed of decisions, and this is where the design review operated as part of a quality management system becomes an essential tool, because it provides regular meetings where all those concerned with the project are brought together. Thus, regardless of which stage the project has reached, the project manager, designer, detailer and construction manager will all be present to contribute to the design and maintain its integrity as it proceeds from conceptual scheme to finished product on site. The case for involving the client or the client's representative in the design reviews is also made.

Advantages

The advantages of the sequential model are that individual skills are maximised and utilised; there are no frustrated designers working on areas in which they are not particularly comfortable or experienced. Designers can concentrate on the latest trends and developments in design, technologists can keep up to date with the latest developments in materials and products and the construction project managers will know their contracts as well, if not better than, the contractor, thus helping to improve communication and reducing the potential for claims. This also allows a more structured approach to the planning of work within the office, since individuals will know how long a particular task will take because they have done similar tasks before. With the traditional team, the project is limited to the speed of the individual, who may be a fast designer but a slow detailer, and as a result the programme may be difficult to manage. Clearly the sequential system can help to produce a more consistent and higher level of both service and product – usually more profitably for the firm and more cost-effectively for the client. Furthermore, quiet periods can be usefully spent researching and updating individual skills, knowing that such effort will be of use on the next job – not something that can be guaranteed with the traditional model, where the next project tends to be given to the individual with the lightest workload rather than the person who is best suited to the job.

Disadvantages

The sequential model has its critics. The factory production-line analogy is often (wrongly) drawn. Architects are still educated and trained on the assumption that they will be 'running the job' and actively involved in all stages of the project from inception to completion. Many designers do not like the idea of losing 'ownership' of the project. Such fears appear to be particular to architects; other creative professions, e.g. advertising, appear to have no difficulty in working with such a model in which individuals with different talents work as a team with clearly defined, yet flexible, boundaries. There may be difficulties with workflow planning when projects vary significantly in size or experience unexpected changes to the programme, i.e. delays or requests to accelerate the work. Such situations can be accommodated relatively easily in the large offices, but may cause problems for the medium-sized to small offices in terms of effective resourcing.

Suitability

The sequential model is most suitable to new-build projects, especially repetitive work, e.g. repeat client and similar building types. It is used mostly by large design offices and some medium-sized offices and is not suited to very small offices (unless work packages are outsourced), although ICTs allow the possibility of solo practitioners joining up and operating as a larger team, with different offices taking responsibility for discrete elements of the project to suit their area of specialism.

Managing design effort

The amount of effort and hence time required to undertake work is related to the way in which people solve problems. Estimating the effort required for a specific project and estimating the amount of time required to complete the work is important for helping to determine fee levels and manage workflow within the design office. Without good estimates it is impossible to determine whether or not a project is within budget and programme constraints. Unfortunately design work is notoriously difficult to quantify, which makes the task of estimating the amount of effort and time required a challenge. In some respects the difficulty of accurately projecting the resources and time required is responsible for programme overruns and resources shortages, which tend to feature more strongly than bringing in the project sooner than expected with fewer resources than estimated. Accurately estimating the amount of work required is important because it relates directly to the cost of labour and hence the project cost. Fee income must be related to the amount of time available for a particular design task or work package, and this must be related to the individual skills available within the office and their charge-out (billable) rate. Recognising patterns of behaviour in individuals may help with the estimating and scheduling activities.

Time and cost control through careful estimating and programming is necessary if the firm is to operate at maximum efficiency. The majority of design managers tend to rely on knowledge gleaned from previous projects as a measure of the resources and time required to complete a new design project. Tools such as work breakdown structure and network analysis techniques can help to make the estimating exercise more accurate, but the very nature of design can render the most accurate of plans obsolete very quickly. This raises questions about the level of detail required when estimating and planning design projects.

Estimating design effort

It is not uncommon for architectural offices to use a very approximate breakdown of design effort related to project stages. The 40/40/20 model (40% up to conceptual design, 40% detailing, 20% realisation) is used, but this does not recognise individual project characteristics and hence is too general to use other than in very early scheduling exercises. To estimate accurately the amount of work required it is necessary to analyse the difficulty of the project in addition to the work identified through work breakdown structures. Individual jobs may vary significantly in size, complexity and the timescale for completion. Past experience of similar types of project and the client is a good base indicator. The following factors are major contributors to variation in effort required for design projects:

- Building size
- Building complexity (layout and design issues)
- Technical complexity (amount of innovation required)
- Unknown/uncertain factors (e.g. town planning conditions)
- Urgency
- Characteristics of the client
- Characteristics of the office design team (skills, experience and attitude)

- Characteristics of the project team (e.g. level of concurrent design)
- Availability of design and communication tools
- Management processes.

Resource allocation takes on even greater importance when dealing with existing buildings. Even where extensive investigations have been carried out, it is unlikely that precise requirements can be established until the building is opened up, i.e. as the work proceeds. Allowance will have to be made for changes (covered by the contingency sum), and the design manager must allocate sufficient time for the designer to deal with such changes (covered by some contingency in the programme). This is important, because the time pressures placed on the designer to make a decision may be more critical than on new-build projects. Depending on the size of the office and the degree of estimating sophistication required, some simple estimation of time is possible. This should be related to the amount of anticipated difficulty:

- Relatively easy (A). Allocate less time (e.g. 5%)
- Not too difficult (B). No special measures required
- Very difficult (C). Allow extra time (e.g. 10%).

Table 11.1 helps to illustrate the relationship between the estimated amount of design effort required and that actually expended, as recorded on staff timesheets. This is a relatively simple table, breaking down projects into three main stages: design work, detailing and realisation. Taken as a whole, these six projects were estimated accurately, with the difference between actual and estimated time within a 5% margin (with the exception of one project). These estimations were worked on a 40-hour week for simplicity, with staff contracted to work a 37½-hour week.

Estimating capacity

Estimation of the amount of work required for a particular project and/or stage of a project will enable the design manager to map individuals' work capacity, and hence the overall capacity of the office. This is needed to help plan the smooth flow of work through the office and to identify periods when staff are underutilised. New projects must not be accepted without first mapping the estimated resource availability. A simple representation is usually adequate for planning and scheduling purposes within most offices, as illustrated in Table 11.2. In this model 10% capacity relates to half a working day, thus 100% capacity equates to a whole working week.

By mapping the capacity of the staff it is possible to see when people are underresourced and plan accordingly. Staff member A is

Project number	Difficulty	Estimated design phase	Actual	Estimated detail phase	Actual	Estimated realisation phase	Actual	Difference
01 New	B	1000	1100	2000	1850	500	470	-80 (2.2%)
02 Existing	B	560	572	600	625	300	325	+62 (4.2%)
03 New	B	240	230	360	355	180	160	-25 (3.2%)
04 New	C (+7.5%)	750	810	1000	995	500	530	+85 (3.8%)
05 New (repeat type)	A (-6%)	140	120	100	98	70	75	-17 (5.4%)
06 Existing	C (+15%)	400	405	500	490	300	420	+15 (1.2%)

Table 11.1 Estimated against actual hours.

Weeks	1	2	3	4	5	6	7	8
Staff A	0	0	0	40%	0	0	0	0
Staff B	10%	10%	0	0	0	0	0	H
Staff C	0	0	0	0	0	0	0	100%
Staff D	0	0	H	H	0	0	0	0
Staff E	0	0	60%	100%	100%	100%	100%	100%

H = holidays.

Table 11.2 Staff capacity mapped over eight weeks.

fully occupied on a project until the end of week 3. Three days have been allocated for CPD activities in week 4, and a new project is scheduled to commence in week 5. Staff member B is fully occupied, apart from a small amount of capacity in weeks 1 and 2. Similarly, staff member C is occupied until the end of week 7, when new work is required. Staff member D is engaged on a large project with no short-term capacity. Staff member E will have no work from week 4 onwards, so new work will need to be found or they will need to be allocated to assist with one of the current projects.

It is necessary to update the schedule at the start of every week by reviewing progress on projects with individual staff, and adjusting the schedule accordingly. It is inevitable that the schedule will need to be revised as work is completed earlier or later than anticipated. Additional factors, such as an unexpected delay to a project owing to factors outside the control of the office (e.g. delay in achieving town planning approval) or clients deciding to accelerate the work, can have a major effect on the planned workflow. The degree of accuracy will decline the further ahead one tries to plan, and for many offices being able to schedule work accurately for four weeks hence may be sufficient to allow the office to function productively.

Achieving a balance between the amounts of time allowed by the client and those required to carry out the work is a difficult but essential managerial task. All stages of the job need to be planned, critical dates identified and design review dates fixed. This then has to be monitored and adhered to as part of a quality service provision. Time management is an important activity for all members of the office, therefore the planning and coordination of all employees' daily activities are essential to the smooth running and competitiveness of the firm. Scheduling of the work needs to be carefully considered; it is just as dangerous to give an employee too little work as it is to give them too much. All programmes should have clear aims and objectives (goals). It is essential to anticipate problems and allow 'time windows' in the programme in which to handle them. A work programme that does not allow for the resolution of some problems will fail and may lead to resourcing problems within the office. If things go better than expected the time window can be used positively, for example for CPD activities.

Staff deployment

From a manager's perspective, it may be useful to consider staff in terms of their experience. A balance of enthusiasm and experience is necessary. Individuals may be classified as inexperienced, experienced or overexperienced in terms of particular project requirements:

♦ *Inexperienced staff.* These are usually students or the recently qualified that are the cheapest resource in staffing terms. However, the need for constant nurturing and supervision makes the true cost of this resource considerably higher than it may appear from a balance sheet. A considered mix of advice from experienced colleagues, combined with an ability to question conventional wisdom, is desirable. Over time the inexperienced staff will become highly valued members of the office.

♦ *Experienced staff.* A design organisation's greatest asset is its experienced and competent staff. Capable of working with minimal supervision they usually produce accurate work fairly rapidly and are able to balance their individual workloads to meet project milestones.

♦ *Overexperienced staff.* Care should be taken to ensure that all staff stay up to date with current developments and do not rely entirely on overfamiliar (and rarely challenged) solutions. Some staff may become bored and complacent. Re-allocation of duties usually dispels any complacency very quickly and tends to mitigate boredom.

What usually happens in a design office is that the design manager has to use the staff available at the time (those who are least busy with other projects). This sometimes means that the most suitable individuals for a particular project are unavailable. The result is to use those who are not most suited or to try and juggle resources. Another approach is to try and programme the project to suit staff availability, but this rarely accords with the client's timeframe. This means that staff cannot be allocated to projects solely on their competences, experience or cost per hour. This situation can be avoided if the office

	Partner	Associate	Architect	Technologist	Trainee
Project 1		X			
Project 2	X	X		X	X
Project 3		X	X		X
Project 4	X		X	X	
Project 5	X		X		
Project 6	X			X	

Figure 11.4 Projects mapped against staff deployment.

is managed using the sequential system, where the job is passed along the supply chain, a systematic approach that can be very cost-effective for some clients and building types. Having an overview of who is working on which project is also useful (Figure 11.4).

Staff holidays need to be managed to make sure that not too many people are absent from the office at the same time. Holiday cover will also be required for the design manager. Assuming sufficient notice is given, holiday cover can be planned in advance and/or programmes planned to accommodate some short-term absences. Sick leave and compassionate leave by their nature are unpredictable and will disrupt most work programmes, especially when offices are running in a very lean mode. Most illness is relatively minor and absence from the office is relatively short term; however, this can still be disruptive to project programmes. Maternity and paternity leave is a little easier to work into programmes. Planning for staff illness, thus ensuring a continual flow of work, is a challenge. Businesses cannot afford to have staff underemployed 'just in case' and so it is necessary to bring in contract staff to cover short periods.

Delegation

Also linked to profitability is the issue of delegation. Delegation of work can only be done effectively if the people employed are capable of doing their job, which implies effective recruitment and continual improvement. All of the firm's employees, from managing director to trainee, should take time to reflect. This must be programmed into the daily routine because it is too easy to be swamped by other (equally important) demands and not do it. Regular, positive feedback sessions are essential if the firm is to grow stronger from its collective experiences. By assigning responsibilities and maximising individuals' different skills to the full, the framework is then in place to look beyond traditional design services to other sources of potential income from a sound financial footing.

Temporary distractions

No matter how well staff timetables and workloads are planned, there are a number of ever-present factors that may cause problems, usually at the most inopportune moment. Thus there will be the need to constantly monitor projects and people, make adjustments and redeploy staff. Unlike machines on a factory production-line, people are rather unpredictable when it comes to performance. Another issue that design managers have to deal with, but that is rarely addressed in textbooks, is staff having a bad day (or two). Our environment and family affect us, sometimes to such an extent that we are distracted from our work tasks. Operating less effectively than normal we are more likely to make mistakes. It happens to us all, although few would admit to it.

Identifying and eliminating waste

One of the most challenging tasks for the design manager is the ability to identify procedures and habits within the design office that are wasteful. Identifying and reducing waste can add to the profitability of a business and can help to reduce the incidence of stress and burnout among staff. To identify waste, design managers first understand how individuals work within the office. This can be achieved through regular interaction with project architects. Designers are quick to complain if they feel that their work is hindered by overbureaucratic administration/management procedures. However, those working on projects are often too busy to identify areas for improvement in daily activities; this needs to be done objectively by someone detached from individual project work. Design managers should allow time in their day to watch and listen to how people within the office go about their business, then analyse and respond. Some staff may complete tasks faster than their colleagues, be able to deal with queries from the site more effectively, etc. To some extent the good and bad practices may be linked to the personality of the individuals, but it is likely that these individuals do something a little different to their colleagues that sets them apart.

♦ *Good habits* that add value need to be identified and discussed within the office, with the aim of disseminating the knowledge to colleagues.

♦ *Bad habits* that create waste need to be identified and miti-gated as quickly as possible.

Adopting a lean thinking philosophy can be very helpful in identify-ing wasteful habits and procedures. The lean approach to manage-ment needs to be applied within the organisation and within individual projects if it is to be successful. Taking a lean approach is not about cutting staff and asking those that remain to do extra work; it is about the clear identification of work and efficient allocation of resources to the task (some of which may be better outsourced). This is partly about office protocols and partly about the working habits of the indi-viduals within the office. Outsourcing work can make a professional office more flexible and more able to accommodate unexpected projects. It can also help to reduce waste in the office, since there is no need to pay staff during less busy times.

Avoiding design errors

Even the most experienced and talented members of the office will make mistakes. Design errors are expensive and time-consuming to correct, with the cost and resources required to correct the error increasing as the design progresses through the detailing phases into realisation. It is imperative that design errors are identified as early as possible, preferably before the information leaves the design office. Design errors tend to result from problems with miscommunication between design team members, and careless work. Failure to com-municate and problems with understanding can be mitigated through regular meetings and the use of design critiques and formal design reviews. Careless work tends to be related to individuals being under too much time pressure and being subjected to too many distractions, which results in incomplete or incorrect work. Carelessness can usually be spotted through quality control procedures and the vigilance of the design manager.

Controlling rework

Trying to predict the amount of work that may need to be revised is very difficult given the collaborative nature of design. Within the office the amount of rework required can be kept to a minimum through careful control of the design work by the individuals involved in the project, access to current information, clear guidance and procedures, learning loops and the support of the design manager. Interaction with other project actors is more problematic, since the design office has very little control over the quality of the work produced by others or their ability to deliver accurate work on time. It is inevitable that a small amount of rework may be required resulting from coordination of design works packages, and this must be included in programmes and factored into work and fee costing. Familiarity of individuals within design teams will have an influence on communications and the ability to develop designs quickly and effectively.

The office to project interface

It is difficult to demonstrate the value of design to clients and other project stakeholders without clearly implemented systems in place to stimulate creative work and control the consistency of the output. There are many ways in which creativity can be transformed into a finished building, and architectural offices differ in their approaches to managing design work. Whatever the approach it is important to recognise that the ways in which design activities and the resulting design information are managed will affect the effectiveness of the process and the quality of the completed building. Consistent approaches to all projects will help individuals and the design manager to work effectively and be better able to deal with unexpected problems.

Architectural offices cannot control the quality of work produced by other offices, but the design manager can influence it through good leadership and the establishment of a project culture that places design quality and client values foremost in the minds of all those contributing to the design effort. Interaction with other members of the project will ease or conversely hinder the coordination of design activities. Members of the office that communicate regularly with others outside the office need to have appropriate interpersonal skills.

Chapter Twelve
Communication and Knowledge-sharing

When people communicate they intend to alter the cognitive environment of the persons they are addressing. As a result, it is expected that the receiver's thought process will be altered. Communication performs much more complex tasks than simply letting someone know that we are about to send information. For understanding to take place, most theorists claim that a background of shared social reality needs to exist. To engage in meaningful communication we need to build on information and develop a context supported by cues and clues. These guide us to use sub-sets of knowledge and help us to link information together. Clues come in many different guises; for example, the appropriate mode of referring to something or someone in conversation depends on what common ground a speaker and addressee share. It is this common ground and the development of a shared understanding that make communication possible. Similarly, a lack of common areas of understanding can create difficulties in communication. When there is a lack of congruent understanding the speaker has to provide an infrastructure of contextual information on to which the new information can be built, developed and hence understood. During interaction the speaker has to access and build a framework of the other's knowledge and influence the way the recipient draws together the sub-sets of knowledge to make communication work. Using clues sent from the receiver of the message the sender may make assumptions of the knowledge a person possesses. This initial and often tentative interaction can be used to check whether early assumptions are correct at a critical stage in the development of a relationship. In practice, offering information, opinions and beliefs and asking questions help to develop an understanding of the other person's knowledge and beliefs. Failure to exchange information and ask questions will decrease a person's ability to use the other's knowledge, and thus considerably hinder effective communication.

Cues and clues that are embedded in the context, body language and emotion play a key part in the development of understanding and relevance of exchanges. Improvements in the effectiveness of communication between individuals and groups can help to increase the performance of projects and organisations.

Key management competences of leadership and decision-making are founded on good communication skills. Effectiveness of communication and knowledge-sharing within the design office is crucial to the health of the business; so too is the ability to share knowledge between projects and make informed decisions. In people-dominated businesses it is the interaction of individuals and their ability to share knowledge through effective dialogue that helps to create a successful business. Design work cannot develop without communication between collaborating team members. Some of this occurs between members of the office, and some between members of other offices via meetings, telephone conversations and the use of web-based technologies. Office culture is very much a product of the communication behaviour – the interaction practices – of its members and the way in which the office is managed. Some design offices are noisy, chatty environments that have a life and energy (a buzz); others are rather quiet and comparatively sober environments in which staff communicate more discretely. Depending on the personal preference of individuals, some environments will be more suitable than others, and it is important to get the right fit. The introvert will not stay long in a noisy office; likewise the extrovert will quickly be ostracised in a quiet environment. Similarly, some design managers are happy working with noisy environments and will encourage open communication and knowledge-sharing through storytelling rituals. Other managers prefer a quiet office, with interpersonal communication and knowledge-sharing facilitated through carefully choreographed meetings and social activities. To the casual observer the quiet office may appear more 'professional' in its approach, but it may not necessarily be the most effective environment for interpersonal communication and informal knowledge-sharing between projects. Owners of the business will also have personal preferences about the way in which the office members communicate.

Lean communication

Given the pressure of time and the desire to make a profit on all projects, it is important that communication media and associated tools are utilised effectively and efficiently. Applying lean thinking to all aspects of office communications may help to attain and subsequently maintain a highly efficient design office. Understanding the value of communication and the value of interaction from the perspective of the office will also help with the implementation and effective use of ICTs. Design managers can help individuals to manage their communications through the use of various controls and procedures. Clear office policies will help to establish a working protocol for all members of the design office; however, individuals must take responsibility for their own interactions and keep them to a controllable level.

Too much casual conversation, too many meetings and unexpected telephone calls and spending too long dealing with emails will result in ineffective use of an individual's time, and will detract from completing tasks. Similarly, poor design office and project communication networks will also result in inefficient use of time. To avoid waste and allow individuals to work without their train of thought being interrupted unnecessarily, some degree of control is required within the office. Obvious areas to tackle include:

♦ *Meetings*. Meetings serve important functions, but they are also highly demanding in terms of the time required to prepare, travel to and attend them. Before attending any meeting individuals, sometimes in consultation with the design manager, must consider the value in attending. This can only be assessed if the agenda and aims and objectives of the meeting are clearly set out and communicated to those invited prior to the meeting. If a concise report is adequate, then this should be sent in lieu of attending.

♦ *Telephone calls*. These are highly disruptive to thought processes and the flow of work in general. People usually telephone because they want something (usually urgently), and expect the receiver of the call to drop everything and respond immediately. Some offices protect their employees from disruptions by operating a time window when employees can make and receive telephone calls. This can be an effective way of concentrating work effort and is necessary in small offices where individuals may share workstations.

♦ *Email*. In a similar way to telephone calls, email can be disruptive and many offices operate a time window when individuals deal with their email.

♦ *Unannounced visits to the office*. Trade representatives and contractors may visit the office on the off-chance of speaking to a member of the design office. These visits can be disruptive and time-consuming; therefore a clear office policy is required and must be adhered to.

It is not uncommon for professionals to work on many different projects concurrently; thus projects may be on site while the architect is developing the design for another project. This requires a degree of multi-tasking and self-management to ensure all tasks are completed without an individual being distracted unnecessarily by the competing demands for their time. Some office members may need a little assistance with their time management from the design manager. The first step is to monitor how individuals communicate during a typical working week, to try and quantify the amount of time spent on income-generating activities. This data will provide a baseline from which to work and a basis for discussion with the individual in question. Agreeing a strategy to reduce unnecessary communication and to make all necessary communication activities more efficient will be helped by the implementation of tools and in some cases additional training and education. Reinforcement of the office policy and sharing of good practices within the office will also help to maintain communication efficacy.

Group and team communication

The importance of group and team development is well documented in management literature and new developments in team-working strategies. Architectural design and construction is often described as a team effort, requiring the input of a variety of individuals from both within and outside the office. For solo practitioners and very small offices, advances in ICTs have made it easier to join project teams in a virtual environment. In medium-sized to large design offices it is possible to put together groups of individuals as a 'project team' in one physical location. A design manager may manage these groups of individuals quite tightly or they may be set up as a self-managing team where managerial interference is minimal. However, as discussed in Part One, the temporary project team is unique to each project and has a complex interaction of formally constituted teams and less formal groups, which makes it particularly difficult to manage and coordinate activities.

In many small to medium-sized practices project architects take a project from inception to completion with additional input coming from persons outside the office. Thus individual projects tend to be a personal crusade rather than a 'team' effort in the true sense of the word. On larger projects small teams may be set up within the office to deal with specific stages of a project, and then disbanded or reallocated once the task is complete. Such groups will be either project-specific or task-specific (e.g. the design group). The manager's role is primarily to coordinate, facilitate and motivate. Control should be firmly in the hands of the professionals, thus the challenge for the design manager or project manager is to stimulate these groups of individuals so that they can grow into cohesive, essentially self-autonomous groups. Good managers need to work constantly to transform a group of people with varying skills and interests into a focused team, and then work hard to sustain the energy and commit- ment – often in a climate of inadequate resources and tight deadlines. Management literature has been advocating the benefits of working in self-managing teams (SMTs) for some time.

Group communication

Research into group communication has shown that social interaction is essential for building and maintaining relationships, and task-based interaction is necessary to accomplish the group goal. Key to project success are the interaction practices that help to establish and then maintain the interorganisational relationships necessary to accom- plish the construction team's goals. The nature of the relationship established through communication will affect the actor's congruent understanding and hence the actor's ability to use information to aid decision-making. The relational qualities necessary to deliver a func- tional building can only be achieved through effective social and task- orientated communication. Improvements in the construction process will only be achieved if we start to understand how we use communi- cation to build and maintain the relationships necessary to undertake multidisciplinary tasks. The success of construction projects seems to be highly dependent on relational and task-based communication. In a construction context these two elements of communication are interdependent.

Groups exhibit patterns of communication that are directly related to their structure and context. Some of the factors that have affected the group and individual communication patterns include reasons for the group meeting; maturity of the group's participants; the par- ticipants' relationships with each other; their professional goals, roles and experience; organisational relationships and experience of the information and communication technologies used. Combined, these factors have implications for team assembly. There are a number of factors common to construction projects. These relate to group development within the temporary project team and the extent and nature of the actors' interaction during the project. Some of the char- acteristics and patterns of communication in a construction context, and indeed other contexts, may remain constant across projects; others may be specific to the context and/or the actors involved. For group communication to occur, the collection of individuals forming the group needs to share common attributes, goals or interest or at least have some common values or norms of behaviour. Small-group communication occurs when three or more people interact in an attempt to adapt to their environment and achieve commonly recognised goals.

Individuals may contribute to group activities for many different reasons, e.g. social or task-based. The context does not always set the agenda for being involved in the group, although they are normally closely related. Involvement in work groups may have greater social attraction than the task for which they are intended. Conversely, people may join a group to sabotage the group's goals (which is not always evident until it is too late). Groups are often said to have a common goal, which is a little misleading. It is important to recognise that the group goal may be both social- and task-based, and this is both conscious and subconscious. Normally groups have a reason, motive or driver behind their communications. At the most basic level people form groups to interact and socialise, gaining comfort and belonging from the group. At much higher levels people gain considerable power from the group and are able to accomplish things that would be difficult or impossible in isolation.

Self-managing teams (SMTs)

The concept of the SMT is not new but has been slow to gain acceptance. To work well the team should be made up of people with different, yet complementary, skills and share a common goal. In the design office these close-knit, self-contained groups need a blend of design, technical and procedural skills. The exact mix will depend on the orientation of the office and the requirements of a particular project; however, a typical self-managed team may comprise an architect (design), a technologist (detailing) and a project manager (procedural). To be effective the individuals must also be compatible, i.e. they must be able to communicate effectively and trust one another, while having operational autonomy to make decisions. Teams must constantly evaluate their actions and evolve as they learn from their collective experience, reflecting on and reacting to events. SMTs have a number of benefits and a few pitfalls to be aware of. Advantages of SMTs are that they:

- ◆ Set and monitor targets within the SMT
- ◆ Increase productivity through a multiskilled approach
- ◆ Tend to generate more ideas than individuals working alone
- ◆ Help to generate, share and utilise organisational knowledge
- ◆ Require minimal managerial interference.

Disadvantages are that they:

♦ Require time to set up for each project
♦ May not function effectively if there is imbalance in the SMT
♦ Have a high dependency on colleagues for their success
♦ May require additional training about team and group dynamics
♦ May have to be reformed for each new project.

Self-managing teams need careful consideration before they are set up, followed by subtle guidance from their team leader once they are operational. Team building is critical since it determines the effectiveness of SMTs, and thus the style of leadership is equally critical. Training may be necessary for the team leader if the team is to maximise its potential. Experience tends to suggest that the teams should have no more than ten members if they are to be effective. The sequential design model (Chapter 11) provides an ideal opportunity for the use of the self-managing team. Such teams also provide a greater degree of consistency, since the start of projects and the end of projects (the most difficult phases to manage) are easier to handle because of the collective knowledge of the SMT; feedback, so often neglected, may be accommodated much more easily.

Self-managing teams are important because they are enablers of information-sharing and knowledge-creation. The team culture encourages information-sharing, and knowledge-generation is continually enhanced. This is an important construct both within the professional office and within the project team. Within the office the link between self-managing teams is potentially the weak link and needs careful management to ensure that work within separate teams is disseminated throughout the firm where necessary. Better integration of teams provides the opportunity for the office to learn from its collective experiences. Within the temporary project team, however, the link between teams (if they exist) is more problematic. Continuous improvement will only come about through continuous learning – a process that must be managed.

Communication within the office

The design manager has to create an office culture in which the members are happy to discuss their projects informally through daily interaction, in addition to the staged knowledge-exchange events built into office procedures. Mutual trust and respect are fundamental requirements here, both of which have to be earned through trans-parent management and reliable actions. The design manager's role is such that he or she will have daily interaction with office members and will be highly visible within the office – essentially management by walking around. During the working day a lot of informal commu-nication will take place between the design manager and individuals as project progress is discussed, problems are aired and solutions agreed. Some of this interpersonal communication will be concerned with maintaining relationships and building relationships with newer members of the office, and some will be more task-related. It is the interpersonal communication that helps to create a buzz within the office and through which professionals are able to share knowledge relatively informally and quickly, i.e. interpersonal communication is a metaphoric glue that holds the office together.

Informal conversations are an important process for understand-ing what are often considered to be 'taken-for-granted' statements; thus conversation is essential to overcome ambiguity. Background information, clues and what may be considered 'small talk' are impor-tant for building relationships and thus crucial for developing an understanding of unfamiliar contexts. Being able to enquire further into subject matter without the fear of embarrassment or ridicule, or risk of offending others, is achieved primarily through interpersonal interaction, which helps to build relationships and hence establish contextual information. In groups it is necessary to know who is most knowledgeable and skilled in specific areas so that people can assume key roles in related tasks. When members freely interact and openly disclose information, other members gain access to, and clues about, a member's knowledge and skills. Such information is key to establish-ing informal group roles and hence the effective use of the group's knowledge in pursuit of the office goals. Over time the knowledge of each member's skills and attributes should make the office more effec-tive. Roles and responsibilities can be assumed and the most appropri-ate person can be quickly allowed to undertake the task, without the need for lengthy discussions to determine who has the necessary skills or knowledge. Effective groups in industrial settings are those that are more productive and meet the organisation's objective.

Groups that have been found to be more productive are said to have a structure that is suited to their function. The high level of productivity is achieved not only because they have procedures for solving problems, but also because the group is stable and less time is devoted to status struggles. Similarly, the members are aware of each other's skills, attributes, knowledge and roles and only a relatively small amount of discussion is required to organise tasks.

Interaction and lines of responsibility

In small design offices the design manager is likely to be a partner or director of the business, and communication between the senior managers and those working on the projects is direct. In medium-sized to large design organisations the design manager will take instructions from the senior managers and translate them into instructions for office members. The personality and managerial approach of individual design managers will influence the manner in which they communicate with their colleagues. The majority of architectural offices rely on relatively informal interaction, with more formal interaction taking place in regularly scheduled meetings. Partners and directors of architectural firms tend to retain a hands-on approach and are highly visible within the design office. Some owners will tend to distance themselves from the daily work and communicate with staff via the design manager. Interaction with fellow architects, architectural technologists, technicians and other professionals working in the office is fundamental to a functioning office, as is the interaction with secretarial and administrative staff. Good secretarial staff that can anticipate the needs of the professional are highly valued by professional offices.

Conflict management

It is likely that there will be occasional disagreements, arguments and conflict within the office. Some of these differences of opinion may be related to work on projects, especially if working to tight deadlines when levels of stress tend to be high. Other areas of disagreement may be personal and relatively trivial, for example two employees arguing about rival football teams. The scale of disagreement is likely to be relatively minor and light-hearted between employees – part of the office banter – but occasionally individuals can become emotive about specific issues they value highly (especially when they feel under too much pressure to perform their work). Design managers will need to recognise disagreements early and, where appropriate, intervene to restore the status quo. When personal differences manifest into situations where individuals are failing to communicate, it is necessary for managers to intervene and resolve the situation quickly. The office culture must remain positive, even in difficult periods.

Communication with other organisations

Communication within projects was discussed in Part One, where the efficacy of communication between offices was also raised.

Communication with other organisations, or more specifically with individuals working in these organisations, is carried out on a number of levels. Interorganisational communication poses a challenge from a management perspective because there is a large volume of informal communication taking place on a daily basis (telephone calls, conversations before and after meetings, etc.) and this is difficult to monitor and control.

The design manager's role here is to communicate with his or her contemporaries in the other offices so that work can be coordinated. Whether these individuals are described as design managers is not important; the important point is to establish who is the official spokesperson for a particular organisation or project. This could be described as formal communication (Figure 12.1). The design manager has no direct influence over the behaviour of staff in other offices. Informal leadership and influence come into play here (Figure 12.2); so does the importance of recognising that different organisations have different values and goals and will give different

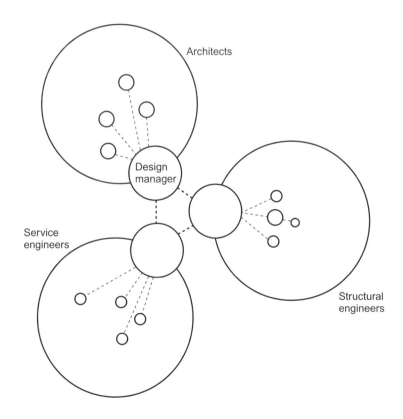

Figure 12.1 Formal communication with other organisations.

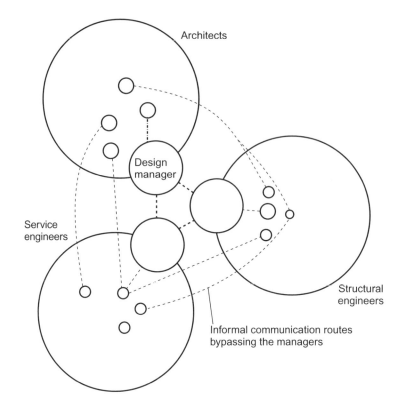

Architects

Design
manager

Service
engineers

Structural
engineers

Informal communication routes
bypassing the managers

Figure 12.2 Informal communication with other organisations.

priority to projects. Thus those interacting from other offices may have other priorities and this particular project's priority may be low – but it is difficult for the design manager to know this.

Managing disagreements and conflict between project participants was discussed in Chapter 3. The problem for the design manager is that he or she has no direct managerial control over team members employed by other organisations. Thus design managers need to try and influence the culture of projects by encouraging an open and trusting relationship with the other project participants. Maintaining an overview of the development of interrelated work packages has been made easier by the use of project web-type tools.

Controlling what we give to whom

Controlling the quality and content of the information issued by the office may influence the profitability of the design office. A protocol must be established for each project and clear procedures established for issuing information. Some projects will be developed under collaborative and relatively trusting relationships; others will not. Thus there will be a need to control what is given to whom on a project-to-project basis. Ideally this strategy should be discussed and agreed with the client at the start of the project, although there may be cause to revise the policy as the project evolves (for example, if the project culture develops in an unexpected manner).

Drawing registers are an essential tool for monitoring the current status of drawings and associated documentation. All projects should be allocated a number as soon as the initial contact with the client has been made. This allows all time and expenses to be allocated to a specific project. A record of what was issued to whom, when, and the status of the document (e.g. provisional, approved) is a fundamental element in controlling the development of design and project work. Information systems such as project web tools provide the means to control and track information sharing.

Managing meetings effectively

Meetings can serve a wide range of objectives, from the procedural and practical site progress meetings to the more social and informal team-building meetings. These have already been discussed in Part One. From the perspective of the design office, meetings can be categorised as being internal (office members only) or external to the office (external actors also present). A fairly typical model would involve a regular weekly meeting to discuss progress on projects with members of the office only, and a regular monthly meeting with specific clients and team members to discuss project performance. Both formal, regularly held meetings and informal, impromptu meetings provide effective vehicles to discuss and share knowledge. Meetings may be internal or external to the architect's office.

♦ *Internal meetings.* Internal meetings are limited to the organisation's members (or in large organisations to a particular division's members). In this familiar environment it is possible to be relatively informal and relaxed, since the others at the meeting should be trusted. Discussions tend to be relatively open, with shared objectives. Examples of such meetings are design team meetings (discussed in Chapter 5) and quality circles. Internal meetings can be used to share knowledge within the office. Dialogues and informal meetings can help to share knowledge informally within the office. The use of feedback through 'quality circles' or 'suggestion systems' is central to the Japanese philosophy of TQM. Quality circles are used to bring together employees, managers and directors to discuss and analyse aspects of the firm's service provision through the use of group problem-solving. Quality circles function at their best as small groups (between 5 and 12), where the firm's members meet on a regular basis, often outside regular working hours. In addition to helping to solve job-related problems, quality circles also seem to increase individuals' satisfaction with their firm by increasing participation in important decision-making activities. Quality circles can have a negative effect if ideas and decisions are perceived to be ignored by their managers.

♦ *External meetings.* External meetings include members from other, possibly competing, organisations or divisions. In this environment people are expected to act in a more formal manner and will, naturally, be less trusting of others at the meeting. Discussions tend to be relatively guarded and objectives may well vary between participants. Examples of external meetings include site progress meetings and meetings at which the client is present, for example design reviews. When actors external to the office participate in meetings, the rules change. Communication is with individuals from other organisations and so the type of language used and the openness of discussions needs careful consideration. In partnering arrangements and integrated teamworking the meetings should be conducted in an open manner and there may be a well-developed sense of understanding and trust between members. In competitive situations the communication may be more defensive and closed. If relationships have become adversarial, the communication exchanges will be defensive and closed.

Organising and chairing meetings

Meetings are time-consuming and expensive events. Well-managed meetings are a highly effective forum for group communication, and used sparingly their value to the design organisation and the progression of individual projects will become obvious. Architects will spend a lot of time in meetings and will often be responsible for organising and chairing meetings. To ensure these events are effective it is necessary to:

♦ Establish clear aims and objectives for the meeting
♦ Determine who should attend and why

- Allocate time to suit the purpose of the meeting and stick to it
- Decide on the most appropriate location (e.g. the site or the architect's office)
- Distribute an agenda and associated reports in advance of the meeting (no less then three working days before the meeting)
- Chair the meeting to allow all participants an opportunity to contribute
- Encourage reluctant communicators and limit the contribution of individuals who prove to be too vocal
- Consider phased participation for large meetings
- Build in short refreshment breaks for meetings that are scheduled to last for longer than one hour
- Confirm all decisions and allocate responsibility and timescales for achieving tasks, and confirm these in the minutes
- Distribute minutes promptly after the meeting (within two days).

Generating and sharing knowledge

For the professional service firm knowledge is its key resource; its core knowledge is the specialised knowledge that a professional would claim by virtue of his or her profession. Clients appoint professionals to apply that special knowledge on their behalf, since they do not posses it themselves. An architect's core knowledge is building design. Such knowledge is closely bound up in professional values and beliefs that (either tacitly or explicitly) influence the professional's actions. We are all aware of Francis Bacon's observation that knowledge is power (*Nam et ipsa scienta potestas est*) and there has been a lot of interest in knowledge management. The challenge for the competitive firm is to manage information flow, knowledge and change to the maximum advantage of clients and the architectural business. This means investing in people and providing a creative and supportive environment in which staff can share knowledge.

Knowledge-generation

Architects and fellow consultants draw on their design, technical and managerial knowledge in order to produce new knowledge about a specific problem. The tasks carried out by professionals are accomplished through the application of expert knowledge. This allows the development and production of knowledge artefacts, such as drawings, specifications, schedules and models. The development and continual replacement of professional knowledge has resulted in increased levels of abstraction and the tendency of many professionals to withdraw into their codified world and hence become somewhat isolated from their clients, the public and in some cases other professionals. Most knowledge systems include elements of vertical and horizontal knowledge, which are integrated during work.

- ♦ *Vertical knowledge.* This takes the form of a specialised language and specialised ways of working, and is the foundation of professional work.
- ♦ *Horizontal knowledge.* This is everyday knowledge and is context-specific, tacit and multilayered.

Each member of the office will develop a reservoir of knowledge that serves as the basis for practice. This means that a professional will apply their knowledge in a slightly different manner to that of their colleagues. This needs to be recognised by managers when managing individuals and groups and allocating work. Design offices will develop from the generation, exchange and renewal of knowledge and some attempt must be made to manage these activities to the benefit of the design office and its clients.

Knowledge retention and sharing

Retention of knowledge is a constant challenge for the professional service firm; the majority of knowledge walks into the office in the morning and out in the evening in the heads of individual members of the firm. Knowledge-based systems should make it easier for employees to access relevant information; however, such systems need careful design and consideration before they can be useful. Systems also need policing for accuracy of information and currency of the information, in itself a demanding job that needs managing through the use of regular audits.

Knowledge-sharing is crucial to the development and competitiveness of the office. Staff often fail to communicate with one another, not through any problems with their peers, but from lack of time and lack of managed opportunities to interact. This is true of communication within the office (mainly face to face) and communication with individuals in other organisations (mainly through telephone and project webs). The physical use of space may have some bearing on informal communication via casual conversations during the working day. Open-plan offices may be more conducive to informal interaction than cellular offices. Similarly, the ability to accommodate all designers and the design manager on the same floor may have a bearing on the informality and frequency of communications. This arrangement is not always possible when architects occupy older buildings with small floor plans situated on several levels. Design managers need to encourage open communication within the office. Office members need to be encouraged to talk about progress on their projects and share good and bad experiences. Opportunities for employees to get together and talk about their project experiences must be factored into workload programmes, otherwise knowledge-sharing is unlikely to happen. Similarly, the design manager must have empathy with the staff working on the projects, i.e. he or she must be able to 'talk' the same language and share the same goals. Informal communication will help to develop shared understanding and is crucial to the development of a trusting relationship. The design manager must be respected by the project staff and trusted to look after their interests. Similarly, the senior managers of the design office must trust the design manager. Being able to talk openly and honestly about the development of projects and the manner in which the office is managed is an important requirement.

Although we learn to design via experiential learning and in many cases learn to manage through our good and bad experiences, it is important that the office does not make mistakes. Errors are expensive, therefore learning by trial and error has to be carefully monitored and errors kept to a minimum and within the confines of the office. One way to deal with this is to ensure that knowledge and reflective practice are shared with other members of the office. It is not uncommon for colleagues to be dealing with similar problems without being aware of the fact. This *can* happen when people are sitting close to each other, but it is more likely when individuals are separated due to the architecture of the office and when individuals are working remotely. Knowledge generated through the use of reflective action and quality circles should be incorporated into some form of knowledge base, which is easily accessible to both existing and new staff. It is through shared experience that the firm may be in a better position to compete. Such a strategy will depend on effective utilisation of information technologies and expert knowledge systems. It will also depend on the manager's ability to plan staff time so that they have an opportunity to reflect, both individually and within the team. Thus issues of communication, information management and knowledge acquisition, storage and retrieval deserve special attention.

Strategic management of knowledge-exchange meetings

The size of the office and the manner in which it manages projects will influence the way in which knowledge-exchange events are planned and implemented. Project-related meetings, design reviews and

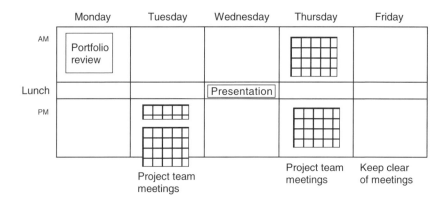

	Monday	Tuesday	Wednesday	Thursday	Friday
AM	Portfolio review			▦	
Lunch			Presentation		
PM		▦		▦	
		Project team meetings		Project team meetings	Keep clear of meetings

Figure 12.3 Overview of knowledge exchange meetings.

internal design critiques are tools to assist in the successful completion of projects; however, there will be a certain amount of informal knowledge exchange that takes place in and around such activities. Strategic knowledge-exchange events should also be built into the weekly schedule. Figure 12.3 provides a representation of a typical weekly schedule for a medium-sized office. In this model Monday mornings are reserved for discussion of projects and allocation of workload. Wednesday lunchtimes are dedicated to informal knowledge-exchange activities. Tuesday and Thursday are used for monthly meetings with major clients. Fridays are kept clear of meetings, since this is normally the day when deadlines have to be met.

♦ *Weekly portfolio review meeting.* The start of the week is a good opportunity to report and review progress on projects. It is also a good time to get all staff together to discuss individual projects and share knowledge between projects. This is a resource-hungry activity, and it is necessary to organise the meeting in such a way that information can be presented quickly and concisely, while allowing time to discuss pertinent issues. The intention is not to discuss the intricate details of projects; this is done with the design manager through daily interaction. Rather the intention is to discuss factors that have some bearing on project success, and which may be of interest to other members of the office. Problems are usually easy to identify, but it is also crucial to highlight good practices and project successes. The design manager should keep a record of the issues raised and analyse the data to see if there are any trends. It may be that a small adjustment to an office procedure would make a big difference to the efficacy of certain work.

♦ *Lunchtime presentations/interaction.* The provision of a communal area for office members to eat together at lunchtime can help to foster relationships and provide the forum for informal discussion about many topics, including work. Some design offices leave this to chance; others have a policy of 'managing' the lunch-break in an attempt to better share project knowledge. Some offices hold lunchtime presentations once a week, which all staff members are expected to attend (if possible) and at which progress on a particular project will be discussed. Given that this is conducted in the staff's free time, the trade-off is that the office supplies the lunch. These staged, but relatively informal, meetings tend to be popular with staff and have proved to help share experiences from different projects. The opportunity to discuss topical themes is also available. Administration staff and partners/directors also participate. These informal presentations should be held in addition to the formally-scheduled knowledge-exchange meetings, not as a substitute for them. The design manager will need to prepare a schedule of themes/topics and presenters. As a general rule it is polite to ask if people would like to contribute and in what manner, rather than dictating a theme or time. Consideration must be given to pressure on individuals, and presentations scheduled to avoid deadlines/project milestones. The time must be kept to one hour, thus the presentations should be short – approximately 20 minutes – with plenty of time afterwards for asking questions and discussion. The short presentation does not place too much pressure or additional work on those presenting. Evenings should be avoided because staff may have private/family arrangements, and are likely to be tired. A typical monthly lunchtime schedule could include project presentations/discussions; partner/ design manager presentations; topical themes (possibly presented by an external speaker); and open discussion.

♦ *Monthly client meetings.* These provide an opportunity to develop the relationship between the client and members of the office, such as the partners, design manager and those staff working on the client's project(s). Such events allow current projects to be reviewed and discussed, as well as introducing and discussing topical issues for possible inclusion. For example, the client may wish to know more about integrated project teamworking and the benefits and challenges such an approach would bring to their portfolio of projects. It is useful to take some time to reflect on these meetings and assess the points discussed, to see how they impact on current practice and their input to future development of the office.

The office to project interface

Construction projects are undertaken in a dynamic social system; nothing is particularly stable for very long and uncertainty and interdependence are constant factors, regardless of project size or complexity. The way in which an organisation is structured and operates, and hence its success, is determined by the communication practices employed. This applies equally to the temporary construction team and to the individual organisations that constitute the various supply chains. Many projects experience problems (both small and large) during their life cycle, despite the best intentions of the actors involved. This may be partly due to insufficient attention to the manner in which organisations and individuals interact during the life of a project, in particular the failure to understand how the participants communicate and how they influence each other through communication. Organisations pay far too little attention to the communication skills of their staff and the interaction practices they employ. Similarly, too little attention and effort is given to the interaction of individuals within a project and the retention of an effective team.

In many respects the issue of interpersonal communication is about developing an appropriate language for use within the office, and one for communication with other project participants. The 'architectural' language used in the office may well be inaccessible to those who have not had an architectural education. Some subtle changes will be necessary when talking to, for example, other professionals, contractors and clients. Similarly, the type of words used on the construction site may need some adjustment, especially with the growing use of migrant labour from Europe and the need to communicate clearly with people whose first language may not be English. The ability to communicate clearly and precisely to a wide variety of actors using a variety of media is an important skill. It is important to recognise that different actors may perceive the meaning of words differently in an architectural environment. Similarly, not everyone has the ability to read drawings; thus the type of media used to convey meaning to others must be considered against the specific context of the communication act.

Chapter Thirteen
Information Management

Computer software packages allow designers considerable freedom in their design approach and have revolutionised the manner in which architects design, and in some cases deliver, buildings. Most obvious developments are the use of CAD software packages, BIMs, visualisation tools, structural modelling, modelling of building performance (e.g. lighting, fire escape) and graphical database software tools. Related areas are electronic filing of project information, database management and tracking of financial affairs. Other tools that help to facilitate the exchange of information are office/project extranets, which allow drawings to be worked on concurrently and issued without the need to print numerous paper copies. Real-time communication through project web technologies is a further help to improved coordination within and between organisations contracted to a project. Digital building has also helped to make the outsourcing of production information to suppliers offshore financially and technically more feasible. In many cases this has led to changes in the type and number of personnel employed in the design office, with less emphasis on the information producers and more on information coordinators.

In many small to medium-sized design offices the design manager role will encompass responsibility for information management. In large offices the information manager may be a separate, yet interdependent, function to the management of design. Effective utilisation and integration of IT is central to the smooth running of the design office. Conversely, if the IT has a poor fit with the skills and working methods of the office, it will be less effective. Considerable time and care must be invested to ensure that the systems used are compatible with the needs and skills of the staff, and are also relevant to the project portfolio. Some clients may insist that the consultants employed to work for them use their ICTs, and compliance with the client's systems may be a condition of engagement. This means that the IT requirements of the office may evolve over time, in response to both new technologies and changes in the project portfolio. A thorough understanding of the information needs of the entire business and the relationship with the client portfolio is necessary before decisions are taken about the systems to be used, i.e. ITs need to be considered strategically as part of the office business plan.

The value of information

Building is concerned with information generation, transfer, exchange, use, storage and retrieval. Much of the mechanics is now dealt with by ITs but the creation and interpretation of the information is still a personal skill, which necessitates an appreciation of the social complexity in which information is exchanged. The problem is not so much with the speed of delivery, but more in the quality of the information produced, exchanged and used. There is a danger in concentrating entirely on the means and not the value of information.

Information is data in a usable form. Information provides a means of communicating with people who do not know one another, and who may have little personal basis for mutual understanding. Information allows people to make decisions and take action. Data has a cost, and information a value. The cost of researching, analysing, using, storing, transmitting, etc. is relatively easy to quantify compared with the perceived value of the information to the user. Information only has value if it is accurate, timely and properly used by the receiver. The value of information depends on the people who are going to use that information, the circumstances in which they use it and their perception of its value to them at any particular time. Meeting the criteria of accuracy, timeliness and appropriateness is a constant concern for design managers, as is the issue of relevance to the intended audience. Once information flow has been mapped and understood, the design manager is in a better position to put in place appropriate frameworks for the management of information. Similarly, an understanding of waste can help with managerial tasks.

Good communication and information flow are essential if a client's requirements are to be translated into a competent design and well-built product. Staff need easy and rapid access to a wide range of up-to-date information. To make informed decisions, vast bodies of information must be transmitted, stored, processed and accessed by many people with differing requirements. Informational needs will vary through the different stages of the project life cycle and must be carefully controlled to ensure that information is both up to date and relevant. Effort is also required to avoid information overload. Speed of access to relevant information is vital to both the efficient management of individual projects and the efficient use and maintenance of the building and its services. The manner in which firms organise and access information will be dependent on the size of the office and the size/complexity of individual projects. A solo practitioner may need information about specific stages of a project a few times per year from a reliable and current source. Large practices tend to implement their own systems and retain much of the information in-house, accessed via an intranet. Here the challenge is concerned with keeping the information current, given a finite amount of time and money.

It is well known that a great deal of uncertainty during the project, and defective work, can be traced back to problems with the quality of the production information. The gulf between designer and builder is evident in the type of information each requires. Information produced by the design team (drawings, schedules and specifications) describes the building as they want it to appear when complete. Such information describes building components and their size, position in relation to other components and quality. The contract documentation does not tell the builder how to assemble the various components; this information is held by specialist contractors and trades as expert 'how to' knowledge. Information that fails to communicate with its user will lead to uncertainty, waste and an increased risk of errors. Effective communication and information management is not only vital to the efficient day-to-day running of the design firm, but also to the daily administration of individual projects. Ineffective use and generation of information costs money and may add unnecessary time and expense to a project. Thus quality control should be a paramount concern for all members of the office.

Making informed decisions

Professionals are paid for making decisions. Information and knowledge are central to the decision-making process; the more relevant and complete the information, the better an individual is able to make an informed decision. It is a little unusual for an individual to have all the relevant information to hand, thus some action is required to obtain further information and hence reduce the level of uncertainty before a decision can be made. Searching for information can be a frustrating and wasteful exercise if the office does not have clear protocols about information storage and access to online providers. Given the amount of time designers spend searching for information, especially in the early stages of a project, it is surprising how little attention and hence support this activity is given in many architectural offices. Typically, the person seeking information has an incomplete picture and may have only partial knowledge of the information he or she wants. When making informed decisions we can decide to:

+ Wait for additional information
+ Act on the information available to us
+ Generate 'new' information, for example produce a drawing
+ Seek further information, i.e. search the office database
+ Opt out of the situation, i.e. delegate the task to someone else.

At all of these stages the individual will be exposed to a variety of messages, many of which will be ignored, i.e. the individual will exercise selective exposure.

Wasteful habits

To understand value also requires some acknowledgement of waste. It is obvious that an incomplete written specification or an unclear drawing will generate waste somewhere in the supply chain as the receiver tries to make some sense of the information. This usually leads to a request to the design office to revisit the information and to clarify any discrepancies, a task that will consume considerably more time than if it had been done correctly in the first place. But there are other habits relating to the production of information that exist within design offices, and which need to be addressed to ensure efficient use of resources. Few staff will admit to the following bad habits, but they are very common in architectural offices:

+ *Overworking drawings.* This is a very common habit among architects and apart from being unnecessary and wasteful it can confuse the reader of the drawings. Accurate allocation of time for completing the work usually prevents too much unnecessary embellishment. Similarly, understanding the needs of those who will use the drawing may help the author to remain focused.
+ *Underworking (incomplete) drawings.* This is less common than overworking drawings and tends to be related to inadequate time to complete a task.
+ *Incomplete written specifications.* This is a very common problem and often a result of poor programming – failing to allow enough time for this activity.
+ *Failure to follow office protocols and accepted standards* for information production. Assuming these have been implemented correctly, there should be no excuses for failing to comply.

- *Searching for information* that should be, or is, located in the office, but is inaccessible. This tends to be related to poor working practices within the office and failure to follow standard procedures.
- *Applying office standards and masters inappropriately* (resulting in errors and rework).
- *Ineffective use of IT.* This is usually related to a lack of knowledge about how to use specific software packages and tools. It is easily rectified through adequate training and regular updating.

Managing information flow

Understanding information flow within the office (and projects) is central to maximising the value of information. A great deal of the information will be transient, with comparatively little retained after completion of the project (for operational and legal reasons). A brief summary of the different categories of information is provided in Table 13.1. Much of this information is also available to competitors. Design typologies and standard details are used frequently by some developers, who hence have little need for the services of a professional designer. Specialist areas (with specific informational requirements) include permission for development (closely linked to design quality), project management, repair and maintenance.

Incoming information

A problem facing individuals on a daily basis, and their managers from a strategic perspective, is the vast quantity of information that is available. The volume of information has increased to such an extent that some form of specialised management structure and technology is required to store, process and retrieve relevant information to avoid a state of information overload. Information overload occurs when an individual or organisation receives more information than it can handle; thus some form of filtering is necessary to allow individuals to perform their work as efficiently as possible. In practice there is a wide range of approaches to information overload. Some design offices operate quite tight controls over who receives what and when; others leave information handling to the individuals in the office with access to the majority of information. Design offices are able to subscribe to on-line information providers that, for an annual fee, provide access to current information such as regulations, standards and manufacturers' information. This helps with the general

	External sources	Internal sources
Business information	Market niche, competitors, collaborators and supply chain partners (consultants, manufacturers, etc.)	Staff records, financial records, individual projects, mission statement, marketing literature, equipment and materials
Design information	Literature from manufacturers, professional journals, academic peer reviewed journals, books; design typologies developed by other design offices, legal (e.g. planning and Building Regulations), guidance documents, e.g., ISOs, health and safety	Standard details and specifications, design typologies from previous projects, design guides developed in-house
Project information	Clients, consultants, contractors, statutory undertakers and local authorities, user groups. Standards and codes	Design typologies, planning and monitoring. Legal obligations to retain information
Product information	Feedback from building performance, client and users	Internal analysis and reviews
Systems and management controls	Management systems, controls and frameworks. Professional code of conduct, guidance and advice via professional journals. Project insurances	Plan of work, office manual, quality management. Professional code of conduct. Professional indemnity insurance and associated insurances

Table 13.1 Information drivers.

informational requirements of the office, but it does not help with the vast amount of project-specific data that is generated throughout the life of a project.

Each project brings with it a new set of challenges and a fresh search for information to answer specific design problems. Consider a designer working in an architectural office. He or she will be engaged in a range of activities concerned with the design, detailing and realisation of a building project. In smaller offices, specifiers may be working on two or more projects concurrently, which may be at different stages. Detailing and product selection is carried out within this environment, and thus the capacity to access relevant information quickly is an important requirement. The individual designer cannot, and should not be expected to, survey the whole body of literature available. An easily accessible, accurate, concise and comprehensive body of information is required. Some of the main sources of technical information for designers working in Britain are:

- Building Regulations and Codes
- British (BS), European (EN) and International (ISO) Standards
- British Board of Agrément (BBA)
- Building Research Establishment (BRE) publications
- Manufacturers' technical literature
- Compendia of technical literature
- Trade association publications
- Technical articles and guides in professional journals
- Building information centres
- Previous projects
- Office standard details and master specifications.

Some of this information is still produced as printed documents, but the majority is available in digital format, accessed on-line via an integrated information provider. Access is quick and, assuming the subscription has been kept up, the material should be up to date and reliable in content.

Internally generated information

Internally generated information tends to be related to specific clients and specific projects. The amount of sharing between projects will depend on the market orientation of the office; for example, specialising in one type of building allows for easier file-sharing between projects compared with a general practice working on many different types of building. The design manager's role is to control the quality of the information created in the office across the various projects.

Externally generated information

Information production outside the design office has been a feature of many design offices for a long time. Before the advent of digital technologies many architectural and engineering offices would outsource packages of information production (mainly detailed drawings) to specialists, especially in busy periods. This was, and still is, done to keep the number of staff employed to a feasible level and to allow for flexibility in workload. What has changed is the scale and ease of outsourcing within the engineering and architectural professions. However, there is still a need to coordinate the various packages of information.

Outgoing information

All information must be checked for quality before it is issued for use by others. Not so long ago it was common for architectural practices to employ someone to check all drawings, specifications and schedules before they were released from the office. With pressures on professional fees and the need for information to be produced more quickly, the checking function has been delegated to staff. It is right and proper that staff take responsibility for their own work and check that it is complete and error free. However, in a busy design office it is often difficult for staff to coordinate their work with others, especially when they may be working on several projects concurrently. Although few design managers will acknowledge that this is a difficult area to manage, some appreciation of the potential problems of self-checking can help to keep staff alert to potential problem areas. Self-checking is potentially suspect and space must be factored into individual work programmes to allow this function to be carried out rigorously, before information is released from the office.

The design manager must take responsibility for ensuring that all information issued by the office maintains a consistent quality, is complete and free of errors. Regular design reviews are one way of bringing project participants together to look at information and sign off the information before proceeding to the next stage or phase. Special attention should be given to new members of staff, since they may be unfamiliar with office procedures and will require some additional time compared with their established colleagues. Extra attention is also necessary for high priority 'rush' projects, which given the speed at which they may be completed may be more prone to errors. Outsourced work will also need to be checked to see that it has fulfilled the specified quality standards and is error free.

Information audits

The value of information held within the organisation should be assessed through the use of regular information audits to weed out unnecessary information. There is no point in storing or transmitting valueless information; it costs money to store and to access and may lead to confusion. The challenge is to be able to distinguish between information that has value and that which may be superfluous. Filters and delimiters are required as part of a management policy and ideally as part of a quality management system. But for many managers the thought of throwing away or deleting information goes against their better instincts; what if there is a problem and we need to check our files? This is a particular problem for professionals dealing with work to existing buildings, where access to old regulations, codes and building product information will be crucial.

Production information

An essential requirement of the professional design organisation is to be able to produce clear, concise and accurate information that can be used to assemble the diverse range of materials and components into a building that meets the client's requirements and expectations. With the exception of artisans and the designer-craftsperson, designers work and communicate indirectly. Their creative work is expressed in the form of instructions to manufacturers, other consultants, contractors and sub-contractors, usually expressed in the form of drawings and written documents, collectively known as production information. Instructions must be clear, concise, complete and free of errors, and meaningful, relevant and timely to those receiving and using the information.

Drawings and written documents are used to describe and define a construction project. At its best, this project information will be clear and concise and easily understood, and the building contract will proceed to programme and to cost. At its worst, poorly conceived and shoddy project information will lead to confusion, inefficiency, delay, errors, revised work, additional expense, disputes and claims. It is a sad fact that very few projects are perfect; many are flawed by poorly expressed requirements. With the advent of computers and digital information, one could be forgiven for thinking that inadequate information would become a thing of the past, but many within the industry have noted a significant increase in the quantity of information provided and a steady decline in its quality. Unfortunately, IT makes it easy to transfer errors from one document to another very quickly. But it would be misleading to blame the technology. The biggest enemy of those trying to produce comprehensive, good-quality information is that precious commodity, time. Downward pressure on professional fee levels has resulted in the need to compress the amount of time taken to produce the project information. Accurate forecasting of the required design effort can help with programming and efficient resourcing, but design managers should still expect some mistakes and omissions and should put appropriate measures in place to spot them before information is issued from the office.

Coordinated project information

Coordinated project information (CPI) is a system that categorises drawings and written information (specifications) and is used in British

Standards and in the measurement of building works, the Standard Method of Measurement (SMM7). This relates directly to the classification system used in the National Building Specification (NBS). One of the conventions of coordinated project information is the 'common arrangement of work sections' (CAWS), which has superseded the traditional sub-division of work by trade sections. Around 300 different classes of work are listed in CAWS, according to the operatives who will do the work; indeed, the system was designed to assist the dissemination of information to sub-contractors. This allows bills of quantities to be arranged according to CAWS. Items coded on drawings, in schedules and in bills of quantities can be annotated with reference back to the specification. Under the coordinated production information it is the specification, not the drawings, which is the central document in the information chain.

Drawings

Drawings are the most familiar medium and are regarded as one of the most effective ways of communicating information. Production drawings ('blueprints') are the main vehicle of communicating the physical layout of the design and the juxtaposition of components to those responsible for putting it all together on site. Referred to as contract information or production information, this set of drawings is usually complex and extensive. Not only does it take a great deal of time and skill to produce the drawings and coordinate them with those produced by other consultants. It is also a skill to read all the information contained and codified in lines, figures and symbols. It is this set of drawings that the main contractor will use to cost the building work and (subject to any revisions prior to starting work) it will be the set of drawings from which the building will be assembled. At their most basic, the contract drawings will comprise drawings produced by the architect, the structural engineer and the mechanical and electrical consultants. Other contributors to this set of drawings may include interior designers, landscape designers, specialist sub-contractors, highways consultant, etc.

Coordinating drawings with other consultants' information and the specification is an important consideration. A drawing system that aims to reduce repetition and overcome defects in less well coordinated systems is the elemental method. This method is based on a four-category system, starting with the location drawings, focusing on the assembly drawings, then the component drawings and finally the schedules. Each drawing has a code and a number relating to the CI/SfB construction classification system. There are four codes: L, for location; A, for assembly; C, for component; and S, for schedule.

This system allows specific reference to drawings and schedules to be easily incorporated in the specification, thus aiding coordination. Another aid to coordination is the use of consistent terminology, clear cross-referencing and avoidance of repetition.

On very small projects and alteration works to existing buildings, it is common practice to write specification notes on the drawings, using a standard written specification to cover only the typical clauses common to most projects. Although widely used as a means of conveying information to the contractor, this is not good practice because the drawing very quickly becomes overloaded with information, repetition is largely unavoidable, and the majority of the notes are rarely descriptive enough to cover all the information required. There is a real danger that those reading the drawing on-site will rely entirely on the (incomplete) notes on the drawing and will not refer to the written specification, as they should. Apart from the obvious dangers of ineffective communication between designer and builder, this means that the drawing must be revised and reissued every time there is a change to the specification, no matter how minor. It is considered best practice to keep notes on drawings to an absolute minimum and keep the written description of materials and workmanship firmly where they belong – in the written specification.

Written documents

Written documents have always taken precedent over drawings. Until relatively recently, it was common practice to award contracts on little more than a written description of what was required (indeed, this is still common in domestic repair and alteration work where the client directly employs an organisation to do work on their property, for example replacing the windows). The advantage of written documents, theoretically at least, is that people can understand them more easily than drawings. Of course, this assumes that the document is well written and easy to read.

Specifications

Drawings indicate the quantities of materials to be used and show their finished relationship to each other. It is the written specification that describes the quality of the workmanship, the materials to be used and the manner in which they are to be assembled. It is a relatively straightforward task to set parameters for achieving quality through the written specification. This is vital because it is the contractor's agent, not the contract administrator, who controls quality of work and materials on site.

Schedules

Schedules are a useful tool when describing locations in buildings where there is a repetition of information that would be too cumbersome to put on drawings. Particularly well suited to computer software spreadsheets, a schedule is a written document that lists the position of repetitive elements, such as structural columns, windows, doors, drainage inspection chambers and room finishes. For example, rooms are given their individual code and listed on a finishes schedule that will relate the room number and use to the required finish of the ceiling, walls and floor.

Schedules of work

It is common practice in repair and alteration works to use a schedule of works. This document describes a list of work items to be done, and is usually appended to the specification. It is a list that the contractor can also use for costing the work.

Bills of quantities

The bills of quantities are derived from the drawings, schedules and specification. Their purpose is to present information in a format that is easy for the contractor's estimator to price. On small projects, it is unusual to produce bills of quantities because the information is usually concise and the estimator can price the project from the drawings, schedules and specification. Bills of quantities are used on medium to large projects. Although computer software packages are available to generate the bills of quantities from the designer's information, it is still common practice for a third party (usually a quantity surveyor) to prepare them. In doing so, the third party frequently finds discrepancies and omissions within the information provided, thus forming a useful (unpaid) crosschecking service for the design team. The contractor's estimator also has a duty to point out any deficiencies in the documentation to the design team when estimating the work.

Preparation of good-quality production information

Production information must convey the intentions of the designer to the contractor. This may appear to be an obvious statement, but those producing the information must constantly bear in mind the fact that readers of the information will not have been party to the decision-making process that led to the contract documentation. The receivers of the information can only read the documentation to see what is required of them.

Designers have their own way of working and many have 'golden rules' that they apply when designing, detailing and writing specifications. In offices where managerial control is not particularly good, this can and does lead to information taking a variety of slightly different forms, reflecting the idiosyncrasies of the authors. The end result can look unprofessional, can lead to confusion and, in the worst case, can result in errors on site. Professionally managed design offices take a much more considered and controlled approach. Designers work to office standards of graphic representation and to a standard approach to detailing, product selection and specification writing. Guidance for members of the design organisation is provided in the office quality manual, with the design manager providing support and encouragement on a daily basis. All members of the office should adopt a lean approach when producing information for others to use, thus helping to minimise waste and maintain quality. There are some golden rules to follow:

- ◆ *Clarity and brevity.* The most effective information has clarity and is concise. This is far easier to state than to achieve because it is impossible to represent everything that is in an individual's mind on a drawing or in text. The skill is to convey only that which has relevance and hence value to the intended receiver. This can be a matter of knowing when to stop drawing and writing. This will help the receiver to avoid information overload and enable them to concentrate on the relevant information without unnecessary distraction.
- ◆ *Accuracy.* It is important to be accurate in describing requirements because confusion will lead to delay and errors on site. Use correct drawing conventions and correct words to convey exact instructions; use correct grammar, units and symbols, and avoid ambiguity. Instructions should be given accurately and precisely and the documentation should be complete.
- ◆ *Consistency.* Whatever the approach adopted by the design office and the individuals within it, it is important to be consistent. Use of graphics, dimensions and annotation should be reassuringly consistent across the whole of the contract documentation. CAD packages and the use of the CI/SfB should both help to achieve this goal.
- ◆ *Avoiding repetition.* Repetition of information in different documents is unnecessary and wasteful of resources, and

when the information is repeated slightly differently (which it invariably is) can lead to confusion. Repetition, whether by error or through an intention to help the reader, must be avoided both within and between different media.

♦ *Redundancy*. There is always a danger that superfluous or redundant material will be included on drawings or in the written documentation. Text from the master specification may be redundant because it is not relevant to a particular project. Rolling specifications from one project to the next invariably result in redundant text.

♦ *Checking*. Check and double-check for compliance with current codes and standards, manufacturers' recommendations, other consultants' details and compatibility with the overall design philosophy. Common problems encountered by site personnel can be reduced significantly through a thorough check before information is issued to the contractor. Drawing offices may employ someone to check all drawings and specifications before they are released from the office. Unfortunately, in the constant drive for efficiency and ever-tighter deadlines for the production of information, such checks are often left to the individuals producing the information. Self-checking is suspect and subject to error simply because of the originator's overfamiliarity with the material. Managerial control is essential in this regard and must be costed into fee agreements. Checking for omissions and errors, accommodating design changes and auditing the process through quality management systems can save time and confusion.

Standards and masters

In the majority of design offices, typical details and specifications are customised to suit the organisation and hence become office 'standards' or 'masters' that are used to save time and ensure a degree of consistency. These are based on good practice (as viewed by the design office) and represent the collective experience of the office. Standards are sometimes developed for repeat clients with repetitive buildings and/or a distinctive architectural image. The disadvantage of using standards and masters is that it can stifle creativity and innovative solutions to detailing problems. This is why some offices work with details from first principles (when the fee justifies the means).

Standard details

Standard details are used to save time and reduce the risk of failure. Not only do they save time in generating the same drawing over and over again, they also encourage good practice since they are usually based on experience of detailing/materials that are known to perform (or more specifically known not to fail). As such, the standard detail forms an essential part of a quality control system. They can be implemented by less experienced staff as long as the process is monitored and checked.

The master specification

The master specification is essentially a library of specification clauses used by the design office on previous occasions that have been assessed for technical suitability, filtered, coordinated and updated on a regular basis. It is not to be confused with rolling specifications from job to job. It is a vital part of the design organisation's expert knowledge system. Maintained and updated on a regular basis, the master specification can save individual specifiers considerable time and effort by reducing repetitive tasks. Correctly managed, over time, the master specification will help to ensure consistency because all project specifications are drawn from it. It will maintain and improve quality through feedback of good and bad experiences, help to keep the cost of production down, and aid the coordination of information. Thus, the master specification is a crucial resource for helping to ensure quality control and also providing a quality assured service to clients. The more effective and easier to use the master specification is, the greater the potential efficiencies and hence profit for the design office. Someone within the office must take responsibility for the master specification. This person's task is to keep the document up to date and record all changes made to it in accordance with the organisation's quality management system.

Advantages and disadvantages

Standard formats can be an effective tool in the quest for consistency of service provision. Standards represent an excellent knowledge base from which to detail familiar buildings, and many organisations try to prevent employees who leave from taking their 'knowledge' with them to a competitor. Effective use of such standards offers a number of benefits, but there are also a number of pitfalls to be avoided.

Advantages:

♦ *Quality control.* Because standard details and specifications have been tried and tested by the design office over a number of years, they should be relatively error free. They will have evolved to suit changes in regulations and to accommodate feedback from site. They provide consistency where there is some turnover of staff, and a pool of experience to guide younger, inexperienced staff. Because they are familiar, tried and tested, standard details represent an effective means of quality control when checked and updated regularly and correctly applied.

♦ *Managerial control.* The use of standard details and specifications can save the design office time and money because common details and clauses do not need to be reworked, merely selected from the design organisation's knowledge base. Indeed, there may be little time available to investigate alternatives.
♦ *Risk management.* The use of tried and tested specification clauses helps to limit the organisation's exposure to risk. Essentially, it is a conservative, or 'safe', approach to detailing the design.
♦ *Benchmarking.* When faced with an unusual detailing problem, the standards form a convenient benchmark from which to develop the detail and help to evaluate its anticipated performance in the completed building.

Disadvantages:

♦ *Perpetuated errors.* Where errors exist in standard details and specifications (and they often do), the errors are perpetuated through reuse on many projects until such time as the error manifests itself, sometimes after a long period. Unless careful checking and updating are undertaken on a regular basis, the use of standards can prove to be a dangerous habit.
♦ *Incorrect application.* Inexperienced members of the design office are often left to apply standards with little or no supervision. Managerial control is essential if costly errors are to be avoided.
♦ *Danger of restricting creative thinking* at a vital stage.

Implementing an IT strategy

Clients expect professionals to utilise the most appropriate and modern technologies to deliver their projects. Considerable financial investment is required for hardware, software licences and updates, security systems, technical support, maintenance, IT consultancy and staff training and updating. Whether systems are purchased or leased, it all adds up to a significant annual investment that needs to be factored into the budget. Typically practices can expect to spend around 5% of annual turnover on IT, although this figure may vary quite considerably between architectural offices. Whatever systems are used they must be reliable and user-friendly. Upgrades and changes to different software packages must be introduced strategically to allow a relatively seamless transition from old to new. Changes also need to be factored into the office work programme, since the effectiveness of staff will be reduced, albeit temporarily, while they familiarise themselves with the new software tools. Office ITs should be integrated as well as possible, and this requires someone in the office to take responsibility for managing the office IT requirements strategically. Someone in a senior position within the organisation must take responsibility for assessing the needs of the organisation and then implementing an appropriate IT system. That person must understand the firm's business and must understand the particular informational requirements of both the design office and individual projects. Understanding and knowledge of IT systems are less important since these can be purchased through IT consultancy as required.

Investment in IT can be expensive. The main expense does not relate to the equipment (hardware and software), but to the maintenance, updating and management of IT systems and associated staff training. Whether or not a specialist information manager is required will depend to a certain extent on the system employed and the volume of information being processed, as much as the size of the office. Managers and staff at all levels in a firm need to be comfortable with the technologies they use on a daily basis. There is a tendency to implement IT without taking adequate steps to ensure that those using the systems are comfortable with them. Persuaded by slick marketing and promises of vastly improved performance, many organisations have invested heavily in IT systems before adequately mapping and hence understanding their organisational needs. The result is a degree of incompatibility between the users and the systems. An ineffective system will never allow the business to reach its full potential and will hinder the organisation in its day-to-day business. There are plenty of anecdotal reports of such problems from businesses large and small. For the solo practitioner the decision-making is relatively straightforward: ICTs need to satisfy personal taste and approach. As the size of the office increases there is a more pressing need to understand how the organisation functions and the needs of those working in the office, before investing in IT. What works for one organisation may cause another some difficulties.

Determining the organisation's requirements

Every IT system, regardless of cost and pedigree, forms part of a social system whose success or failure is linked to the dynamics of the organisations using it. The technology must fit the business objectives and culture of the office. This means that a bottom-up approach to IT and ICT requirements should form part of an effective business strategy. Too often, the decisions on IT and ICT are made by managers who do not use the technology on a regular basis. The architects, technologists and CAD technicians are the people who understand their requirements best; they must be central to decision-making about investment in technology.

The majority of guidance on IT systems for design offices starts with their drawing requirements, e.g. CAD systems and BIM, with other issues considered secondary to this prime function. A more considered and integral view is to look at the informational requirements of the business (not just drawings and production information). Consideration should be given to:

- *Integration and compatibility* (clients, consultants, manufacturers and suppliers, contractors). There are essentially two interrelated factors to consider: the requirements of the organisation (dm) and the requirements of the projects (pm software).
- *Expectations* (realistic or otherwise). Consider benchmarking here – what do competitors use, etc.?
- *Urgency.* Timescale and resources
- *Software and hardware* selection
- *Staff training* and implementation
- *Monitoring and feedback*
- *Future upgrades.*

The office to project interface

Information helps to hold organisations and projects together. Information and its management is a major driver and must be both understood and embraced if competitive advantage is to be secured. Compatibility between the office IT systems and those used by other project team members will influence the profitability of individual projects and hence the financial wellbeing of the office. Coordination problems take time to resolve and usually manifest at the least opportune moment, with the cost of resolving the difficulties eating into the firm's profits. To ensure an effective process and to help provide an excellent service to the client, it is crucial that IT is completely integrated. This means dealing with integration of people and technology early in the project team assembly stage (discussed in Chapter 3). Compatibility problems may be resolved, or at least identified early, and their effects mitigated through effective management of the process.

Temporary project teams cannot be left to evolve; they must be designed and managed so that information is used effectively. Understanding the needs of other project participants – the way they like to work and their preference for certain software and communication media – can help to improve understanding and hence reduce waste. For example, the ability of staff to interact with actors in other organisations through real-time communication technologies may allow more effective use of staff time. This may also help to reduce uncertainty and to limit coordination problems.

Chapter Fourteen
Financial Management

A smooth-running business must have a constant supply of money passing through its books to pay its staff, service its overheads and generate profits. It is an area of architectural practice that many designers feel uncomfortable with, but with the right advice from a good accountant there is no reason why the design office cannot function effectively and profitably. Too many architects earn a poor living through inadequate attention to the factors that determine the amount of money generated, and hence the health of their business. Financial management and accountancy tend to be associated merely with bookkeeping and completing the appropriate tax and VAT returns. But they form a much richer process that relies on the ability to estimate design effort relatively accurately and hence resource projects efficiently, which allows cash to flow into the business. This requires a thorough understanding of the factors that influence the profitability of individual projects. Financial management of the architectural business is about maximising financial opportunities; it is finance that drives the business and hence provides the opportunity to practise architecture. To create and maintain a profitable business it is necessary to:

- ◆ Charge realistic fees for the services provided
- ◆ Ensure a consistent cash flow
- ◆ Use simple accounting systems to allow the effective management of finances.

It is also necessary to seek appropriate advice from professionals with financial and business expertise. Banks offer excellent advice and help packages for new businesses, much of which is provided free of charge. Advice should also be sought from an accountant before the business is launched, with measures implemented to help make the business profitable from the start. Accountants can, for example, provide advice on how to benefit from taxation law and hence reduce the tax burden on the business. This may be something as simple as how the architectural business is legally constituted and the financial benefits of one type of arrangement (e.g. a limited company) over another (e.g. a partnership).

The relationship with clients and the ability to attract and retain profitable clients is a fundamental concern for professional service firms. Cash flow projections for the short, medium and longer term need careful consideration, monitoring and occasional adjustment. It is not uncommon for professionals to carry out a considerable amount of work 'up front', before they invoice and subsequently receive payment. Often the timeframe between starting a package of work and receiving any income may be several months. During this period money is required to pay staff salaries and service office overheads. Forecasting both workload and cash flow are very important tasks, but given the nature of the work both can be challenging to achieve with any degree of certainty. However, forecasts allow financial objectives to be set, resources allocated and progress monitored.

Ensuring profitability

Profitability is important and some attempt to manage cash flow and staff workload is needed on a regular basis. There is a simple relationship between the income generated from each client and the costs incurred in servicing that client. The main expenditure is staff time; thus understanding how people spend their time is a crucial step in assessing profitability. On a simple level, client profitability is the amount of money received from the client minus the cost of staff time and associated overheads (Figure 14.1). The cost incurred in servicing the client comes directly from the time spent in completing work for that client, as recorded on staff timesheets. Cost is calculated by multiplying the number of hours spent by the total cost of employing the members of staff who are working on that project. The operating profit over a 12-month period is the amount of income received from all clients minus the total expenditure over the same period. Profit is the surplus income after all costs have been deducted and before any taxes have been paid. Given that partners or directors privately own the majority of architectural offices, the profit may be defined as the surplus payable to the owners. The profit is purely an accounting exercise that can and will be manipulated (within the law) to make the most out of personal and corporate tax rates.

The profitability of the office may fluctuate over a given timeframe, depending on the strength of the market and the demand for

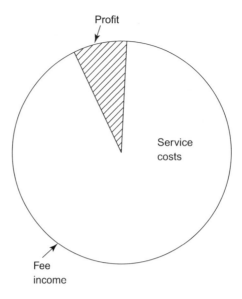

Figure 14.1 Servicing costs and profit related to fee income.

services. Architectural firms are particularly vulnerable to shifts in the output of the construction sector, which tends to swing from one extreme to the other relatively quickly. Given such dependency and uncertainty about clients commissioning services, it is necessary to have some degree of flexibility in the firm's biggest expense, staff costs, if profitability is to be maintained. This means that the business must be designed to accommodate a certain degree of flexibility, able to respond to economic upturns and downturns quickly without damaging the financial health of the business. Profitability is also influenced by the contribution of its employees. The better-managed firms provide bonus schemes for staff who contribute to the profitability of the business through having the right attitude. Profitability is influenced by staff morale, leadership and managerial controls. Management systems cannot help to generate good morale, but they can help to provide a working environment that helps members of the office to do their job more easily.

Financial management systems should be simple and transparent, helping to maximise cash flow and facilitate effective financial management of the business. Accounts are used to provide a record of all financial transactions. This includes the income and expenditure of the business over a 12-month period, known as the profit and loss account. It also includes details of the firm's assets and liabilities at a particular date, known as the balance sheet. The accounts will show whether the business has made a profit or a loss over the accounting period. In addition to any legal requirements, the accounts are necessary for determining tax liabilities and distribution of dividends to shareholders, and as proof of financial standing to clients and suppliers. The accounts will also be necessary when seeking a financial loan from a bank and to determine the value of the business in the event of a sale or change of partner.

The profit and loss account is essentially a simple spreadsheet that lists the income in one column and the expenditure in another. This is usually compiled on a monthly basis. By deducting the total expenditure from the total income it is possible to see if the business has made a profit or a loss during the month. Income is from the fees received. Expenditure largely covers salaries, cost of the business premises, cost of equipment necessary to run the business, insurances and an allocation for depreciation of furniture and office equipment. Data from the profit and loss account can be used to compare the financial performance of the business against the projected performance (the budget).

The balance sheet provides a record of the assets and liabilities at a particular date. Assets include fixed assets (such as buildings, fixtures and fittings, equipment, company cars, etc.) and current assets (which include cash deposits at the bank, fees due from work in progress and debtors). Liabilities are the money owed by the business to suppliers and banks (loans). The balance sheet will also list the capital invested in the business, for example the partners' capital or capital raised from the issuing of shares.

Sources of income

Professional design offices are able to generate income from a variety of sources. The most obvious is from architectural work and the associated field of project management. Less obvious sources may include areas such as architectural photography, technical writing for product manufacturers, building product invention and design, teaching and commercial research activities. Depending on the market orientation of the firm and the collective skills of its members, some avenues of income may appear more attractive than others and should be reflected in the business strategy.

It is the ability to attract work continually that ensures a constant income stream. How, what and when a firm should charge for its services has caused a lot of angst over the years, as architects have been forced to drop their mandatory fee scales and experiment with different means of generating income. Competition from other players has also placed downward pressure on fee levels. As a general rule the amount of fee charged will depend on market conditions, i.e. the fee charged is that perceived to be what the market can stand or, more specifically, what the client can afford. It is usual to find regional variations and variations within specialised building types. A particular skill of senior partners and directors is being able to pitch the fee at the right level, which requires a considerable amount of knowledge, experience and negotiating skills. The fees charged should be adjusted annually to reflect inflation and wage increases, thus helping to retain an appropriate profit margin. All changes in fee level must be communicated to clients well in advance of any proposed rise. On projects that are expected to last over several years, it may be possible to include a defined amount of price adjustment within the client agreement. If this is not possible, the fee agreement should include some provision for rising costs over the period of the project.

There are a number of ways to charge for the services provided. The benefits of one method over another will depend on the type of services required, the preferences of the client and the design office and the project context. Whatever fee agreement is entered into, it is crucial that the architects and clients are absolutely clear what services are to be provided (and what are excluded) and how much they will cost. This helps to avoid any confusion, disputes and excuses to delay payment of fees at a later date. The most common methods of generating fee income are through percentage fees and time charges. Lump sum fees and conditional fees are also used. Additional costs, such as travel to the construction site to attend meetings and cost of printing drawings, will usually be charged to the client in addition to the agreed fee.

Percentage fees

Percentage fees are based on the final cost of the building work, the contract sum. They are the most common type of fee charging when providing a full service. Percentage fees will be discussed with clients and agreed on a project-to-project basis to reflect the extent of work required. As a very general guide the percentage fee may be between 5 and 8% of the contract value for new-build commercial projects, and between 10 and 15% for more complex work such as small domestic-type projects. If there is a high degree of repetition in the design the fee percentage may be reduced to reflect the reduced amount of work in relation to the final cost of the building work. Work to existing buildings tends to attract higher fees because of the additional amount of work involved, and somewhere around 15% is not uncommon. The RIBA publish indicative percentage fee scales based on average costs and building complexity. These may be of some assistance to those less experienced with percentage fee negotiations. As the contract sum increases, the level of fee will be reduced. Fee income will decrease if the final contract sum is reduced; conversely the fee will increase if the final cost of the project is greater than that budgeted. Critics of percentage fees claim that it is in the designer's interest to allow the contract sum to increase because they will then be entitled to more money. This tends to overlook the fact that architects are professionals, and thus must apply integrity to all aspects of their work. Exceeding the contract sum is not a good advert for any of the actors involved in the project and a great deal of effort will be spent in trying to deliver the building within budget. It is usual for percentage fees to be paid in instalments based on the estimated final cost, with the requisite adjustments made to reflect the final agreed contract sum.

Time charge (hourly rate)

Hourly rates are often disliked by clients because the time can (and often does) add up to a large fee that may be unexpected. It is good practice at the start of a project to agree a time limit that cannot be exceeded without the client's permission, thus giving both client and designer some degree of certainty over expenditure and income respectively. Charging an hourly rate would be appropriate to the provision of partial services, additional services, specialist consultancy and additional work beyond the architect's control (e.g. additional work requested by the client). Architectural practices will charge different hourly rates for different members of staff, based on the level of experience and perceived value of the work. Different rates may also apply to the type of work required. For example, legal work would normally attract a higher hourly rate than, say, more usual architectural consulting. As a general rule of thumb, the minimum charge-out rate for a member of staff should be no less than three times their gross salary (including pension and National Insurance (NI) contributions). Based on a 35-hour week, for 45 weeks per year (1575 hours) and a gross staff cost to the office of, for example, £50,000 per year, this would equate to $3 \times £31.75$, approximately £95 per hour. Hourly rates reported in 2006 typically range from £80 to £150, with senior staff in the area of £180. Complex, specialised and legal work would typically attract fees somewhere around £250 per hour. In situations where work is required urgently and the staff is working overtime, the hourly rate would need to be increased (say by 50%) to reflect the increased salary costs. This would need to be agreed with the client in advance. It is usual to invoice clients on a monthly basis for the time spent.

Lump sum

A lump sum fee is a figure agreed with the client in advance of the work and is not negotiable. Some clients favour this type of arrangement since there is no risk of the fee increasing, unless they request additional work for which there will be an additional fee. In a lump sum arrangement the client has cost certainty, but the architectural practice carries an increased degree of risk compared with other fee arrangements. It is essential that the architects include a contingency within the lump sum to allow some provision for uncertainty. Calculations to establish a lump sum are usually made on the number of hours anticipated to complete the work (which can also be checked against a percentage fee and adjusted accordingly). A contingency figure of, say, 10% is then added to the final figure to allow for inaccurate estimating. Lump sum fee arrangements should not be entered into unless the extent of the work is well-defined and the timescale is fixed, both of which will need to be agreed with the client. The architectural practice will also need to make clear the exact nature of the services provided for the fee. To aid clarity it is also common to define the services not provided within the lump sum agreement. For small projects the lump sum may be paid in one instalment on successful completion of the project, although it is more common to agree a series of staged payments.

Conditional fees

Conditional fees are otherwise known as 'no hay, no pay' or 'no win, no fee' arrangements. The payment of an agreed fee is conditional on achieving a successful outcome for a defined project. There are situations where such arrangements may be entered into: for example some clients will commission professionals to prepare designs so that they can try and buy a site and/or achieve planning permission. An estimate of the risk involved (resources committed balanced against the prospect of no income) needs careful consideration before such an agreement is entered into. In such arrangements the fee will only be paid on successful completion of the project; that is the condition. Because of the risk involved for the practice, the agreed fee will be higher than would normally be charged for such work. Conditional fees are a high-risk strategy and some architects do not regard this method of generating fee income as befitting a professional firm. If payment is forthcoming it will be in one instalment. In addition to getting a fee, the hope is that the project progresses further and the client commissions additional services under more standard forms of agreement.

Fee bidding and negotiation

Whatever fee system is agreed with a client, it usually follows a period of discussion and negotiation to find the best approach for both parties. Following the abolition of the RIBA's mandatory fee scale in 1986, it has become common for clients to invite design organisations to tender for work (submit a fee bid) or negotiate the fee. Many professional firms do not like fee bidding since it is often perceived as unprofessional, although they still expect contractors and sub-contractors to tender for work. On a more practical level, fee tendering is unpopular because it requires the architectural office to carry out a lot of work in preparing the fee bid, without any guarantee of success. This places additional pressure on the firm's resources. It is not unusual for a client to invite tenders from at least three firms with specialism in the same area, thus firms find themselves competing against one another. Depending on the size of the project and the client's requirements, it can take a great deal of staff time to prepare a well-presented tender document. The amount and type of information required for a fee bid will vary between different clients. There are essentially two methods of submitting a bid:

♦ *Fee only.* The title is a little deceptive because the firm will also be expected to submit details of their firm's track record, details of their quality systems and often the qualifications and experience of the staff, in addition to their fee for carrying out the specified work and a programme for completing the work.
♦ *Fee and design.* This usually requires the same information to be provided as for a fee only bid, but will also involve some design work. The scope and nature of the design work will vary between clients and building types, but it is not uncommon for clients to request plans and elevations for commercial projects. Clearly this involves a lot of work for which the firm will not be paid and as a general rule of thumb, fee and design tenders will take at least three to four times the effort to prepare compared with the fee only bid.

Fee tendering is a time-consuming activity but can be carried out relatively efficiently if the office has a good database of past projects, is able to estimate design effort relatively accurately and has a database of associated financial data. For small design firms fee tendering has to be accommodated within the fee-generating work; for larger firms it is often possible to employ at least one person to spend their time on fee bidding, falling within the firm's marketing activity and costed accordingly. There is a common misunderstanding that the cheapest fee bid wins. All clients will require a mix of experience, expertise and creativity, in addition to some assurance that the office can execute the project efficiently and professionally. Negotiation of the fee can also be a time-consuming activity, but less so compared with fee tendering.

Clients will balance cost against likely performance because it generally holds true that you get what you pay for. In general a client's assessment, and subsequent decision, is based on the organisation's:

◆ Past experience (demonstrated through past projects)
◆ Current expertise and creativity (demonstrated through current projects)
◆ People to be allocated to 'their' project (experience, expertise and balance of creative, technical and managerial skills)
◆ Management acumen, the ability to execute the project effectively (within time and budget and to specified quality standards)
◆ Financial stability.

Clients will want to know what value the architectural office can add to their project. The fee is not necessarily significant in this decision-making process because it is usually discussed in detail after a decision to use a particular firm has been made, i.e. the fee will be negotiated. From the architect's perspective the skill is trying to match the client and their requirements to the level of fee charged. Architects will also need to assess the client's intentions and the pros and cons of working with them. Meeting to discuss fee levels is a good opportunity to make an initial assessment of the client and if there are concerns that the client is likely to be unprofitable, then the job should be declined.

Fee invoicing and cash flow

Attempts must be made to plan the start and completion of projects in relation to office resources, thus ensuring a steady supply of work for staff as well as a relatively constant income stream. Prompt invoicing will help to facilitate cash flow and reduce the need for borrowings. It is highly likely that different projects will have different arrangements for when fees are scheduled for payment. Typically invoicing is related to achievement of project milestones or by regular (monthly) instalments. Generating and maintaining a regular schedule of payment dates will considerably aid financial planning and workload planning

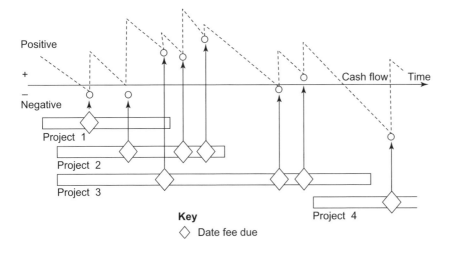

Key

◇ Date fee due

Figure 14.2 Relationship between the project portfolio and cash flow.

(see Figure 14.2). Making some effort to ensure a relatively regular income each month will also help to ensure salaries and suppliers can be paid without the need for a loan from the bank.

Management of the fee income is influenced by the way in which the firm is managed, and the partner/client relationship. It is clearly in the interests of the business to maintain good client relationships through regular dialogue and the provision of an excellent service. The senior partners and directors must ensure that their clients fully understand and agree with the fee-charging arrangement and the dates of stage payments. Each office should also have a clear policy on its terms of trade, which may help to achieve prompt payment.

All architectural offices require a simple and clear accounting system. Fee invoices must clearly and simply state the work done, the amount owed and the date on which payment is due. Invoices must be issued promptly (on the agreed date if applicable) and any late payments flagged up immediately. Some firms charge interest on late payments as a standard policy; others are reluctant to apply such a policy for fear of damaging client relations. Whatever the policy, it should be communicated plainly and clearly to the client at the time of the fee agreement, not afterwards. It is unfortunately common for clients to question even the most straightforward of invoices, thus delaying payment. To help avoid, or at least limit, such behaviour it is crucial that the invoice is not presented in an incomprehensible fashion, but simply states the work done and the amount owed.

Debt recovery

Too many small businesses fail because of cash flow problems caused by late payments. This applies to all businesses, from architects and engineers through to contractors, sub-contractors and tradespeople. Research has shown that only around one-third of clients will settle their account within 30 days, with large companies taking somewhere between 45 and 60 days. Some clients will delay payment for as long as possible, even when there is no good reason for doing so. This means taking a realistic view of cash flow and utilising reliable accounting systems in an effort to track the amount of debt. Businesses also need to take positive measures to ensure that as much money as possible is paid within 30 days to assist cash flow and minimise borrowing. Debt collection needs to be planned and an agreed strategy employed for all clients. Accountants will provide advice and guidance on this area. Businesses must be prepared to take legal action and not back down. The general advice is that administration staff should undertake debt collection, not the fee-earning partner or director. Architects and designers will be emotionally involved in their projects and this does not make for good debt collection, besides which their skills lie elsewhere. In medium-sized to large offices it may be possible to justify the part-time or full-time employment of a financial administrator; for smaller firms it may be necessary to outsource this task. When dealing with repeat clients, previous experience of their payment habits may make it a little easier to predict how quickly the debt will be paid. Known bad debtors should be avoided if possible, since it is unlikely that they will ever become profitable clients.

Controlling expenditure

Income generation has to be balanced against expenditure. The aim is to make a profit and hence stay in business, and this can only be done through careful control of expenditure. This means taking a considered approach to how staff are employed and utilised, how space is used and how office overheads are kept to reasonable limits.

Staff utilisation

Skilled, dedicated and enthusiastic architects, technologists, technicians, project managers, design managers, administrators and secretaries are an expensive resource and it is crucial that their time is utilised effectively. This means engaging in some form of time planning and management as well as thinking very carefully about the number of staff required and how they are to be employed. For many small design offices it may be a sensible policy to employ staff only when the need arises, by outsourcing some of the work or employing staff on a temporary (fixed term) basis. The use of contract staff is very common in the architectural and engineering sectors. Working over-time is another way of coping with temporary increases in workload, but this must be paid for by giving staff time off in lieu or by paying overtime for the additional hours worked. Costs related to salaries include NI contributions, pension scheme, private health insurance and payment of professional subscriptions (e.g. Architects Registra-tion Board (ARB), CIAT, RIBA) as well as the provision of specific perks, such as company cars.

The number of hours that can be invoiced to clients in a year will depend on the salary paid to the employee, their position within the firm and their effective utilisation. This is usually referred to as the number of chargeable hours, or the firm's capacity. The number of chargeable hours provides a useful indication of the amount of fee income likely. Take the example of a five-person office, each member working a 35-hour week for an average of 45 weeks per year, a total of 1575 hours per year. The utilisation rate of each employee would be something similar to that shown in Table 14.1 for a 12-month period.

The partner would be expected to spend a large amount of time on attracting new business and strategic management work, thus utilisa-tion would be, say, 30%. (Some offices assume that the senior partner will not generate any chargeable hours and factor this into their overheads.) The associate would have an office/design management function, and utilisation is likely to be around 50%. The architect and the technologist would be expected to be the most highly utilised in

	Utilisation rate	Chargeable hours	Hourly rate	Projected fee income
Partner	30%	472	£160	£75,520
Associate	50%	787	£120	£94,440
Architect	80%	1260	£95	£119,700
Technologist	80%	1260	£95	£119,700
Trainee	50%	787	£30	£23,610
			Total projected fee income for 12 months	£432,970

Fee income = chargeable hours (capacity) x hourly rate (price)

Table 14.1 Staff utilisation.

terms of chargeable hours, both around the 80% mark, allowing 10% of time for administration and 10% for training/professional updating. The trainee will be relatively poorly utilised in the first few months, but this should grow quite quickly to somewhere around 50% given adequate support by the design manager. The problem with this plan is that it does not allow for staff being sick, nor does it allow for clients not paying their invoices in full. So the figures above could be seen as an optimistic forecast of fee income. However, it is a very useful way of helping to ensure a good balance of staff in terms of the financial health of the business.

All staff should try and identify waste and eliminate it from the daily routine, thus making the whole process more efficient and allowing all members of the office to be more productive. Areas where time, and hence money, is wasted can be found in everyday activities. The 'classic' is time wasted trying to find project files and repeating work already done by someone else. This can be addressed by good data management systems, monitoring data from timesheets and by the design manager walking around and looking at what is happening. In well-managed offices all staff are aware of their charge-out rate and the number of hours they have to work on specific jobs. This makes it easier for individuals to manage their workload to agreed targets.

Cost of space

The environment in which individuals work will influence their productivity, creativity and sense of wellbeing. Physical office space has to be paid for. Space planning and management is a useful exercise to help keep the amount of space within workable and economic limits. Flexible working and careful design of the office can greatly assist in keeping the cost of space to a sensible level and, hence, can help to keep the business financially competitive. A number of options include:

- Purchase of office space (a building or part of a building)
- Leased office space (with shared facilities may be a cheaper option)
- Work from home (may suit very small businesses and some staff)
- Work as a virtual office (with a small head office).

Overheads

In addition to staff costs and the cost of office space, there is the equipment necessary for the business to function. This includes basic essentials such as fixed telephone lines and mobile phones, internet access and the hosting of a homepage, computer hardware and software, the cost of maintaining intranets and project websites, pens, paper and drawing equipment, office furniture, filing cabinets, etc. Cars are another expense, whether leased or purchased. Small practices usually require staff to provide their own car, which must be insured for business purposes. Financial reimbursement is based on the number of miles travelled each month. Larger businesses usually provide company cars.

Insurances are a legal necessity and their combined cost can add a significant amount of expense to the cost of running the business. Architectural firms must have professional indemnity (PI) insurance, public liability insurance, employer's liability insurance and premises and contents insurance. Additional insurance costs relate to company car insurance and staff benefits, such as health insurance. Premiums are usually increased on the anniversary of the insurance and will certainly increase following a claim.

Financial monitoring and evaluation

Monitoring and evaluation of financial data are an important activity for which time must be allocated. The performance of the firm should be evaluated at planned intervals against the strategies previously agreed. Adjustments may be needed to suit changing circumstances. Most offices will monitor the economic pulse of the office on a weekly basis, updating the budget to include new projects, delayed projects, completed projects and problematic projects/clients, as well as changes to staff costs and overheads. Evaluation and financial monitoring should aim to:

- *Assess the extent to which projects have achieved their stated objectives*. These should be related to previously determined standards of design, programme, resources, budget, profitability and client satisfaction.
- *Consider the improvement of working methods*. Objectives may have been met, but there may be scope for improving the way in which future projects are managed more effectively, and hence more profitably.
- *Optimise the use of resources*. Has the firm been managed effectively given the resources available? Have the individual talents of the firm's members been optimised?
- *Assess the current standing of the business* in the market in terms of market share.

Collecting data – the timesheet

Well-designed costing systems are important to monitor the prog-ress of individual jobs, assessing the efficiency of the design firm as a whole and helping to identify areas for improvement. There needs to be a mechanism for collecting and analysing financial data, which will enable a calculation of client (or project) profitability to be made. The most common tool used to collect information is the staff timesheet. The historical data collected from timesheets provides useful information to inform the estimating of design effort, budgets and fee levels.

There is considerable variation in the use of timesheets within design offices. A small minority of firms do not use them, preferring to monitor costs based on the amount of income entering the prac-tice minus that expended, and relying heavily on subjective decisions. In some cases this is a sign of poor financial management, although some very small offices can and do operate quite happily in this way. Some offices use timesheets but fail to use the information collected to their best advantage. They simply use the timesheet as a crude way of ensuring employees have put in the requisite number of hours each week, which is to miss the point. At the end of the project the data may be analysed, although it is more likely to be ignored unless there has been a problem and/or the project has lost money; again this is not a particularly good use of the information collected. Efficient design offices recognise the benefit of analysing the data collected on timesheets to monitor the financial pulse of the firm on a regular basis.

The format of the timesheet should be as simple as possible without losing information on critical areas. The amount of time an individual spends on a particular phase of a project is easy to collect, input to spreadsheet and then analyse. Similarly, the time spent on other matters such as professional development, holidays and sick leave needs to be recorded to give a complete picture of an individual's billable hours. Analysis of the data collected should be undertaken on a regular basis (e.g. monthly) to assess the profitability of clients and staff.

Client profitability

Analysing the amount of time spent servicing a client provides a cost (including all overheads) that can be compared to the fee income. Some care is required in the timing of such calculations because there are different phases in the office/client relationship. Taking a snapshot at one point during the project is likely to be misleading. Putting aside marketing costs (included in overheads), there is the cost of pitching for work, the preliminary client contact and the exploration of interests and values to ensure a good fit between the client and the office. Time is also required to understand the client and to secure the commission. In many situations this can be a lengthy process, as clients assess various options and place demands on the office prior to any income being generated. The second phase relates in many respects to the early team composition and early briefing phases, where client and project members are getting to know one another. This, like the start-up phase, involves senior staff whose time is expensive, and these are areas where many design offices underestimate the amount of time required to cement relationships and build trust. Once through this stage the project proceeds to the design and construction phases. Here the level of client input and the agreed level of service agreement need careful monitoring (Figure 14.3). During the life of a project many factors are outside the control of the client and the design office. For example, a delay in gaining planning permission and requests for additional information can consume unplanned resources, so too can disagreements and disputes with contractors.

Clients vary in their demands made on a design firm, with some demanding considerably more attention than others. Clients new to the office and those experiencing their first building project will

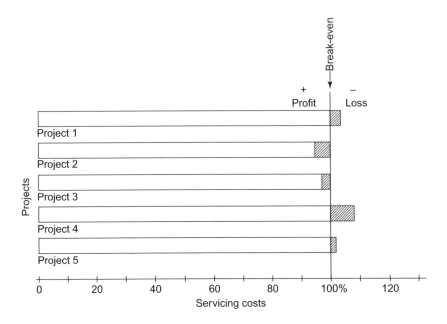

Figure 14.3 Client profitability.

usually require more attention than more experienced clients who are already known to the office. This means that the fee level must be set at an appropriate level to allow time for increased or decreased levels of interaction. The vast majority of clients are honest, enter into a project with good intentions and act with integrity, usually paying their invoices on time. There are a few clients that are not so well intentioned and are better avoided, although they may be difficult to spot until it is too late. Some unscrupulous individuals will try to make money by exploiting professionals, making excuses not to pay for work and threatening legal action. Fortunately, the managers of architectural offices tend to be good at warning their peers in other offices about such individuals.

Staff profitability

Staff costs may account for up to two-thirds of a design firm's expenditure; therefore thorough analysis of timesheets is needed to monitor the amount of time spent on fee-generating work (that chargeable to clients) and that spent on tasks associated with overheads. Some members of the firm will be more efficient at certain tasks than others (a point that applies to all staff, including the senior managers and support staff). The point was made earlier about the ability of the design manager to allocate the right staff to the right task, hence ensuring staff satisfaction and helping to ensure the office makes a profit. This job is made easier with accurate information on which to base those decisions (Figure 14.4). Each member of staff will have a target number of hours for each phase of a project, which must not be exceeded. Data should also be analysed from a staff-specific view to identify which staff do particular tasks quicker or more slowly than others, with a view to reorientating their duties. For example, a comparison of the hours spent per stage by individual architects and technologists on their past five projects may be revealing. Individuals tend to differ in the amount of time they spend on certain stages of each job. On the assumption that the competitive firm maximises its strengths and seeks to minimise its weaknesses, it may be sensible to allocate staff to the aspects of the job at which they are most proficient and/or provide additional training and education. This can only be done if the data is available on which to base informed decisions.

Crisis management

It is impossible to avoid the odd crisis or two, so it is necessary to be prepared. A contingency plan will help to mitigate the financial

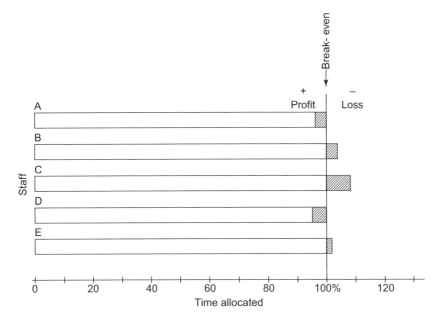

Figure 14.4 Staff profitability.

impact of the disaster and allow the business to function as normally as possible. Clients going into liquidation, the loss of a key member of the organisation because of sudden illness or serious accident, and damage to office space because of fire or theft, are all examples of unexpected events that will have a major effect on the business. We tend to be relatively resourceful when faced with an unexpected crisis; however, it is prudent to plan ahead so that the continuity of the business may be maintained. Problems tend to occur at the most inopportune moment and fall under three broad areas: economic, human and physical.

♦ *Economic.* Economic disasters are often caused by events over which the organisation has little control. Typical examples would be a rapid economic downturn in the national economy resulting in a downturn in client activity, or a client going into liquidation and not paying their fees.
♦ *Human.* We try not to think about staff being away from the office for a long time due to sickness, nor for that matter about the untimely death of key personnel. Given the importance of staff to the wellbeing of the business, it is crucial to have a contingency plan to allow the organisation to function until a suitable replacement can be found. Staff on

long-term sick leave will need to be replaced with temporary staff, which is both disruptive and costly. The death of a director or partner will have implications for the constitution of the business that can take a long time to resolve.

♦ *Physical.* Other disasters may be relatively innocuous in nature. A storm-damaged office roof may just allow enough water into the office to destroy a large quantity of drawings and/or important equipment. More obvious threats are theft of equipment and damage from fire, vandalism and terrorism. Temporary failure of a computer system may cause considerable disruption and result in missed deadlines.

The majority of clients, suppliers and staff will be sympathetic and understanding, if a plan is in place to resume normal service as soon as possible. They will be less accommodating if there is no up-to-date contingency plan and their project is perceived to suffer.

Crisis recovery plans

Contingency plans need to be agreed, implemented and reviewed periodically for their applicability to changing conditions. A crisis management group needs to be set up that consists of those in the office who best understand the whole of the business. An individual should be put in charge and a plan formulated which is then communicated to all members of the organisation. As a minimum the following should be considered:

♦ Where the business will operate from if the physical office space becomes unusable
♦ Access to telephone lines and computers
♦ Hard/digital copies of essential information held off-site and easily accessible
♦ Someone delegated to take charge if key personnel are suddenly incapacitated
♦ Strategy to cope with the inability (or refusal) of a client to pay the fees due.

Hard copies of the following should be kept in an alternative location to the main office:

♦ Contact details for all staff, suppliers and customers
♦ Copies of all information on the organisation's IT system
♦ Copies of financial and tax matters relating to the business
♦ Legal documentation relating to individual jobs
♦ Legal documentation relating to the business.

All of this information must be kept up to date and a planned periodic review must be agreed and adhered to. Rather than regarding this task as a time-consuming burden, it should be seen as an opportunity to periodically review business plans and look towards new technologies for automatic replication of data. There is the potential for cost savings, which can offset the cost of disaster-recovery planning. Organisations with clear plans may also benefit from reduced insurance premiums.

The office to project interface

Profitability of the design office will be determined to a large extent by the performance of people working on individual projects. Smooth-running projects will consume fewer resources (staff hours) than projects that are fraught with difficulties. Smooth-running projects also allow invoices to be issued to schedule and there is a higher chance of being paid on time if things are progressing well. When unexpected problems arise during the life of the project, time will be required to resolve them satisfactorily; this often involves the input of other, more experienced (and more expensive) members of the office whose time has not been factored into the calculations. This will impact on other projects as individuals are reallocated, albeit temporarily, to try and solve the problem quickly. Occurrence of problems also tends to result in delayed invoicing for payment and (not surprisingly) reluctance on behalf of the client to pay promptly. Thus the success of individual projects will have a positive or negative effect on cash flow. This relates to the success of the early stages of the project in which the project team is assembled and the brief developed. Assessment of projected client profitability and job profitability is required before committing to a project. It takes a lot of nerve to say no to a client, but this may be necessary in the longer-term interests of the office and its continued profitability.

Chapter Fifteen
Attracting and Retaining Clients

It is of little use developing a creative, dynamic, competitive and well-managed design office if clients are unaware of the services on offer. Effective promotion of the organisation and the services provided are fundamental to the attraction and retention of profitable clients. Promotion of a strong individual message (a brand) is a key requirement for effective marketing and relies on communication of the firm's culture and values to its clients. This is not a one-way process; clients actively seek out information about professionals they feel will help them to realise their dreams. Marketing activities should be integral to the organisation's business strategy and also to its organisational culture. Everything a firm does will have a secondary function related to the promotion of the office image. The manner in which designs are presented to clients, meetings administered, problems attended to, etc. is all part of the promotional initiative. Every letter, every telephone conversation, every drawing says something about the design office. Combined, these messages provide people outside the firm with information about the firm's approach to every aspect of its business. The term 'client' is used in this chapter to refer to the individual or organisation that commissions work from the architect's office. This may be the sponsor of the building project or it may be an independent project manager or contractor acting on behalf of the building sponsor.

All clients, regardless of their level of experience, will have a perception of what it is an architectural firm does, just as they will have a perception of what the structural engineer or general contractor does. Their perception will vary depending on the amount of contact a client has had with architectural practices and the type of practices with which they have communicated. For many the word architecture is synonymous with design; as such, the architectural firm offering a diverse range of services that includes management, either as a one-stop shop or as discrete packages, may find that marketing their services to clients meets with some resistance because the service is unfamiliar to them. In a highly competitive environment in which professional boundaries are fluid, it is crucial that the architectural practice is able to distinguish itself from the competition.

The unique relationship between the client and the design office is akin to a courting ritual – a process in which attention is sought, and once contact has been established there is a period of tentative interaction during which the parties try to establish common values and establish a basis of trust. Hopefully the outcome of the courting ritual will be the start of a working relationship in which both parties grow to trust and respect one another. This relationship is subsequently formalised in some form of contract for services, but continues through the project and beyond, often into new projects. Over time, design organisations will develop a portfolio of projects and cement relationships with a variety of clients.

There are four interrelated stages in the development of a client's relationship with the design office:

- *Marketing activity before initial client contact.* To a large extent businesses are reliant on clients seeking them out, and marketing activities are necessary to help raise the profile of the office within targeted niche areas. This stage is about visibility in the market and giving out an attractive message to clients so that they make contact with the architectural practice.
- *After client contact but prior to entering into a contract for services.* This is a crucial stage during which client and architect are trying to match values and the level of service required. This relies on interpersonal contact between client and senior staff in the practice. Dialogue is used to test each party's ability to perform specific functions within given parameters.
- *During the project timeline.* Interaction with the client during the development and realisation of the project is important in maintaining a sense of ownership and mutual respect. Close contact can help in discussing and resolving problems as they arise.
- *After completion of the project.* Establishing repeat business will be very closely related to how the office (and other actors) performed on the project. Repeat business will also be affected by the frequency with which the architectural practice retains contact with the client and the users of the building post-completion.

The client's perspective

Expending effort on communicating a consistent image is a fundamental task; however, before embarking on a range of marketing activities it may be useful to look at the architectural business from the perspective of clients. Members of the design office should be familiar with the services on offer, but it may be less clear to those without intimate knowledge of the office. What sort of image is the design office communicating to people outside the firm? Clients will be looking at the overall profile of the firm and the decision to short-list may be made on first impressions. Thus the firm has to be visible in the market and think very carefully about the type of image it wishes to be associated with, which requires a considerable amount of planning and effort.

Clients discriminate. They are expending a lot of money and emotional energy on a project and naturally they will require some form of reassurance before committing to a binding contract. Clients will also expect excellent performance for a fair fee and the majority of clients will put a lot of effort into narrowing down the choice of consultants to a small number of potential project partners. In researching the market, clients expect to see evidence of well-managed, coherent, consistent and reliable businesses, not a group of professionals pulling in different directions. The image communicated by the office to clients will be instrumental in the client's decision to enter into a dialogue with that office. The client will be looking not just at the main contact with the firm, usually the principal, but also at the staff who will be engaged on his or her project, i.e. the profile of the whole firm. The messages that the firm gives out to its external environment need to be managed, ranging from the drawings produced to the decor of the office and the manner in which telephone calls are dealt with by the office receptionist. Typically clients will want to see details of:

- ◆ *Track record of the firm.* Length of time in business, reputation for creativity and delivery, relevant benchmarking and other performance indicators for projects, references from previous clients, etc.
- ◆ *Project portfolio.* This will include details of completed building projects, including the budget and timescale, supported with drawings and photographs. Current design and construction projects (with particular reference to the client) should also be included.
- ◆ *Client portfolio.* List of clients that the office has worked for in the past and current clients (where appropriate). Client testimonials are useful in helping to provide evidence of excellent service provision.

- *Staff portfolio*. This should include academic qualifications of all staff, and details of training and professional updating. Special skills and competences should be highlighted.
- *Communication skills* (and speed of response to enquiries).
- *Experience, motivation, maturity and emotional ability* (mainly perceived through meetings with the members of the office).
- *Evidence of lean processes and procedures.*
- *Financial security of the office*. Demonstrated with bank references.
- *Health and safety policy.*
- *Insurances.*
- *Quality management systems.*

Some of this information will be available on the office web-based homepage and via other promotional sources. More detailed and commercially sensitive information will only be released after the client has entered into a dialogue with the office.

Approved lists

A great deal of care is required in the selection of the most appropriate consultants. Some may be known to the client organisation from previous project work and through strategic partnering initiatives; others may be new and hence constitute an unknown entity in terms of behaviour and performance. Clients with large property portfolios usually operate an approved list of suppliers and set out specific entry requirements that must be met before a consultant will be considered for work. For example, the use of a recognised quality management system is likely to be one of many conditions.

- *Existing consultants*. Performance needs to be demonstrated, i.e. measured and analysed. Consultants will be evaluated on their ability to provide value for money, the way in which they resolved problems during the project, their level of creativity and willingness to innovate, and general enthusiasm for the work.
- *Potential consultants*. New consultants regularly face two hurdles; not only do they have to prove their credentials to the client, but they often have to dislodge an existing supplier of services. Thus clients will want to see what the new consultants can offer that is better or uniquely different to that already provided. Previous performance can be checked through references and benchmarking information.

The architect's perspective

In addition to trying to look at the business from the perspective of clients, it is important to ask a few questions about the client portfolio, both the existing client base and those that the organisation wishes to attract. A balanced portfolio of clients can help to spread the risk of a sudden downturn in a particular sector, helping to spread the financial risk to the business. This means that marketing activities need to be targeted at different niche markets and/or client types, which means that effort needs to be expended to attract new clients operating in unfamiliar market niches. Marrying service provision with client wants is fundamental to the development and retention of a profitable business. There are two distinct client groups to consider: existing clients and those the firm would like to attract – their potential clients. The issue of client profitability (discussed in Chapter 14) will need to be assessed before marketing is directed at specific interest groups. If the client is unlikely to be profitable it is clearly a waste of resources trying to communicate with them.

- ♦ *Existing clients.* Marketing to existing clients is often taken for granted by professional firms, yet these represent the most probable source of new business. Existing clients need to be nurtured and much of the effort of developing the business around existing clients will be of an interpersonal nature, supported with targeted promotional material. Of course, this works both ways; many clients do not want to go through the time-consuming process of selecting new consultants every time they wish to build, and so they too will be keen to retain relationships in readiness for new projects. This is especially true where the design office seeks to make the client a cohesive element of the firm's culture, requiring input from the client as well as the firm. Similarly, the close involvement of the client is an essential requirement of long-term relationships based on mutual trust, such as strategic partnering and alliances.
- ♦ *New clients.* Attracting new clients takes a different form of effort and is more demanding of resources. Some studies have suggested that attracting new clients consumes as much as ten times the resources needed for existing clients, although this is very difficult to quantify with any accuracy. Many potentially profitable clients may already have an established network of contacts, so the firm must recognise that it will be trying to dislodge a competitor. For professional firms such as architects, care

is required not to compromise the Code of Conduct, which clearly states that architects must not attempt to take work from other architects; other professionals are of course fair game.

New clients are an unknown entity. There will be some uncertainty about what information they require and how they will interact with the office. As a rule of thumb, the new clients will require at least twice the effort to develop a working relationship with after initial contact, compared with existing clients. Clients will expect the professional firm to deliver what it promises, so the promotional campaign must match the service delivered. To deliver less than an excellent service every time can cause a lot of damage, regardless of the effectiveness of the promotional activities. Retaining and enhancing reputation is critical to the success of a professional service firm and is at the heart of the promotional effort.

Communicating with clients

Architects, along with many other professional service firms, have experienced a considerable amount of criticism for their complacency when it comes to marketing. It is an area too often taken for granted, yet the consistent communication of a corporate image is one way of distinguishing the firm from others offering similar services, and in recent years the subject has been given much more priority. The organisation must 'know its business' before any marketing strategy can be designed and implemented. Or, more specifically, the firm's culture must have been designed and its aims, both short term and long term, agreed before a strategy can be put in place. Every firm has its own culture, which has evolved through a mixture of deliberate policies (by design) and circumstance (by accident). This is reflected in the communication of the organisation's corporate image or identity. Corporate identity is concerned with how the firm is perceived by its clients (both existing and prospective), its employees and service providers, competing firms (architects and other professional service firms), project stakeholders, the architectural profession, and the public. Perception will be based on the experience of the service provided, the appearance of the buildings it designs, the firm's culture and the manner in which it presents itself through marketing activities; it goes much deeper than the firm's logo and web-based homepage. The face needs putting to the name constantly and consistently.

Graphic communication is the trademark of the architectural firm and often forms part of its brand image. Its culture and corporate image are reflected in letters, reports, presentation drawings, detail draw-ings and contract documentation as well as in specifically designed marketing material. As part of the corporate image the standard of graphic communication should be high, but more importantly consis-tent. Many firms are aware of the importance of corporate identity through their graphics and operate a house style. Other firms are less precious and have an inconsistent (one might argue amateur) approach to the material that they produce, i.e. they are putting out a potentially confusing message that may be perceived by clients as representative of a poorly managed firm. Building designers spend an enormous amount of time on producing information from which others construct the physical artefact. Yet it is the completed building that usually figures prominently in the graphics used to promote the design organisation's services to existing and potential clients, not the drawings and specifications.

Corporate identity should link all of a firm's activities into one easily identifiable and memorable image. Establishment of a corporate iden-tity takes time and inevitably will change as the firm itself responds to changes in the market and interaction with its clients and project partners. Once a corporate image has been designed and agreed, a variety of promotional tools can be employed to raise awareness and communicate beliefs and values to existing and potential clients. Public relations, marketing and advertising efforts are complementary and interdependent forms of external communication.

Public relations

Public relations are concerned with the management of external com-munication channels, of which marketing and advertising are key elements. Public relations should be seen as the management of communications between a firm and its clients, which is a complex and demanding activity. To be effective, public relations informa-tion must be carefully considered, well designed, planned and well implemented. Public relations are most commonly associated with press relations in the form of press releases and feature articles. Press releases are essentially news items, such as an announcement about a new commission or completion of a project, and are usually directed at local audiences and specialist interest groups. These pieces of news must have some degree of interest for the readers of the newspaper or journal for which they are intended, otherwise they will be rejected and effort wasted. Feature articles are longer than press releases and can cover a topic in greater detail, usually in the specialist press. Articles may be submitted on a speculative basis although sometimes they will be commissioned by the journal. Another form of public relations covers the sponsorship of events or causes associated with any specialist areas of the firm's activities. These events are usually local to the physical base of the architectural practice or associated with a specific market niche. Sponsorship of events and causes may help to raise the profile of the firm through the associated marketing activities; they also provide a forum in which to interact with people on a face-to-face basis, and this may lead to new commissions.

Marketing

The main purpose of marketing is to bring the design firm's services to the attention of clients. In architectural circles this activity is usually described as 'attracting' or 'getting work'; other sectors are more familiar and comfortable with the terms promotion and marketing. Marketing comprises strategies for identifying and developing services to match (or create) market demand. It is a business philosophy based on the orientation of the firm to the wants and needs of its clients. The aim is to achieve client satisfaction and to make a profit. This includes the use of market research to help target new markets, identify new services and identify competitors, and hence adapt to changing market conditions. In professional service firms marketing is influenced by the market awareness of the practice managers, the partners and directors.

Advertising

The implementation of creative communication strategies, often in media communication campaigns, to bring services to the attention of clients is known as advertising. Advertising is primarily concerned with raising awareness, from which clients may or may not decide to contact the office. Advertising campaigns should be designed to reflect the general marketing strategies and be consistent with the firm's image. Advertising can be used to establish and maintain the firm's image by raising its profile and separating it from its competitors. Until 1986 the architectural profession was restricted by its own Code of Conduct, and even now many within the profession feel that advertising is not something professionals do. Such caution is understandable, but carried out with the same professionalism that is reserved for other activities, advertising is an essential part of a professional service firm's competitive strategy and survival in a highly competitive market. Advertising campaigns can be expensive and there is some debate as to their effectiveness.

Promotional tools

Promotional tools help to bring the attention of the firm to potential clients and also to reinforce its image with existing clients. Bringing about and raising awareness is particularly important, since if a client is unaware of the firm or the firm's range of service provision, it will not be considered. A number of tried and tested marketing tools are available, ranging from the corporate brochure to newsletters and direct mail campaigns. Web-based homesites are a popular way of communicating information about the practice, although these rely on clients actively seeking out the homepage and taking time to read the information posted on it.

Paper literature costs money to produce, although with advances in printing technology a modest-sized brochure or newsletter need not take up a significant part of the marketing budget. Electronic newsletters and homepages provide another outlet for promoting the firm, although similar rules apply in terms of their accessibility and relevance. The strategies listed below rely on the prospective client becoming aware of the literature, taking note of it and deciding to make contact with the architectural firm, i.e. they rely on a certain amount of luck (e.g. landing on the client's desk at the right moment or being easily found by search engines when surfing the World Wide Web). Whatever strategies are used the corporate image must be consistent. The firm's name and any corporate logos should be included on both the front and the back of any literature, along with the firm's address and telephone number (and where appropriate a contact name). The quality of the literature sent out and posted on the homepage will influence whether or not it is read, and will also influence the reader's perception of the firm. Literature is a part of the firm's ongoing communication effort and needs careful consideration since it is widely accepted that it has less than ten seconds to convey a message. This literature should also be sent to the local branch of the RIBA for inclusion in the database of the Client Advisory Service (CAS).

Another important factor is the speed with which the office responds to enquiries from clients. This is usually done by a senior partner (assisted by secretarial staff) and can be very quick when the relevant information is available in electronic files, e.g. PDF. This is an important first contact, which will say a lot about the practice to the enquirer.

Homepages

There are few businesses that exist without a web-based homesite, and clients expect to see one. The design, maintenance and updating of the site is crucial to the message given out to viewers. Similarly, the ability of search engines to find the homepage when people conduct a search on the web is crucial. Clients can tell a lot about the practice from its website. A slick, visually attractive, easy-to-navigate, informative website with up-to-date information is a sign of a well-managed office. Poorly designed, difficult-to-navigate sites with outdated information give out a bad message and do little to attract clients. It may be a useful exercise to check what the competition is saying and how easy their sites are to navigate, before launching or updating the homesite. Good websites need considerable investment in resources and for many offices it is usually prudent to outsource the design of the website to website designers. Although this may appear an expensive option, it does free up staff time to do more productive, fee-generating, work. As with the printed information, the firm is reliant on a potential client or client's agent searching for information, and therefore it is critical to get the keywords right; the danger is in remaining invisible simply because a search engine cannot find details of the homepage.

Maintenance and regular updating of the site should be assigned to a competent member of the office and resources (especially time) allocated to the task. Old news will need to be updated, project descriptions, drawings and photographs added, and achievements/awards updated to reflect the continuing evolution of the business.

Practice brochures

The practice brochure is one of the most important promotional tools used by architects and many offices still use the brochure as their first point of contact with potential clients. It is common to provide printed brochures to support interpersonal interaction with the client. The practice brochure is tactile and according to many offices it is a useful tool; however, it is expensive to produce given that the content will be tailored to suit a specific client. An alternative approach is to place the practice brochure on, or incorporate it into, the firm's homepage (and print it out when necessary). It is essential that the brochure is well designed and carefully targeted at prospective clients. Brochures should include a brief history of the practice, a statement of the firm's corporate values and mission, details of significant projects and an overview of the services offered. A statement on design philosophy and possibly the firm's mission statement (sometimes combined) should also be included. Text should be concise and direct. The firm's competitive advantage to the client should be clearly identified so that the unique approach of the practice is evident and the practice is distinct from the other players.

Newsletters

Direct mail is a promotional tool targeted to a specific audience, examples being sales letters (whose use may be questionable for the professional service firm) and the newsletter; they work best when followed up by telephone calls. Newsletters are cheaper to produce than brochures and are most effective when they are focused and interesting. Thus the content of the news and the target audience need some thought. The common mistake is to try and say too much to too wide an audience. The purpose of the newsletter needs to be established. Is it to keep existing clients informed of developments within the firm or is it intended to raise awareness among new clients/ markets? It is an important question because the content may need to be subtly different for defined audiences. If newsletters are used it is important to maintain the frequency, e.g. twice annually, so that clients know that the practice is still in existence. Suddenly stopping the newsletter can have a negative effect on clients; the perception may be that the firm no longer exists.

Directories

Entries in printed and web-based directories may also help raise awareness, although it is usually necessary to pay a small annual fee to be listed in many of these publications. The more space required for text and images, the greater the fee. Architectural practices registered with the RIBA will have an entry in the Directory of Practices. Entries in directories aimed at a niche market may be a worthwhile investment.

Architects' signboards

Erecting the standard practice signboard on new developments is a cheap and effective way of communicating with those passing the site. The sign will be one of many, but clients thinking of building will be looking at developments in their locality and will be taking notice of the name of the project team as communicated on the various signboards.

Client presentations

Clients may invite a select number of consultants to demonstrate their suitability for a particular project by making a presentation. This is done as a means of narrowing down the short-listed consultants. Clients will be looking for consultants, or more often a point of contact within the firm, that they feel comfortable dealing with. The interpersonal skills of those doing the presentation will be under close scrutiny. Client presentations need to be conducted professionally and should reinforce the corporate image promoted through marketing activities. Emphasis should be on what the firm can do for the client. Presentations should be open and honest representations of the firm based on its collective experience and qualifications. It is common for presentations to be rather formal events with the architects presenting to a panel of representatives from the client organisation. However, some clients prefer a more informal arrangement and so it is necessary to check the format before preparing the presentation. As a general rule at least two members of the office should attend to make the presentation and to answer questions.

Architectural competitions

Architectural competitions are usually seen as a good way of raising awareness of the practice. They are best suited to strong design practices and even then the success rate is likely to be low. Putting together a design for an architectural competition will involve the commitment of considerable resources, and many practices may simply find it too expensive and/or too time-consuming to engage in competitions. Time may be better spent on activities more likely to generate financial income.

Community involvement

Despite the increasing globalisation of services many architectural practices concentrate on serving the needs of their local community. Competitive advantage is achieved through knowing the local customs, values and needs of the area, something businesses from outside may find difficult to access quickly and effectively. Building a good reputation for good work takes time and many professional service firms still rely on word of mouth for their business (usually combined with involvement in local activities and sponsorship of events). Giving short talks to local interest groups and business groups about a new project or a topical issue concerning architectural design and the built environment can be an effective way of raising the profile of the business. Similarly, writing articles for targeted magazines and local newspapers provides another means of raising awareness with the public.

Managing marketing activities

Managing the client relationship is essential in helping to achieve maximum value for the client and also for the design office. Responsibility for client relationships and marketing activities must be delegated to those most suited to doing the job. In small offices this will be the principal architect, but in medium to large offices marketing will be undertaken by a marketing manager and/or outsourced to marketing specialists. This may be in addition to other duties. Activities need to be planned, adequately resourced, monitored, systematically evaluated and maintained. Time must be found to consider, agree and implement suitable activities, set realistic budgets and achievable timescales, then monitor, evaluate and adjust as required. This can only be carried out once the core values, and hence the purpose of the business, have been clearly defined and understood by all employees.

Outsourcing marketing activities

Whether marketing activities are undertaken by someone in the office or outsourced is a prime consideration. There are a number of benefits and challenges in using an external consultant to deal with public relations and the design of the firm's website. Similarly, there are advantages and disadvantages associated with using resources from within the office. For small to medium-sized offices it is highly unlikely that the resources or skills will be available in-house to deal with communications. It is more cost-effective to outsource marketing and web-design activities to experts. In larger offices there may be the resources to employ full-time marketing experts, although many large offices still outsource their web-design to attain and maintain a professional image.

Planning

A well-planned and managed marketing strategy will allow time for concentrating on the development of the business and serving clients' needs. Marketing activity must be adequately resourced and monitored. Different strategies are required for marketing to existing clients than those employed to attract new clients. Marketing activities should take into account:

- Identification of new markets and opportunities
- Identification and awareness of shrinking markets and reduced opportunities
- Retention of existing clients
- Promotion to potential clients and securing new business
- Client profitability.

The firm's marketing strategy needs to consider the services to be promoted and should identify and promote its competitive advantage to clients. Bringing the services of the firm to the attention of potential clients can be looked at as passive and active strategies.

- *Passive strategies* rely on potential clients approaching the firm after they have received information from a third party, for example a recommendation from an existing client, consultant or the CAS, from information on completed jobs featured in magazines, or from the architect's signboard erected on a building site.
- *Active strategies* rely on the firm courting and nurturing clients, for example sending company promotional material to carefully selected clients and doing client presentations. The active strategy is more expensive in terms of resources than a passive approach, but is more likely to result in new business.

Resourcing

Adequate resources are required to do the job properly. That means setting a realistic marketing budget and allocating sufficient time to manage the activity. In small firms it is very tempting to cut the number of hours allocated to marketing when additional work pressures increase, and to 'borrow' from the marketing budget in tough times. Such tendencies must be resisted, since the modern professional service firm is dependent on effective marketing for continuity of business. A marketing budget is required to cover:

- Design and distribution of publicity material
- Design, maintenance and regular updating of the web-based homepage
- Corporate entertaining, presentations and attendance at events
- Entering design competitions
- Training and education (marketing activities)
- Time to manage the marketing activities.

Depending on the size of the firm, the budget may be concentrated on one of these areas. For example, some small firms may spend the majority of their budget on interpersonal means of promotion, using corporate entertaining and presentations. Others may rely heavily on the distribution of publicity material, through advertising, direct mail and the design and maintenance of active websites. Whatever a firm's individual strategy, it is important to remember the importance of training and continual updating so that the marketing strategies retain their currency.

Monitoring, evaluation and maintenance

Management of the marketing activity is based around monitoring and evaluation. All leads generated from promotional activities should be followed up and monitored as part of a systematic plan. All leads to potential work, whether they lead to a commission or not, should be evaluated to see how they were generated. This provides valuable feedback about the effectiveness of certain promotional strategies and helps with the planning and targeting of future resources. It may be difficult to identify clearly which marketing activities were more successful than others, but unless some attempt is made to monitor and evaluate the marketing activities, it is impossible to make judgements about the effectiveness of marketing activities. Some practices will encourage all staff to try and bring new business into the office, offering a financial bonus for new contacts that lead to work and financial income.

Once a marketing plan has been put in place, it is important to retain the momentum, thus helping to maintain an image in the market. It is of little use embarking on a promotional campaign and then, for whatever reason, ceasing abruptly. A sudden reduction in marketing activity will usually be perceived negatively by clients, so it is important that initiatives are capable of being maintained over a long period. Emphasis should be on a consistent image and a consistent level of marketing activity.

Managing change

A well-designed and planned promotional campaign will consider the impact of change on the business, for example introducing new service provision, and the manner in which it is communicated to clients. As a general rule it is better to keep clients informed of intended changes before they are implemented, so that clients are prepared. For example, the implementation of quality assurance will place additional burdens on the firm initially (until its members are comfortable with the system). Most clients will understand, especially if they know that they should get a better service from the firm in the long term. Therefore, it is important to involve the client and to keep them informed at all times through a suitable communication medium; such a strategy also helps to generate client input and feedback, in line with the philosophy of ownership and partnering.

Crisis management

The firm's ability to deal with unexpected events quickly and effectively should be part of a comprehensive public relations package.

A key function of public relations is to manage a crisis and try and turn negative events into positive opportunities. No matter how well managed the design office, there will be occasions when problems arise, however ordinary the building or familiar the client and consultants. The fact that every site, and hence every project, is unique means that unexpected events may happen, often more frequently than anticipated. It would, however, be unrealistic to expect things to run smoothly all of the time, because clients may change their minds, other consultants may make mistakes and builders may get things wrong. Public relations can be used to avoid (or at least minimise) damage to the firm's reputation in a crisis, an activity usually known as crisis management. Damage to the firm's reputation and loss of confidence in the organisation on the part of its clients may harm the long-term viability of the business. Furthermore, time spent on litigation would be better spent on more creative and rewarding endeavours. Timely, careful and sensitive public relations efforts should be used to respond to crisis situations. Just as it is essential to keep the client informed of progress, it is also important to keep the client informed of any unexpected events. A well-designed and implemented quality management system provides the framework in which to do this.

The office to project interface

In a multiproject environment all clients will expect their project to take priority within the office. This demand can pose problems for the design manager if clients and projects are not dealt with fairly and equally. Clients need to understand how the office functions and the effect that prioritising can have on the other projects in the office. Tension between available resources and client requirements will always be present; however, this can be mitigated through good communication with the client and sensitive programming of work.

Interaction between clients and the design office will determine the success of individual projects and hence the profitability of the architectural business. Regular interpersonal contact with clients and other stakeholders at regular progress meetings and design reviews may provide an opportunity for informally updating clients of developments and for strengthening interpersonal relationships. Feedback visits (postoccupancy evaluation) offer another opportunity for interaction and rekindling of social networks if managed well. Regular visits not only provide feedback on how the building is being used and is weathering, but will also help to demonstrate the architects' passion and commitment to their client and the building.

During the project lifeline, the architectural office will also come into contact with a variety of actors and organisations, ranging from planning consultants and landscape architects through to specialist subcontractors and craftspeople. Although it may not be obvious at the time, other contributors, keen to put together an effective team for a new project, may be assessing the performance of the office. Thus the way in which key members of the office interact with other actors can make the difference between getting and losing new work. Similarly, interaction with project stakeholders forms an ideal opportunity for the architects to assess the performance of other actors, especially those they find themselves working with for the first time.

The increasing commercialism of clients in all sectors and their willingness to consider a wide range of procurement routes emphasises the need for professional marketing activities. Similarly, the changing face of architectural practice has to be communicated to clients so that the value to be delivered through design is foremost in early decisions.

Appendices

Appendix 1
Typical Complaints and their Avoidance

The Architects Registration Board (ARB) published a list of the ten most common complaints it receives from clients in its annual report 2004/5. In the report the ARB advises architects to adhere to the Architects Code as one way of avoiding the pitfalls that can result in an appearance before the Professional Conduct Committee. Following good management practices and procedures also helps, since all of the complaints listed by ARB are concerned with management (and the failure to communicate). These complaints are listed below with a brief comment on how to avoid them.

1. Excessive delay in the project being completed.

The problem here is primarily related to poor predictions of project duration and the failure to discuss with clients the potential reasons for delay. Architects must make it clear to clients how the project duration has been calculated and by whom. They must also explain the measures put in place to try and ensure projects will be complete to the planned timeframe. If progress starts to suffer then the architect must be proactive and advise the client, and if necessary take measures to get the project back on programme.

2. Client expectations were raised too high.

Raising client expectations too high can occur as the architects discuss design possibilities that are beyond the scope of the budget. Having a good knowledge of realisation costs can help to mitigate unrealistic expectations. Similarly, bringing specialists into the design phase can help with the realistic estimation of construction costs.

3. The client was expected to pay for mistakes/errors made by the architect.

Architects must be open with clients and acknowledge when they have made a mistake. Using quality management systems and good design management practices will help to mitigate the number and extent of errors, although it is impossible to eliminate all problems. Tracking the cause of design changes and variations will help to identify those that were a result of an error and those requested for other reasons. Adopting a collaborative approach may go some way to sharing responsibility for errors and the cost of rectifying them.

4. Contract papers were not clear.

There should be no excuse for failing to set out fees, roles and responsibilities clearly and concisely before work commences. This is required by the client and also for the smooth running of the office. A short meeting with the client to discuss contract papers before the project starts can help to avoid uncertainty and problems at a later date.

5. Attempted work outside area of competence.

Architects must clearly state the extent of services that they are experienced and qualified to undertake. This varies considerably between architectural practices, and clients cannot be expected to know the scope and limitations of the services on offer. Open and frank discussions with the client can help to explore areas of uncertainty and identify the need for additional services from fellow consultants.

6. Failure to reply to the client's letters/emails and or telephone calls.

According to ARB, communication problems are the cause of many complaints. One of the biggest complaints is the failure to advise clients about increased costs. All professionals should have a clear policy on how they respond to communications from clients and project participants, and this should be set out in the quality plan and/or office manual. Failure to reply is unprofessional and bad business practice. Good architectural practices tend to be proactive in tackling problems and taking the initiative to contact clients before they discover the problem from another source. This is about managing the client/architect relationship and can be helped by bringing the client into the project at strategic intervals, for example at design reviews.

7. Failure to deal with post-completion issues.

The failure of architects and other project team members to deal with problems that arise after completion of the project and the payment of fees is not a sensible policy. The level of 'after sales' service quality will be instrumental in helping to retain the architect/

client relationship and will influence the possibility of future work. The problem is usually that the fee has been spent and the resources are not available to deal with the problems. Accurate estimation of design effort and the allocation of resources to post-completion issues are necessary if a professional service is to be maintained after project completion.

8. Clients given bad advice.

This tends to relate to architects advising the client on matters outside their scope of expertise, for example on engineering matters and financial/VAT issues. This can be avoided by clearly setting out the extent of the services provided and also defining areas that are not covered by the fee agreement. This is best done via face-to-face discussion, and confirmed in writing.

9. Conflicts of interests.

All business relationships, for example with contractors, must be declared to clients early in the appointment process. Clients expect their professionals to be open about such matters and with many architectural practices working with formal and informal alliances, it is particularly important to be clear about how such relationships may influence the client's project.

10. Work delegated to juniors.

It is common for projects to be secured by partners and directors, and after some initial involvement by them, for the work to be delegated to less senior members of the office. This is common practice in all professional service firms, but the failure to explain how the work will be handled within the office can cause problems with the client, who may be expecting the partner to work on the project, not a junior.

Appendix 2
Guidance for New
Design Managers

Many architects develop management competences as their careers develop, with some moving into formal and informal design management roles. The formal design management role carries a considerable amount of responsibility and can be a highly rewarding career move, in terms of both job satisfaction and financial reward. Some architects will be promoted to a design management role by their current employer, while others will move to a new employer to take up the position. In both situations is important to define your management style and make sure that the owners of the business and the staff understand how you intend to operate.

There are some golden rules to follow if entering a new design office. The design manager will initially be perceived as an outsider and also as 'management' by the designers. It is highly likely that the design manager will be greeted with a degree of caution in the first few weeks and that the staff will be defensive. New design managers should expect to take somewhere between three and six months as a minimum to get to know how the office and the staff work and start to develop empathy and trust. The challenge is slightly different for those promoted internally. They will be familiar with office systems and the staff, which makes the job a little easier at the outset. However, they may be too familiar with office systems, which makes it difficult for them to see what needs to be improved. Similarly, they may be too friendly with some of the office staff, which makes treating everyone equally as a manager quite a challenge. Moving from being a member of the design office to a management role will put the individual in a different position and relationships with staff will change. All new design managers should:

- ♦ *Observe*. Watch how the members of the design office work and interact with their colleagues. Listen to the hum of the office as designs are conceived and developed, since it is the informal conversations that reveal how well the office procedures fit the working methods of the staff.

♦ *Develop*. Develop empathy with all staff and build trust. Try to get to know individual strengths and weaknesses as fast as possible, since it helps with programming and allocation of duties. Find out what each member likes doing and also what they dislike about their job function.

♦ *Discuss*. Discuss individual workloads and existing procedures with all staff members. Try and encourage an open communication culture in which individuals are happy discussing difficult issues, confident that the design manager will try and help them.

♦ *Act*. It may be possible to make a series of minor and incremental changes quite quickly to help improve the effectiveness of the design studio. However, all changes must be discussed with the staff and adjusted to accommodate feedback, before they are implemented.

♦ *Feedback*. The design manager acts as an interface between staff and the owners of the business and must develop a team ethos. Strategic feedback helps to share knowledge and keep all members of the business up to date with developments.

Appendix 3
Suggested Reading

Instead of listing many additional sources I have picked out three books and three peer-reviewed journals as a start for further reading. I have also provided details of the CIB W096 research network for those who may be interested in discussing design management issues in a supportive and knowledgeable environment.

Books

Chappell, D. and Willis, A. (2005) *The Architect in Practice* (9th edition), Blackwell Publishing, Oxford. This is essential reading for all architectural students about to go into practice.

Littlefield, D. (2005) *An Architect's Guide to Running a Practice*, Architectural Press, Oxford. Provides some sound, practical advice on the business side of architectural practice, supported with case studies. The thrust is firmly on making architecture a profitable occupation.

Maister, D. H. (1993) *Managing the Professional Service Firm*, The Free Press, New York. Very few management books deal specifically with the management of professional service firms. This is a comprehensive and inspirational account of how to manage professional service firms.

Peer-reviewed journals

Three journals that include research work directly relevant to this book are:

- ♦ *Engineering, Construction and Architectural Management*
- ♦ *Architectural Engineering and Design Management*
- ♦ *Design Studies.*

Research network

The CIB W096 Architectural Management research group includes members from practice and academe from around the world. The group has been active since 1992 and meets regularly to discuss developments in design and architectural management. CIB W096 publishes its work through conference proceedings and peer-reviewed articles. Further information is available via www.cibworld.nl

Notes and additional references

The first book that addressed the synergy between the architectural office and projects was *Management Applied to Architectural Practice* by J. Brunton, R. Baden Hellard and E.H. Boobyer (George Godwin for *The Builder*, London, 1964). The development of architectural management and an argument for architects to adopt management practices can be found in *Architectural Management in Practice* by S. Emmitt (Longman, Harlow, 1999).

Additional information on value and risk management can be found in *Value & Risk Management: a Guide to Best Practice* by Michael F. Dallas (Blackwell Publishing, Oxford, 2006) and further guidance on effective communication in design and construction teams is provided by S. Emmitt and C.A. Gorse in *Construction Communication* (Blackwell Publishing, Oxford, 2003). Comprehensive coverage of construction activities can be found in *Construction Planning, Programming & Control (Second edition)* by B. Cooke and P. Williams (Blackwell Publishing, Oxford, 2004).

Index